THE PERSON
AND WORK OF
THE

The Holy Spirit
Effects In Us
What Christ Has
Done For Us

DONALD T. WILLIAMS

BROADMAN
& HOLMAN
PUBLISHERS

Nashville, Tennessee

© 1994
by Broadman & Holman Publishers
All rights reserved
Printed in the United States of America

4210-48
0-8054-1048-1

Dewey Decimal Classification: 231.3
Subject Heading: HOLY SPIRIT // TRINITY
Library of Congress Card Catalog Number: 93-48106

Scripture quotations are from the *New American Standard Bible,* © the Lockman Foundation, 1960, 1962, 1963, 1968, 1971, 1972, 1973, 1975, 1977; used by permission.

Library of Congress Cataloging-in-Publication Data
Williams, Donald T., 1951–
    The person and work of the Holy Spirit / Donald T. Williams.
       p. cm.
    Includes bibliographical references and indexes.
    ISBN 0-8054-1048-1
    1. Holy Spirit.   I. Title.
BT121.2.W538   1994   93-48106
231'.3—dc20   CIP

To Marsha,

Than whom only the Holy Spirit is more mysterious
and
Than whom only the Holy Spirit has contributed
More to my growth in Christ.

—D.T.W.

Commentary, Acts 2:1–4
Sonnet LIX

For many days the little band had stayed
    Together, meeting daily in the room
    While time grew heavy with a sense of doom,
And every moment that it was delayed
Seemed an eternity—but they obeyed.
    To waver would be rudely to presume;
It seems they'd learned their lesson at the tomb,
    So patiently they waited and they prayed.

That morning seemed no different, much the same . . .
    Then unexpectedly there came a sound,
    A hurricane of wing-beats, tongues of flame,
Which blew them out into the streets around
    Articulating praises to the Name
When, swifter than a hawk, the Dove came down.

—D.T.W.

CONTENTS

INTRODUCTION

"Of the making of many books there is no end," wrote Solomon, and his words have never been truer. Unfortunately, to be made is not necessarily to be needed, and to be made and needed is not necessarily to be read. So, as a good steward of my time, why should I write this one? And as a good steward of yours, why should you read it?

In the last twenty years we have seen, if not a great outpouring of the Holy Spirit, at least a great outpouring of books about Him. But most of these books have approached the doctrine of the Holy Spirit piecemeal and polemically. We have almost reduced the whole discussion of His work to the question of how to handle the experience of glossolalia (speaking in tongues). We have made the controversial aspects of His ministry the focal point of the discussion. It was a natural mistake, but one with disastrous consequences, for it has produced in many Christians an unbalanced and incomplete understanding of His role in God's work for our salvation. And that situation, I believe, has led to a great impoverishment of the Christian lives of both traditional evangelicals *and* charismatics.

This book intends to do two things which few recent books on the Holy Spirit have attempted. First, it seeks to look at the doctrine of the Holy Spirit and His work as a whole, letting Scripture and the rich heritage of Christian history set the agenda, not today's controversies. There is a need for controversial books, but there is also a need for a book that helps intelligent laypersons and students to set the controversies in their broader biblical context. So we will treat the issue of tongues—whether they have ceased, what they mean—but we will treat it as it appears in the structure of a holistic understanding of the Spirit's work: as a sub-point, perhaps even a sub-sub-point, not as the central focus. Second, we will view the whole work of the Spirit in terms of the central focus which *should* unify our understanding of His work. Who is the Holy Spirit? What principle underlies and unifies all of His activity? *He is the personal Agent and Representative of Jesus Christ who acts for Him to glorify His name by making Him real in our lives.* That sentence is the thesis of this whole study.

Why do we need to study the doctrine of the Holy Spirit? Four reasons come immediately to our attention.

1. *We need to study the doctrine of the Holy Spirit because this doctrine is important.* The Holy Spirit is God; He is the Third Person of the Trinity. The Westminster Catechism is correct in saying, "Man's chief end is to know God, and to enjoy him forever." Jesus taught us that the very definition of eternal life is knowing God (John 17:3). This means that every believer has a built-in motive for wanting to know God better, and knowing God involves knowing the Holy Spirit. It also involves knowing everything we can find out *about* Him. It is true that personal, experiential knowledge of God is our goal, not simply the possession of information. But the two cannot really be separated. Suppose I told you that my closest friend from childhood is a man named David Gordon. "What does he do for a living?" you ask me. I don't know. "Where does he live?" "What are his favorite foods?" "What are his hobbies?" "Who is his favorite author?" I don't know. How far down that road do you think we could go before you would conclude that

I didn't know this alleged best friend at all? Having a close relationship with a person involves being interested in that person and knowing about him or her. That is why God's people have always understood that serious Bible study is indispensable to the knowledge of God. So we will study the doctrine of the Holy Spirit because we want to know God better.

2. *We need to study the doctrine of the Holy Spirit because the work of the Spirit is necessary to salvation.* It is true that we are saved by the work of Christ, and that His finished work on the Cross is the sole ground of our justification. But apart from the work of the Holy Spirit, Christ's supreme sacrifice would do us no good at all.

If the Holy Spirit had not inspired Scripture, how would we have any sure and accurate knowledge of what Christ has done? If the Spirit did not illumine the minds of believers as they read the Bible, how would we understand such mind-boggling truths? If He did not convict us of sin and call us to faith in Christ and then regenerate us, making us new persons who now want to follow Christ and love Him instead of fleeing from Him, how would we ever come to believe and be saved? If the Holy Spirit did not sanctify us after conversion, gradually transforming us into the likeness of our Redeemer; if He did not keep us through that same work in the faith, how would we ever persevere in faith to the end of our lives and be saved? The biblical answer, as we shall see, is that fallen humanity could not do any of these things apart from the work of the Holy Spirit. He is absolutely indispensable to our salvation; without Him no one could be saved, and the death of Christ would be in vain.

By the same token, the work of the Holy Spirit is of supreme importance to us because apart from Him there would be no such thing as the Christian life. Growth in grace, effective ministry and service, indeed even fellowship with Christ and God the Father would be totally impossible without the work of the Holy Spirit. As we are interested in these things, we will want to study every-thing the Bible has to say about the doctrine of the Holy Spirit.

3.   *We need to study the doctrine of the Holy Spirit because it has, paradoxically, been a greatly neglected doctrine.* That is, we have said a lot about it, but only to prove a point in contro-versy. We have neglected the study of it for its own sake.

We have done so, in the first place, because it is a difficult subject. The Holy Spirit is surely the hardest Person of the Trinity to understand. I once heard a child refer to the Trin-ity as "The Father, the Son, and the Other One," and it is easy to see why this is so. The Lord Jesus is perhaps the easiest of the Persons to relate to because He became a man, took on our own nature, in order that we might be able to relate to God. The Father is ultimately incompre-hensible, but He has revealed Himself to us in terms we can comprehend. The best analogy He could give us was to call Himself a *Father*—and we know what a father is, and we know something of how to relate to one. It is not that difficult to take a good human father and imagine him without any of his imperfections, and with omnipotence, omniscience, etc. What you have when you do that is a very imperfect concept of God, but it is true as far as it goes. We have God's own authority for thinking of Him that way, and it is something we can handle. But what happens when God tries to describe the Holy Spirit in terms of something we can hold in our minds? You get a dove, the wind, a flame of fire, yet some One who is also somehow personal. This is much harder to grasp. There is a certain mysteriousness here beyond what we encounter in the other Persons of the Godhead. But we must not be deterred; the very difficulty requires us to give this doc-trine our full attention.

Another reason for our neglect of the doctrine of the Spirit is the very fact that it has become controversial for us. Emotions run high precisely because the work of the Spirit is frequently the place where doctrine meets inner experience. Viewpoints on such questions as the "second blessing" or the gift of tongues seem to carry with them almost of necessity an insidious temptation to spiritual one-upmanship. "Only *we* have the *full* gospel!" "Your experience is of the Devil!" Negative experiences with such attitudes have made many of us afraid to touch the doctrine of the Spirit at all lest we open up the proverbial can of worms. But if the Bible is really the Word of God it is a grievous sin for us to neglect any of its teaching. And if the ministry of the Holy Spirit is as central to the whole Christian faith as we have been suggesting, we can ill afford to let the excesses of others deprive us of a right appreciation of it. The right response to a badly handled controversy is not to close our Bibles but to open them and to address the issues biblically and responsibly, without fear. Caricature, imbalance, and polarization can only be countered by a fresh and positive presentation of the truth in all its wholeness, sanity, and splendor. Instead of being frightened into silence, we have to get back to our biblical business of speaking the truth in love.

4.   *We need to study the doctrine of the Holy Spirit because it is controversial.* This, I think, is not the primary motivation we should have for any study, but it is an important one nonetheless. Precisely because polarization has occurred, irresponsible teaching has been put forth, and churches have been split, we need to know where we stand and have the confidence that we are on biblical ground in order to minister effectively in such times. Faithfulness to our Lord demands it.

So our need for such a study as this is great in every way. But before we open our Bibles and begin, there is one last caution we need to consider. We are entering holy ground and must do so with some awe and trepidation. The very essence of the Holy Spirit's work is to glorify the Lord Jesus Christ (John 16:14), and this should tell us something about the seriousness with which we should approach our work. John the Baptist is the only man of whom it was said that he was filled with the Holy Spirit from his mother's womb, and we know that this is so not only because the Bible tells us but also because of what John said of Christ: "He must increase, and I must decrease" (John 3:30). This is the authentic voice of the Holy Spirit speaking, and such an attitude toward Jesus is the authentic mark of a person in whom the Spirit dwells in His fullness.

Perhaps the Holy Spirit Himself is somewhat uncomfortable with the idea that we should undertake a study of Him, for His sole purpose and desire is to focus our attention, not on Himself, but on Christ. And if we are to study the Holy Spirit rightly, that is exactly what we must ultimately do. I have a feeling that the Spirit watched me closely as I wrote this book—and will watch you as you read it—and that He will be pleased only if the end result of writing and reading is that glory and honor and majesty and dominion abound in our lives to Jesus Christ. I pray He will be pleased.

1

AGENT OF CHRIST

In the nineteenth chapter of Acts, Paul found a group of people in Ephesus who were trying to follow Jesus but who seemed rather confused. "Did you receive the Holy Spirit when you believed?" he asked them. They had never even heard of the Holy Spirit, and they certainly didn't know who He was. Most of us have heard of the Holy Spirit, but the first thing we need to get straight about Him is just exactly who this strange Personage is.

The first thing to understand about the Holy Spirit is that He is the Third Person of the Trinity. I was once asked to critique a gospel song a young lady had written. "It has a good message," I said, "except that in the second verse you seem to commit yourself to the Sabellian heresy." "What?" she replied. "You seem to imply," I explained, "that 'Father,' 'Son,' and 'Spirit' are just three different names for the same Person." "Oh!" she gasped, somewhat surprised, "I thought that's what they were!" I have since discovered that she is far from alone in that assumption. And this view is not only heretical but, followed to its logical conclusions, robs us of some of the deepest blessings of the Christian faith.

If Father, Son, and Spirit are not just three different names for the same Person, what are they? The answer to that question is the doctrine of the Trinity, one of the most difficult ideas in all of Christian theology, but also one of the most important. This doctrine affirms that the following statements are all true at the same time and are not contradictory: that there is only one God; that there are three Persons in the Godhead; that these three Persons are distinct from one another. While the Father is not the Son nor the Son the Spirit, they constitute not three gods but one God. One Being, three Persons, not just three different ways of talking about one Person: We stretch our minds to their limits and still can't quite grasp the idea. But we must at least make the effort if we want to understand who the Holy Spirit is.

Since *Trinity* is not a biblical word, why did the church ever come up with such a difficult concept? Basically, the church needed this word in order to account for everything the Bible was affirming about who God is. It was the only way the church could work in all the facts without contradiction. Notice that the doctrine of the Trinity is not contradictory. This doctrine does not simultaneously maintain that there is only one God and that there are three Gods; that would be irrational. The doctrine of Trinity says that there is one God who is tri-Personal, which is merely incomprehensible. Yet there is a great difference between being irrational and incomprehensible. We must frequently believe things we cannot comprehend, but never under pain of insanity, the truly irrational.

The best way for us to understand why the doctrine of the Trinity is so necessary is simply to examine what the Bible says about the Person of the Holy Spirit. The early church fathers were driven to formulate the doctrine of the Trinity by wrestling with what Scripture teaches about the Person of the Son. Once they worked out the relationship between the Son and the Father, the Holy Spirit fit right in. But you can start with any of the Persons and get the same results. The biblical teaching about the Person of the Holy Spirit can be stated in four simple propositions.

The Holy Spirit is God.

The Holy Spirit is a Person.

The Holy Spirit is not the Father or the Son.

The Holy Spirit is subordinate in function to the Father and the Son.

If these four statements are true, they summarize the Person of the Holy Spirit and the Trinitarian nature of God.

The Holy Spirit as God

The first thing Scriptures teaches us about the Holy Spirit is that He is God. The mere fact that He is called the Spirit of God, or God's Spirit, strongly implies His divinity (see, for example, Matt. 12:18, 28). Clearly, the spirit of man or woman is a human spirit; by the same token, the Spirit of God must be a divine Spirit—a Spirit who has the nature of God. But we are not left with just inference; the Bible explicitly states this. Acts 5 tells the story of Ananias and Sapphira who sold some property and gave some of the proceeds to the church. The only problem was that they pretended to be giving the whole price. Peter asked Ananias what ever put it in his heart to lie to the Holy Spirit; Peter's conclusion was "You have not lied to men, but to God" (v. 5).

So the Holy Spirit is God: He has the nature of God, and what you say to Him you say to God. This means that the Holy Spirit has all the attributes of God: He is omnipotent, omniscient, and omnipresent; He is good, wise, gracious, and just; above all, He is holy, that is, totally separate from all that is evil. The work He does in us is God's work. Such is the nature of this Being who is said to indwell believers. Quite clearly, people cannot have the Holy Spirit resident in their hearts and be the same people they were before. Do we realize what it means to be convicted by— regenerated by—empowered by—indwelt by—filled with such a Being as this? Whatever all this strange New Testament language means (and it would sound very strange indeed if it were not so familiar), it must refer to something dynamic, life-giving, and life-changing.

The Holy Spirit as Person

The second fact which is revealed about the Spirit is that He is personal, in fact that He is a Person. The phrase "Spirit of God" is not just another way of talking about God's power, or God in action. This truth is never stated in so many words, but it is implied so unmistakably in so many passages that there can be no doubt whatsoever.

In Matthew 10:20, for example, Jesus promised His disciples that they would not be on their own when facing persecution. They would receive extraordinary aid indeed, for "it is not you who speak, but it is the Spirit of your Father who speaks in you." In the epistle to the Hebrews, the Holy Spirit "says" (3:7), "signifies" (9:8), and "bears witness" (10:15). In 1 Peter 1:11 He "indicates," and in 2 Peter 1:21 He "moved" the prophets so that they "spoke from God." The undeniable implication of these passages (and many others like them) is that the Holy Spirit is articulate: He is able to speak intelligibly, to use language. If He can speak, it follows that He also possesses intelligence. Surely these are attributes which imply personality.

In 1 Corinthians 12:11, the Holy Spirit distributes His gifts to believers individually, "just as He wills." So He is not only articulate and intelligent, but He is also purposeful: He has a will and is able to make decisions. Furthermore, we discover in Romans 15:30 that He loves and in Ephesians 4:30 that He can grieve. Without a doubt, a Being who possesses intelligence, speech, a will, who loves, and can grieve is a personal Being, in fact, a Person—no less so than the Father or the Son.

The personality of the Spirit is something we should ponder for a moment. One often hears people who would never deny that the Holy Spirit is a Person but who speak of Him as if He were some sort of cosmic vending machine, responding mechanically with power or blessing if only we insert enough coins of faith. But the Spirit who indwells believers is a Person. He has His own will and His own ideas. He has his own agenda, which does not necessarily coincide with ours. He distributes His gifts according to His own purposes rather than according to our expectations. He has plans for us: He wants to make us holy. More than anything else He wants to glorify Jesus Christ, and so He wants to make us Christlike. Consequently, He is deeply grieved by our sin and by our flippance and self-centeredness, for un-Christlike Christians do not glorify Jesus Christ.

The Holy Spirit has His own set of priorities for us, and He is absolutely committed to achieving His goal of bringing all those whom Christ has saved to real personal holiness, no matter what the cost. He loves us with the toughest of loves. He is God, and He is a Person. It is an awesome thing to be indwelt by such a One as this. Are we daily conscious of the real meaning of what we believe?

The Spirit Distinct from Father and Son

The third foundational fact about the Holy Spirit is that He is not the same Person as the Father or the Son. Many Christians become confused at this point. It is when this fact is combined with the first two, along with the realization that there is and can be only one God, that the doctrine of the Trinity becomes necessary. But Matthew 3:16–17 makes this clear.

> And after being baptized, Jesus went up immediately from the water; and behold, the heavens were opened, and he saw the Spirit of God descending as a dove, and coming upon Him, and behold, a voice out of the heavens, saying, "This is My beloved Son, in whom I am well-pleased."

Here we have the three Persons clearly distinguished: the Son coming up out of the water, the Spirit descending, and the Father speaking from Heaven. Other passages make similar distinctions, showing the necessity of holding to three separate and distinct persons in the Godhead: The Father gives the Son and begets Him as well (John 3:16); the Spirit leads the Son (Matt. 4:1); and the Father and the Son send the Spirit (John 15:26). The Son prays to the Father many times. Such interactions between the Persons are not presented by Scripture as a charade; when Jesus prayed to the Father He was not just talking to Himself. When Jesus sends the Spirit He is not just talking about coming to us Himself. For the Spirit to come, Jesus had to go away (John 16:7). And when Jesus returns it will not be like the coming of the Spirit but in like manner as the disciples saw Him go; in the meantime they were to wait for the Spirit (Acts 1:4–11).

We see then why the ancient church was driven to formulate the perplexing doctrine of the Trinity: Nothing less could accommodate all the facts. And we also see why this teaching is essential to Christianity. For if we give up the Trinity, the plan of salvation comes apart. Our salvation depends on God's becoming a man to die for our sins. How could this be if God were a simple monotheistic deity like Allah? If the Godhead had died when Jesus died, the universe would have immediately ceased to exist. If the whole Godhead had taken on the limitations of human nature in the Incarnation, how could God be present in the lives of all His people at once? Simple monotheism is just too simple. Only the Tri-unity of the God of the Bible allows for human beings to be saved by Christ and united to Him by His Spirit.

The doctrine of the Trinity may be incomprehensible, but accepting it allows us to comprehend everything else—including the Person and work of the Holy Spirit. For unless Jesus can send the Spirit to us, the whole plan of salvation simply cannot work.

Spirit as Functionally Subordinate to Father and Son

This brings us to the fourth important fact regarding who the Holy Spirit is. The Holy Spirit is God; He is a Person; He is not the Father or the Son; finally, His role is functionally subordinate to that of the Father and the Son. This assertion may seem at first to contradict the previously established truth that the Holy Spirit is God. How can God be subordinate to anything? But before we jump to conclusions, let's see what the Bible has to say.

The subordination of the Spirit is the place where we really begin to understand His function and role in God's work in our lives. The Spirit proceeds from the Father and is sent or poured out by the Son (John 15:26; Acts 2:33). Without controversy, the lesser is sent by the greater. If the president of the United States cannot attend the funeral or wedding of the leader of another nation, he may send the vice-president as his representative. The vice-president does not send the president. This illustration represents the relational roles of the Son and the Spirit.

Because He has permanently taken on our human nature in the Incarnation, the Son cannot be personally present with believers all around the world at the same time. That personal presence now involves a physical presence in His resurrection body. That is why Jesus said that it was to our advantage that He go away; through His personal Agent and Representative, the Holy Spirit, Jesus is now intimately present in the lives of each of His followers (John 16:7).

The Holy Spirit is the personal Agent and Representative of Jesus Christ, who serves the Lord by representing Him in the lives of His people between His ascension and His return. The Spirit is just as much God as Jesus is, and He is equal to Him in essence, power, glory, and honor; but He voluntarily adopts a lower position of service because of His love for the Son and His desire to see Him glorified. The Holy Spirit is equal to the Father and the Son in being or essence, but subordinate to them in function because of love. That, in brief, is the doctrine of subordination in the Trinity.

It is of the utmost importance that we understand this glad submission in equality exemplified by the Holy Spirit. As we will see in the next chapter, this is the key to understanding every aspect of His ministry, and it is a tremendous example to us as we seek to serve the Lord.

It is hard for our secular age to understand how God can set up an order of authority in which, for example, the husband receives headship in the home, without implying a difference in honor, value or worth between husband and wife in particular, or men and women in general. (Scholars debate the precise range of meaning possible for the word translated "head" in Eph. 5:23, but there is no doubt that, in context, a leadership role is being discussed.) God had no problem with such an order at all, for He models for us, at the Trinitarian heart of His Being, that there is no conflict whatsoever between submission and equality. If we could grasp this principle in our homes and in our churches we would go a long way toward realizing that oneness in the Spirit which Paul often urged on the churches under his charge.

Summary

The Holy Spirit is the third Person of the Trinity, God, and the personal Agent of Jesus Christ sent by Him to us as His Representative, whose work is essential to salvation and indispensable to the Christian life. In the next chapter we will examine more closely the nature of His commission as Jesus' Agent, sent to complete and apply Jesus' work in the lives of His people.

Questions for Further Study

1. We developed the doctrine of the Trinity from New Testament affirmations about the Holy Spirit. Make a similar outline of passages which would show how the affirmations about the Son lead to the same conclusions.

2. Look up words like *God, Trinity, Holy Spirit*, etc. in a good theological dictionary (*New Dictionary of Theology, Evangelical Dictionary of Theology, Moody Handbook of Theology*, etc.). How does what you learn there fit in to our discussion?

3. The early church fathers were driven to formulate the doctrine of the Trinity when they approached biblical teaching about Christ with two assumptions: (a) Every statement about Jesus in the Bible is true; (b) None of these statements is contradictory. Are these assumptions still valid for doing theology today? Why or why not? What are the consequences of giving them up?

4. Can you explain in simple terms

    A. The concept of the Trinity?

    B. The evidence for the Trinity

    C. The relevance of the Trinity for theology and Christian living?

5. Look up the words *procession* and *Filioque* in a good theological dictionary. You will see them often in more technical discussions. How do they fit into our discussion in this chapter?

2

HE SHALL GLORIFY ME

The Holy Spirit is responsible for many operations in the whole plan of God's work for the glory of His Son and the salvation of His people. It is the Holy Spirit who inspired Scripture, who illumines the minds and enlightens the hearts of believers as they read it, who convicts of sin, regenerates the believing sinner, sanctifies him, and keeps him for final salvation. The Holy Spirit also indwells believers, empowers them for service, helps them to pray, seals them as the earnest of their inheritance, and equips them for service with spiritual gifts. He brings forth in their lives the fruit of love, joy peace . . . (Gal. 5:22–23). Some of these categories may overlap—there may be more than one way of describing the same ministry in some cases. Still it is apparent that the work of the Holy Spirit involves a varied and perhaps confusing array of jobs.

Before we attempt to examine the different facets of His work, it will be useful to try and see it as a whole. We are less likely to become bewildered if we can see the forest before we encounter the intricacies of the trees. So we must ask: Is there in Scripture a unifying perspective, a general principle which governs every aspect of the Spirit's work? Several New Testament passages which present, as it were, a summary of His commission suggest that there is.

The Spirit's Mission

The Gospel of John records more of Jesus' teaching about the Spirit He was to send than any other Gospel, and some of those passages speak of His work in general terms. One of the most important for our purposes is John 16:13–15.

> When He, the Spirit of truth, comes, He will guide you into all the truth; for He will not speak on His own initiative, but whatever He hears, He will speak; and He will disclose to you what is to come. He shall glorify Me; for He shall take of Mine, and shall disclose it to you. All things that the Father has are Mine; therefore I said, that He takes of Mine, and will disclose it to you.

The Spirit who is to come will not act for Himself, but for the One who has sent Him. His primary mission will be to glorify the Lord Jesus Christ, and the primary way He will do that is by communicating to Jesus' disciples that which He receives from Jesus. The Spirit seems to be essentially an Emissary of Jesus Christ, representing Him in His absence (v. 7). And He is the ideal Emissary. Being God, He is omnipresent, always available to those to whom He is sent; He never says anything except what He is told to say; and everything He does honors and glorifies the One who sent Him.

We get a similar perspective in John 14:16–18.

> I will ask the Father, and He will give you another Helper, that He may be with you forever; that is the Spirit of truth, whom the world cannot receive, because it does not behold Him or know Him, but you know Him because He abides with you, and will be in you. I will not leave you as orphans; I will come to you.

Again, what is emphasized here is the Spirit's role as Representative, Deputy, or Agent. Christ is going away to prepare a place for us (vv. 2–3), but we are not to worry—in the meantime He will send another Helper. The idea is that this Helper will take Christ's place until He returns. And He will be a replacement like the original. Greek has two different words which can be translated "another," one of which is used when the other is of a different nature, and one of which is used when the other is another of the same kind. (You see both words in Gal. 1:6–7, where Paul spoke of a "different [*heteros*] gospel" which is "really not another [*allos*]" one at all.) It is the second word which is used here in John 14:16: Jesus' stand-in will be Another of the same kind as He is Himself, One who is able to represent Him perfectly—so well in fact that Jesus says we will actually be better off under the new arrangement (John 16:7).

Another passage which speaks of the same basic idea, but in different words, is John 7:37–39. On the last day of the feast, Jesus cried out,

> "If any man is thirsty, let him come to Me and drink. He who believes in Me, as the Scripture said, 'From his innermost being shall flow rivers of living water.'" But this He spoke of the Spirit, whom those who believed in Him were to receive; for the Spirit was not yet given, because Jesus was not yet glorified.

In chapter 6, Jesus had just given His famous "bread of life" discourse, in which salvation is described in terms of eating His flesh and drinking His blood. The full meaning of this symbolic language is difficult to grasp, but clearly it speaks of Jesus Himself as the source of eternal and spiritual life. Now the invitation to that life is still presented in terms of thirst, a thirst which will be quenched abundantly by the Holy Spirit from within. Since Jesus Himself has already been established as the Source of life, what the Spirit ministers to the soul in these living rivers must in some sense be the Lord Jesus Christ, who is made abundantly present by the communication of His Spirit. Note also that, once again, the connection is made between the Spirit's being given and Jesus' being glorified. It is not certain whether "glorified" here refers to the crucifixion, the resurrection, the ascension of Christ, or perhaps all three. He received glory in all three before the Spirit came. The point is that everything about the Spirit's coming centers on the glory of Christ, which is both the prerequisite and the purpose of the Spirit's ministry: "He shall glorify Me."

Five Summary Statements

We can summarize the teaching of these pages in five brief sentences, five propositions which will give us a convenient handle on the essence of the Holy Spirit's ministry.

To Glorify Jesus

The ministry of the Holy Spirit is to glorify Jesus Christ. This is basic to everything that He does, and there is nothing He does which does not contribute to this overarching goal.

To Be Jesus' Personal Agent

The work of the Holy Spirit is to act as the personal Representative, Deputy, Envoy, or Agent of Jesus Christ, carrying out Christ's work in His absence. An envoy does the work of the one who sent him, not a different work of his own. The Holy Spirit is not a free-lance operator.

To Unite Us to Jesus

The work of the Holy Spirit is to serve as the link between Jesus Christ and His people until the second coming. The Spirit is the Agent who effects and is the Medium of our personal union with Christ during this age.

To Apply Salvation

The way in which the Holy Spirit glorifies Christ and carries out His mission is by taking the blessings and gifts won and purchased by Jesus on the cross and applying or communicating them to our hearts.

To Make Jesus Real to Us

The ministry of the Holy Spirit is, finally, to make Jesus real to us. Is that not the central difference between the Christian and the non-believer? To the average person Jesus is just an idea; the unbeliever hears the gospel, but the gospel is just words and ideas to be debated. For some people, however, the idea that *I* have sinned and really deserve to go to hell and Jesus died for *me* hits home. Faith becomes not just a casual and flippant response to an idea, but a life-or-death issue, a real commitment to a real Person. These people are true Christians, and the difference between them and the others is the work of the Holy Spirit in their lives, making Jesus real to them. Thus the Spirit brings glory to His name.

Implications of the Spirit's Mission

This understanding of the underlying purpose and nature of the Holy Spirit's mission has several interesting implications for our further study of His ministry.

For Our Theology of the Spirit

In the first place, it is important to see that the Spirit is the key to understanding each and every aspect of Christ's work. The work of the Spirit is not something different or extra added on to the work of Christ for our salvation; it simply *is* the work of Christ, carried on in His name and on His behalf by His officially appointed Representative. Whether we speak of inspiration, illumination, conviction, calling, regeneration, sanctification, or whatever, the question we must constantly ask is, "How does the Spirit's activity here carry on the work begun by Christ? How does it glorify Christ by making Jesus real to us even in His physical absence?"

It seems to me that the failure to keep this perspective constantly before us—indeed, to make it our central concern—has been the greatest weakness in all our discussion of the Spirit's work on both sides of the charismatic issue. I believe that restoring it to a central place in our study of the doctrine of the Spirit and His work throughout will be the source of our deepest insights as we proceed. It is the key that opens the whole topic like nothing else.

For Hermeneutics

A second important realization as we study the Scriptures is that if the work of the Holy Spirit has the kind of character we have been indicating, it follows that the Holy Spirit does not have to be specifically mentioned in order to be involved in the work described as applier and communicator. What Jesus does in this age of the world, He does by His personal Agent, the

Holy Spirit; and what the Spirit does, He does for Jesus Christ. If the general principle is sound, then the involvement of the Spirit in Christ's work may legitimately be inferred even if it is not specifically mentioned in a given passage. The Holy Spirit is the One in general who applies the things of God to our hearts and makes them real in our lives.

For Spiritual Discernment

The third implication which flows from an understanding of the general character of the Spirit's work is if any teaching, experience, or practice does not glorify Jesus Christ, it is not of the Holy Spirit, and consequently it is not of God. The question is: Where is the primary focus? When a gift is practiced in such a way that our attention is primarily focused on the gift itself, or the people who do or do not have it—when certain kinds of experiences become an end in themselves—when teaching finds its unity and constant theme in anything other than Jesus Christ, including even the work of the Holy Spirit Himself—in such cases the people of God are entitled to be suspicious. The existence of such problems does not in and of itself invalidate the particular gifts or experiences being claimed. However, it does cast severe doubt on the validity of the claims in the particular instance in question, for the Holy Spirit is not in the business of hindering His own ministry.

Failure in the final analysis to glorify Jesus Christ and keep Him in the center of our thoughts is evidence of counterfeit spirituality. We must be slow to judge in specific cases because many factors—immaturity, lack of sound teaching, confusion, pride—can dim the glory of Christ in work the Spirit may actually be doing. Which of us could ever claim that his or her own work and teaching is ever totally free from all such imperfections? But if our spiritual experience does not glorify the Son, it is not of the Spirit.

Conclusion

The understanding of the work of the Holy Spirit to which we are coming tells us something of how important the Spirit's ministry should be to us. It is of the utmost interest to us precisely because we are Christ-centered people. If the ministry of the Holy Spirit is to glorify Jesus Christ—to communicate to us that which He has purchased for us with His blood, to bring us into fellowship with Him, to make Him real to us—then disciples of Jesus Christ have the highest possible personal stake in that work. To the extent that we love Jesus, we will value the ministry of the Holy Spirit. Let us therefore pursue these studies with all diligence, in a spirit of prayer and dependence on Him.

Questions for Further Study

1. Can you state the general principle of the Holy Spirit's ministry in one sentence? in five?

2. What are some practical benefits of understanding the general principle behind the Spirit's work? Can you think of others not mentioned here?

3. How can it be better for Jesus' disciples for Him to go away (John 16:7)?

3

THE HOLY SPIRIT
AND INSPIRATION

The Spirit of Christ Within Them

A systematic study of the work of the Holy Spirit in the lives of New Testament believers must early deal with the inspiration of Scripture, for that aspect of His work precedes all the others both logically and (in the case of believers alive today) temporally. Every other aspect of His work we will study is one in which He is still engaged, but the inspiration of Scripture is a job He has finished once and for all. And the inspiration of Scripture is also the basis for the rest of the work the Spirit does in the church, for the Bible is the primary means He employs in everything else that He does.

The work of the Spirit in general is to glorify Jesus Christ; to act as His personal Representative/Deputy/Agent and carry on His work in His absence; to serve as the link/liaison between Christ and His people until the second coming; to take the blessings purchased by Christ on the cross and communicate or apply them to the hearts of His followers; to make Jesus real to us. In the inspiration of Scripture, the second of those summary statements is the one which is most immediately applicable, though all of them will apply before we are done. The place to begin the doctrine of inspiration is to ask, "What is the ministry of Jesus Christ in the area of truth?" Whatever it is, the work of the Holy Spirit in inspiration is simply an extension and particular application of that ministry of Jesus Christ.

Jesus' Work of Revelation

The idea of Jesus playing a key role in God's work of revealing Himself to mankind is a theological commonplace, but one which deserves attention. The work of Christ is traditionally summarized in the three offices of Prophet, Priest, and King. As Prophet He is God's ultimate and final Spokesman and Revealer. As Priest He made atonement for our sins through His blood and lives to make intercession for us. As King He rules at the right hand of the Father.

The author of the Epistle to the Hebrews tells us that God, after speaking to us in the ancient prophets in many ways, has in these last days spoken to us in His Son (Heb. 1:1–2), who is the "radiance of His glory and the exact representation of His nature" (v. 3). The Gospels stress the fact that representing and revealing the Father was one of the primary functions the Lord fulfilled in His earthly ministry. He claimed that "he who beholds Me beholds the One who sent Me" (John 12:45) and that "He who has seen Me has seen the Father" (John 14:9). In other words, Jesus revealed God to human beings just by being who He was: if you want to know what God is like, look at Jesus. But He also revealed God to us by what He said. In His high-priestly prayer He told the Father that "I have given them [the disciples] Thy word" (John 17:14). Then in Luke 24:44–45 we have a summary of Christ's ministry as Prophet and ultimate Spokesman and Revelation of God:

> "These are My words which I spoke to you while I was still with you, that all things which are written about Me in the Law of Moses and the Prophets and the Psalms must be fulfilled." Then He opened their minds to understand the Scriptures.

Here we have two distinct ministries connected with the impartation of God's truth: *revelation*, the giving of His Word, and *illumination*, helping us understand it. Both are supremely the ministry of Jesus Christ.

The Spirit's Role in Jesus' Work of Revelation

Jesus came to reveal God to us: His nature, His will, His ways, His purposes, His plan of salvation, His promises. And being Himself the exact representation of God's nature and the ultimate expression of His purpose, Jesus did a perfect job of it, the best that could ever be done. But it was not a job that He finished during His time on earth. His words and deeds would have to be recorded for future generations in an accurate, trustworthy, and permanent manner. The meaning of His death, burial, and resurrection would need further explanation, elaboration, and application to meet the needs of the church which would be founded after His departure.

If the job of revelation He had begun was to be completed, the end product would have to be completely authoritative and trustworthy so that His followers could refer to it with confidence as the basis of their faith as long as the earth endured. In order to accomplish this great work, Jesus commissioned the apostles to be His special spokesmen, empowered to speak for Him as He spoke for the Father. And to enable them to carry out their humanly impossible task, He promised them the aid of the same Spirit who had inspired the prophets of old when they laid down the preliminary Scriptures as the preparation for His coming. These promises are recorded in John 14:26 and 16:13, and the product of the Spirit's labors through those apostles (with a little help under their auspices from Luke and Mark) was the New Testament, which still allows the Father to be revealed through the Son to this day.

The Spirit's Role: Inspiration

The next question we must ask is, "What is the exact nature of the Holy Spirit's work through the apostles (and prophets before them) that enabled them to complete the work of Jesus Christ in revealing God to us?" The classic text which answers that question is obviously 2 Timothy 3:16: "All Scripture is inspired by God. . . ." The word translated "inspired" is the Greek word *theopneustos*, which means literally "God-breathed." To be inspired is to be breathed, or spoken, by God. And grammatically, what is inspired is properly not the mind of the apostle or prophet, but the writings, that is, the words produced by means of those minds. Therefore, we may define inspiration as that work of the Holy Spirit by which He produced the Word of God using human minds as instruments, so guiding, influencing, and superintending their activity that the words they wrote were the very words of God. That is why the *words* of Scripture—the language, the grammar, the context—are so important to us; the words, not just the thoughts of their writers, are an effect produced by the Spirit of God Himself.

The Bible has a great deal to say about the relationship between the Holy Spirit and the words of Scripture which can help us fully understand the doctrine of inspiration. David, the psalmist, said that "the Spirit of the Lord [literally, the Spirit of Yahweh] spoke by me, and His word was on my tongue" (2 Sam. 23:2). Isaiah claimed the same kind of inspiration in Isaiah 51:16 when he recorded the Lord's saying to him, "I have put My words in your mouth." In Scripture God speaks through the language of His human servant; specifically the Spirit of God puts God's words in the mouths of men; and He does this in the Old Testament no less than the New.

Beyond doubt, the apostles viewed the Old Testament as having been spoken by the Holy Spirit in order to reveal Jesus Christ. Peter noted that the Scripture "which the Holy Spirit foretold by the mouth of David" had to be fulfilled; the Spirit's activity in its inspiration gave it a kind of necessary truth (Acts 1:16). The whole Jerusalem Church had the same view of the Old Testament as shown by the way they refer to it in Acts 4:25. Examples could be multiplied (Heb. 3:7; 9:8; 10:15) to show that the early Christians viewed the words of the Old Testament to be the very words of God through the Holy Spirit, all pointing inexorably to Jesus Christ.

Casual references, which reveal that faith, appear on almost every page of the New Testament; and the apostles also make it a matter of explicit teaching. Paul's statement of the doctrine in 2 Timothy 3:16 has already been mentioned. Peter also has two fascinating summaries. In 1 Peter 1:10–11 he told us that it was "the Spirit of Christ within them" who predicted "the sufferings of Christ and the glories to follow." Then in 2 Peter 1:20–21 he laid down the principle that "no prophecy of Scripture is a matter of one's own interpretation" because those prophecies cannot be accounted for by human nature alone. Rather, "men moved by the Holy Spirit spoke from God."

The Product of Inspiration: Scripture

This Spirit Christ promised to His apostles would enable them to complete the task of writing down the revelation begun in the Old Testament and culminating in the life, death, and resurrection of the Lord Jesus Christ Himself. One would expect that, with Christ now having been revealed in all His glory, the Spirit of Christ would speak of Him and for Him no less wonderfully and infallibly through the writings of His apostles now than He had done through His prophets of old. Their writings would be Scripture, like the writings of Moses, David, and the prophets—words spoken by the Holy Spirit Himself, and therefore the very words of God. And this is not just a reasonable expectation; it is a historical fact.

Peter, referring to the letters of Paul, clearly classed them with "the rest of the Scriptures" in 2 Peter 3:16. And that is the way the church has received the New Testament to this day, as books which fulfill Jesus' mission of revealing God to us in a way which simply cannot be accounted for on the basis of human literary and theological genius alone. They have impressed themselves on the minds of God's people by the sheer weight of glory inscribed on their pages by their divine Author as works uniquely inspired, absolutely authoritative, and wholly trustworthy, full of the glory of God in the face of Jesus Christ.

The Mode of Inspiration

"But *how*," the question comes irresistibly to our minds, "did the Holy Spirit accomplish this work of inspiration?" Did Paul, Peter, Mark, Luke, and John go into a trance as the Holy Spirit took over their writing hands? Did they simply act as secretaries to the Spirit, writing down the words He dictated to them? How else could the Spirit guarantee the inerrancy of what they wrote? In fact, we seem to have given the impression that we hold to such a naive view of inspiration, to judge by the straw men some opponents of inerrancy argue against.

If we had been left to ourselves to produce a human writing which was the Word of God, that is probably how we would do it: by having the Spirit employ what is usually called "mechanical dictation." But no one who is at all familiar with the Bible should ever imagine that it was written mechanically. The diverse personalities of the human authors are as evident on every page as the majesty and unity of the content. Mark and Luke have different approaches to telling a story; Matthew and John manifest different interests as they select from their memories of Jesus' sayings. Paul and James have different theological concerns; and each one has his own individual vocabulary and style. Yet these highly individual writers produced a collection of books which display a unity of spirit and content which simply cannot be explained apart from the other single Mind which was also at work. What the Holy Spirit did in the inspiration of Scripture was something far more marvelous and mysterious than we ever would have guessed.

Fortunately, we have statements from the human authors which tell us what it was like to write inspired Scripture. The most detailed passage is found in 2 Peter 1:13–21, and it deserves to be quoted in full.

> I consider it right, as long as I am in this earthly dwelling, to stir you up by way of reminder, knowing that the laying aside of my earthly dwelling is imminent, as also our Lord Jesus Christ has made clear to me. And I will also be diligent that at any time after my departure you may be able to call these things to mind. For we did not follow cleverly devised tales when we made known to you the power and coming of our Lord Jesus Christ, but we were eyewitnesses of His majesty. For when He received honor and glory from God the Father, such an utterance as this was made to Him by the Majestic Glory, "This is My beloved Son with whom I am well-pleased,"—and we ourselves heard this utterance made from heaven when we were with Him on the holy mountain. And so we have the prophetic word made more sure, to which you do well to pay attention as to a lamp shining in a dark place, until the day dawns and

the morning star arises in your hearts. But know this first of all, that no prophecy of Scripture is a matter of one's own interpretation, for no prophecy was ever made by an act of human will, but men moved by the Holy Spirit spoke from God.

Peter here ascribed the highest authority to his own writings, not simply by claiming that they represent the testimony of an eyewitness, but by associating them with the Old Testament prophets. In those writings the human will was not finally determinative, but holy men spoke from God as they were moved by the Holy Spirit. That in itself should make us sure enough, but the things Peter saw and wrote about make the prophetic word even more sure. There is implied here what logicians call an *a fortiori* argument: if the Holy Spirit's inspiration of the old Scriptures made the message of the prophets "sure," then how much more trustworthy is the testimony of the eyewitnesses to the fulfillment of those predictions? If the Old Testament was a lamp, the New is the dawning of daylight itself; and even of the Old we can say that the Holy Spirit determined what was said.

Inspiration: The Human Factor

Yet, as Peter wrote these words, with an inspiration like unto or greater than that characteristic of the Old Testament implied, he was fully conscious of the fact that *he*, Peter, was doing the writing. He was conscious of a set of perfectly reasonable motives: the fact that the original eyewitnesses were dying and there was a need for their message to be preserved in more permanent form. He was aware of the effort involved. He intended to be diligent in the performance of his task. And he was conscious of the source of his information: not the Holy Spirit immediately in some kind of dictation, but his own memory as an eyewitness. Writing Scripture felt like work, in which Peter's own mind was fully engaged. The Holy Spirit inspired the words Peter was writing, not by circumventing Peter, but by using his mind, will, and concern for the church.

Luke confirmed this view of the mechanism of inspiration in the insights he gave us into the composition of his Gospel. He told us that he did research into the life of Christ (1:3). He "carefully investigated" everything from the beginning, probably interviewing Mary and the other original surviving disciples and participants in the events during the course of his travels with Paul.

Perhaps one of the most interesting statements of the relationship between the Holy Spirit and the human authors of Scripture is David's in 2 Samuel 23:2: "The Spirit of the Lord spoke by me, and His word was on my tongue." David was from the tribe of Judah, which settled in the southern part of Palestine and later became the heart of what we call the Southern Kingdom after the secession of the ten northern tribes. So when David recited his psalms, the Holy Spirit spoke with a particular accent: His word was on David's tongue! And not only David, but every biblical writer had his own individual style which easily can be recognized by real connoisseurs of the biblical text. Paul's long sentences, piling subordinate clause upon subordinate clause; Mark's simple and straightforward narrative punch; Luke's Greek, flowing with almost classical elegance; John's unique blend of the profoundest thought and the simplest language; God through the Holy Spirit breathed out the very words of Scripture in the unique personal idiom of each of these men, not bypassing or overriding, but using their peculiar personalities as the vehicle for divine revelation.

The Spirit's Contribution

This mysterious manner of working is one which is characteristic of the Spirit's approach to other areas of His ministry as well. It forms a pattern we will see again and again: The Spirit works through concrete human personalities in such a way that those personalities are not suppressed or submerged in the process, but rather are maintained inviolable in their integrity. To bring a sinner to repentance, the Spirit has to bring about a radical change in that sinner's will. Somehow He does it, not against the sinner's will, but through it. He does not make you repent against your will but He enables your will to repent. In sanctification He conforms you to the image of Jesus Christ, and in order to do that He must transform your personality. But somehow in the process your unique personality is not lost. The unique traits which make you different from all God's other children are not flattened out, but enhanced, as the Spirit brings you into conformity with Jesus Christ. Holiness makes you free to be the unique self you were meant to be.

Is this not a great mystery: that the path to true individuality should be conformity to Christ? Yet such is the work of the Holy Spirit in our lives. And there is a reason behind the mystery, for the infinite excellence of the character of Christ could never be cloned in one finite human being. The Holy Spirit is working to glorify Jesus Christ by creating a vast number of portraits of Him, each one specially designed to bring out some aspect of His majesty and beauty which no other can capture quite as well. Together the saints will be a grand reflection of the glory of the Son, bringing out the infinite beauty of His glory and grace to angels and archangels, cherubim and seraphim—and to one another—for all eternity (Eph. 1:10; 3:8–11). Nothing less than this is the goal of all the Holy Spirit's work, and nothing less than this is the destiny of every true child of God who is redeemed by the Son and regenerated and indwelt by the Spirit.

But to return to the doctrine of inspiration: if the human writer used his own will, energy, memory, and style, and wrote out of his own motives, and if his own personality comes through unimpeded in what he wrote, the obvious question which comes next is, what difference did the inspiration of the Holy Spirit actually make in the whole process?

David told us in Psalms 12:6 that "the words of the Lord are pure words; as silver tried in a furnace on the earth, refined seven times." Inspiration removes the dross of sin and error that would otherwise be inevitably and inextricably mixed in with any extended writing by fallen people. The picture is that of the refining of silver ore by fire, and the number seven is the Hebrew symbolic number of perfection. So David is saying that the ore of Scripture has been perfectly refined, completely puri-fied. David wrote his own words, and they were truly his; but when he wrote under inspiration they were also truly the Spirit's. The Spirit so guided, moved, and supervised the natural processes of David's mind that, when the finished product was on the page and in the canon of Scripture, it was exactly as the Spirit desired. The same can be said of each of the other biblical authors. They were fallen and imperfect; but when they wrote Scripture, their words were perfectly refined and purified of all error by a mysterious process wrought by the Spirit of God. Therefore, it was the Spirit of the Lord who spoke by them, and God's words which were on their tongues.

Effects of Inspiration

While the first quality given to Scripture by the Holy Spirit's role in its production is purity of content, the second is usefulness. Since the words of Scripture are inspired by the Holy Spirit, since all human imperfection has been removed so that they can be said to have been breathed out by God Himself, and since they are in fact not just words about God but God's words, then they are by that very fact the most relevant words to the human condition ever written. Nothing is more needful to be known than what the Scriptures can tell us, for they are the key to meaning, purpose, and fulfillment for us. That is why Paul, after asserting their inspiration in 2 Timothy 3:16, drew the conclusion that they are therefore profitable for teaching, reproof, correction, and training in righteousness. It was the Spirit of God within those holy men who was the ultimate source and guarantor of both the truth and relevance of what they said. And every word of it draws our attention, in one way or another, to the glory of God in the face of Jesus Christ.

Implications of Inspiration:
The Trustworthiness of Scripture

There are some tremendous practical implications of the biblical teaching about the work of the Holy Spirit in the inspiration of Scripture. Surely the first is that we should have great confidence in the trustworthiness of the Bible in all that it teaches. To the extent that we understand what the Bible says, we understand what God says, and the words of Scripture therefore have God's authority behind them. We should obey the teachings of the Bible just as we would the Lord Jesus Christ Himself if He appeared to us in bodily form and spoke to us, for its words were inspired by His personal Representative and Agent, the Holy Spirit. Therefore, we should believe its teachings and obey its commands as if they were the very words of His mouth. This does not mean that there will never be any apparent errors or contradictions in the text. But many of the ones alleged evaporate once we come to the text without a bias against the supernatural, and the few remaining problems have at least a possible resolution. The bottom line is that if we believe in the Lordship of Christ we must also accept the authority of His chosen Spokesman, the Holy Spirit; and if we believe He did anything like what the inspired biblical authors describe, then the text must always be given the benefit of the doubt.

Is it intellectually dishonest to insist that the text of Scripture always be given the benefit of the doubt? Not at all. It would be arrogant, not to say dishonest, to claim that in our present state of knowledge we are able to solve every problem the text presents, reconcile every seeming contradiction, and adequately explain every apparent discrepancy. The doctrine of inerrancy does not rest on our ability to do so, but on the teaching of Scripture concerning the nature and extent of inspiration, the authority of Jesus in words inspired by His personal Agent, the Spirit.

In a book so old, so large, and so complex, it is not surprising that there are some things we are unable to explain. But because we trust Jesus and His Emissary the Spirit, because Scripture teaches that its words are inspired by that Spirit, because we have found it to be generally trustworthy where we can independently verify it, and because we have seen so many acclaimed "errors" disappear before increased knowledge, we are justified in adopting a firm policy of always ascribing whatever problems we encounter to our own limited understanding rather than to the text itself. It seems to us that to confidently speak of Scripture as erring is just as dishonest (for a believer) as to claim that the text presents us with no problems. We are inerrantists because, in the light of the whole doctrine of inspiration, to speak of errors in Scripture seems to manifest an arrogance toward the Spirit unbecoming in followers of the Son.

The Applicability of Scripture

Christians should have great confidence in the applicability of Scripture. Paul stressed that inspiration makes the Scripture profitable (2 Tim. 3:16). The Holy Spirit did not inspire the text for nothing. If God saw fit to exert His mysterious supernatural power in order to inspire Scripture so that it could reveal Jesus Christ, we must believe that every word in the text is not only true but also useful. That is exactly what Paul said: "All Scripture is inspired . . . and therefore profitable." Consequently, the doctrine of inspiration means that the relevance of Scripture is axiomatic. If we cannot see the relevance of a particular text or teaching to our lives, it is up to us to keep digging. We have already seen how a seemingly abstract and esoteric doctrine like the Trinity has astoundingly practical implications for salvation and for personal relationships. The same is true for every teaching and every book of the Bible because it was inspired by the Holy Spirit.

The Sufficiency of Scripture

The inspiration of Scripture by the Holy Spirit should give us great confidence not only in its accuracy and its applicability, but also its adequacy. Scripture is inspired and therefore profitable so that "the man of God may be adequate, equipped for every good work" (2 Tim. 3:17). We sing a chorus which says "Christ is all I need," and if God reveals Himself by giving us Jesus Christ, and Christ is what the Scriptures are all about, and if the Spirit so inspired them that they reveal Him perfectly, then it follows that there is nothing lacking in the Bible which we need to know in order to find our ultimate purpose and fulfillment. It is not the only book we need, or the only one we should read. However, there is nothing we need to know in order to be saved, to please the Father, or to glorify the Son, which is not adequately revealed in its pages. But it also follows that in order to be the adequate and equipped servant Paul described, we need the whole Book. Mature believers with a good understanding of the Holy Spirit's work of inspiration are characterized by a concern for the whole counsel of God and a hearty appetite for the meat of the Word.

The Study of Scripture

Since a full and accurate understanding of the Bible is such a pressing need, it is well that the doctrine of inspiration also gives us some excellent practical guidance in how to approach the task of Bible study. The Bible is, as we have seen, both like and unlike other books. It was written in normal human language by people who used the normal processes of composition and employed the normal grammatical constructions, figures of speech, and techniques of rhetoric used by other writers of their day. In this, the Bible is a book like any other. But the Holy Spirit so guided these writers that all error and imperfection were refined out, and they were led into all the truth as they wrote. Their words are the very words God wanted written to convey His Word to all people. In this, the Bible is unlike any other book. Both of these facts must be kept constantly in mind as we study the Bible, for they mean that its interpretation must also be pursued in a manner both like and unlike the approach we use to any other book.

The object of inspiration was the words, through the instrumentality of the human mind of the author. In other words, the only way an interpreter of Scripture has of knowing what the author of a biblical text meant is by analyzing what he wrote. You examine the choice of words, the use of grammar, the literary and historical context, the style, and the presence of any figures of speech or structural devices. These are the only clues we have as to what any given text means. In this, the study of the Bible is like the study of any other piece of literature. So to say that the Holy Spirit inspired the words, and that in those words he let the personality, style, and interests of the human author come through, is to say that in the Bible the Holy Spirit says what the grammar and context say when all other factors are taken into consideration—nothing more and nothing less. The Spirit chose to speak through concrete texts written by concrete people who chose specific combinations of words, and in our interpretation we must honor that choice. But doesn't He super-

THE HOLY SPIRIT AND INSPIRATION

naturally illumine our minds as we read those texts? Yes, of course. That is the subject of our next chapter. But He never does it apart from the text which he originally inspired. To suggest that the Spirit says to us anything beyond what the words say is to exalt His work of illumination by impugning His competence in inspiration, which seems a rather self-defeating way of honoring Him. Let us rather strive to be honest interpreters of the words He actually gave us.

So the interpretation of Scripture is like that of any other book; but it is also very different. Some of the differences will be best discussed when we come to illumination in the next chapter, but there is one which we can mention here. We have no right to dissent from the teaching of Scripture at any point, because its words are not just the words of human beings but the words of God. And this fact is a most useful tool for interpretation, for any interpretation which causes one passage of Scripture to contradict another is one we can with confidence reject. It gives us a most useful check on our interpretation which we do not have in other books; the interpretation which says that a human author has contradicted himself just might be correct. Everything the Bible says, on the other hand, is assuredly true.

The Importance of Scripture

Jesus Christ is the ultimate revelation of God and the ultimate source of all life, meaning, and purpose. His work of revealing the nature, will, and plan of God was completed by His personal representative, the Holy Spirit, in the inspiration of Scripture. Therefore, Scripture is now what reveals Christ to us. The Holy Spirit continues to represent Christ, to act for Him, and to bring Him into the lives of His people. He ministers Christ to the whole person, including mind, emotions, and will—and these can never be completely separated. The connection we have seen between the Spirit and the text of Scripture suggests that both will be intimately involved at every step of that ministry— that, having inspired the Bible to bring Christ into our lives, He will not now normally act apart from Scripture in bringing Christ's life into ours. The Bible will in fact be the primary tool or means used by the Spirit to carry out His mission of making

Jesus real to us, the primary channel through which He brings us into contact with our Lord.

This expectation is confirmed by several explicit statements. How does the Holy Spirit call us to repentance and faith? "Faith comes from hearing, and hearing by the word of Christ" (Rom. 10:17). How does He sanctify us, bringing us into conformity with the character of Christ? "Sanctify them in the truth; Thy word is truth" (John 17:17). How does He give us guidance? "Thy word is a lamp to my feet and a light unto my path" (Ps. 119:105). How does He train and equip us for service? "All Scripture is inspired by God and profitable for teaching, for reproof, for correction, for training in righteousness, that the man of God may be adequate, equipped for every good work" (2 Tim. 3:16–17).

The Holy Spirit did not inspire Scripture for no reason; He inspired it that He might use it. And He uses it as the primary means by which He accomplishes His work of bringing Jesus Christ into our lives and bringing glory thus to Him. Whether it be conviction, calling, sanctification, assurance, or empowering, we will never find the Spirit working without finding that in some way He is using the Word He inspired to accomplish that work. You can read the Bible without knowing the work of the Spirit, but you cannot know the work of the Spirit in your life without finding that He is applying to your heart the message of this great Book He inspired to make known the glories of Christ.

The writer of the Epistle to the Hebrews liked to quote the Old Testament and credit the Holy Spirit as its author. The capstone of the doctrine of inspiration is that he does not use the tense you would expect. Clearly, Moses or David or one of the prophets said these things a long time ago. But the Holy Spirit says them today (Heb. 3:7; 9:8; 10:15). There is an immediacy about it. He was not satisfied simply to ensure that these words would be true, and then leave them in the text for us to take them or leave them. He still works through the text He inspired, and what He said then He says today. He still speaks for the Lord Jesus Christ. Jesus of Nazareth said, "Come to Me, all who are weary and heavy-laden, and I will give you rest" (Matt. 11:28). He said, "The one who comes to Me I will certainly not cast out" (John 6:37). And through the Holy Spirit, He still says these things today when we read them or hear them proclaimed in faith. The deep gap and abyss of time which yawns between us and the first-century Carpenter is obliterated by the Holy Spirit who still speaks for Christ in the words of the text, speaking them directly to the hearts of those who listen with the ears of faith. How does He do that? An excellent question. The answer is called the doctrine of illumination, and it deserves a chapter of its own.

Questions for Further Study

1. Can you give a concise definition of inspiration in your own words?

2. Describe how the Son and the Spirit cooperate to reveal the Father. What does each contribute to this one work?

3. Look up the words *inspiration* and *Scripture* in a good Bible dictionary or encyclopedia; Greek students can look up *theopneustos* and *graphe* in Kittel's *Theological Dictionary of the New Testament* or the *New International Dictionary of New Testament Theology*.

4. Carefully delineate the roles of both the human author and the Holy Spirit in the production of Scripture.

5. In what ways is Scripture both like and unlike other books? How is this question related to the answer to question 4?

6. What are some implications of the doctrine of inspiration for personal Bible study? What changes should you make in your own approach to the Bible as a result?

4

THE HOLY SPIRIT
AND ILLUMINATION

The Holy Spirit did a marvelous thing when He inspired the words of Holy Scripture: to so work through the mind of the human authors that, without doing any violence to their individual wills or personalities, He could lead them to write the very words God wanted to convey His message to humanity. The Bible clearly teaches that He did His job so well that we can accurately call those words the words of God. They are the perfect vehicle for God's purpose of revealing Himself through revealing Jesus Christ. When interpreted naturally in their total linguistic, historical, and literary context, they say exactly what God wanted them to say and can be trusted implicitly to teach only the truth.

Yet this wonderful and miraculous work of inspiration was not enough to achieve God's purpose of bringing us to salvation and to a personal knowledge of His character, will, and glory. Though the words of the Bible are infallible, sufficient, and incapable of being improved on, the process of getting them off the page and into our hearts is more complicated than we might expect. God's purpose for His Word will not be fulfilled until it is inscribed, not on tablets of stone or pages of parchment or paper, but on our hearts (Jer. 31:33). For this transfer to take place, a further work of the Holy Spirit is necessary: the work of illumination.

Definition

Inspiration is that work whereby the Holy Spirit produced the words of Scripture through the mind of the author. Illumination is that work whereby He produces right and helpful understanding of the words of Scripture in the mind and heart of the reader or hearer. In illumination as well as inspiration, the Holy Spirit continues to carry out the work of revelation begun by Jesus Christ, who not only gave His disciples the word of God but also explained it to them. On many occasions He answered their questions about the meaning of His parables, and on one pivotal occasion He "opened their minds to understand the Scriptures" (Luke 24:45). He devoted Himself to that work for forty days between His resurrection and ascension, and He commissioned the Holy Spirit to carry it on in His absence until He returned.

The Need for Illumination

That we should need supernatural aid in understanding the Bible should not be all that strange a notion to us. After all, when we proclaim the Word of God to people, we are asking quite a lot of them. We are asking people whose only experience is of earth to understand heavenly things; we are asking those whose lives are like a wisp of smoke blown away by the wind to understand eternal things; we are asking those whose hearts are desperately evil, deceitful, and corrupted by sin to understand holy things; we are asking human beings whose minds are prodigious breeders of clever plans by which they think to grasp success to accept the grace, the unmerited favor, of God; we are asking those whose every thought is for their own advancement to accept as their highest good the glory of God. Without the aid of the Holy Spirit, what we are asking is nothing short of impossible. That impossibility is explicitly recognized by Scripture: "A natural man does not accept the things of the Spirit of God; for they are foolishness to him, and he cannot understand them, because they are spiritually appraised" (1 Cor. 2:14).

This absolute impossibility of reading or proclaiming the Word of God profitably apart from the work of the Holy Spirit is a truth that needs to be burned deep into the consciousness of every believer, and especially every pastor and Christian worker. The temptation to proceed on our own steam is too insidious and too deadly; nothing saps the church of power for witness and Christian living more than this. It is not possible by the length of time we spend, the correctness of our methodology, the sincerity of our motives, or the intensity of our desire for the truth, to understand and rightly appreciate the teachings of Scripture. It is not possible for our pastors by the clarity of their illustrations, the incisiveness of their logic, the eloquence of their diction, or the power of their rhetoric, to drive home to our hearts these celestial truths. The Holy Spirit will indeed use all these things; but unless He blesses them they are in themselves absolutely impotent. We must learn well the lesson of our dependence on Him. If you are at all like me, it is a lesson you will have to learn and relearn.

Where the Need Does Not Lie

Where, precisely, does this impossibility lie? Of what does it consist? It is helpful, first of all, to see what it does not consist of. It does not, in the first place, flow from any lack of clarity or intelligibility in the biblical text itself. (Though not all texts are equally clear, this is not the ultimate source of the problem.) The Bible is written in normal human language, with all the grammatical and lexical cues used in a normal way. God said to Moses in Exodus 4:11, "Who has made man's mouth? Or who makes him dumb or deaf, seeing or blind? Is it not I, the Lord?" God, who made the organs of human speech and implanted in the first man the ability to generate language (indeed an irresistible impulse to do so), is certainly capable of using it to achieve His purposes.

Nor does the impossibility proceed from sheer intellectual inability to comprehend the concepts, though it is true that some of them will stretch our minds to the limits of their capabilities and beyond. Peter said that Paul's letters contain "some things hard to understand" (2 Pet. 3:16); but he did not say impossible to understand. The problem is not the abstract, esoteric, and complicated nature of the teaching so much as a tendency in untaught and unstable readers to distort what they are reading "to their own destruction." That phrase leads us to the heart of the issue. The exalted nature of the ideas makes some, though not all, of the teaching difficult; what makes it impossible is a perverse, rebellious, and sinful indisposition to the truth built into our natures since the fall.

Where the Need Does Lie

In 1 Corinthians 2:14 Paul made two separate statements about the natural man (that is, humans as they are by nature since the fall apart from the intervention of God's grace). Man does not accept the things of the Spirit, and therefore he cannot understand them. In other words, he is guilty of a willful rejection of the truth. It has been well-said that people do not reject the Bible because it contradicts itself, but because it contradicts *them*. They are unsympathetic to the message of Scripture because it is contrary to several prior commitments which their lives are based on—primarily their own autonomy and self-sufficiency. They simply cannot allow these presuppositions to be challenged, because the result of that is to admit they are sinners before a righteous and holy God and face the necessity of bowing before Him, giving up their own rebellious claims to sovereignty over their lives.

Yet Scripture does challenge these commitments, in a way which makes people extremely uncomfortable. It answers to their own consciences and to the reality of the world in which they must live in a way which cuts the ground completely out from under them. Unless their whole nature is to change, this is a situation which sinners will find literally intolerable. They find in themselves therefore an impulse, sometimes conscious, sometimes unconscious, but operating with irresistible force, to turn a blind eye to the truths which Scripture forces on their consciousness. Their only defense, if they cannot avoid contact with the Bible altogether, is to misinterpret it, to twist its message into something they can live with. Peter said they "distort" it (2 Pet. 3:16); Paul said, they "suppress" it:

> For the wrath of God is revealed from heaven against all ungodliness and unrighteousness of men, who suppress the truth in unrighteousness, because that which is known about God is evident within them; for God made it evident to them. For since the creation of the world His invisible attributes, His eternal power and divine nature, have been clearly seen, being understood through what has been made, so that they are without excuse. For even though they knew God, they did not honor Him as God, or give thanks; but they became futile in their speculations, and their foolish heart was darkened. . . . Therefore God gave them over in the lusts of their hearts to impurity. . . . For they exchanged the truth of God for a lie. (Rom. 1:18–25)

Here we see a detailed analysis of the effects of the deliberate refusal to face the truth which is the essence of sin. Deep down we know that the message of nature is true, that there is a God to whom we are accountable, and that He is holy, righteous, pure, and powerful. Yet we suppress that knowledge, "evident" though it is within us, because we will not honor God. The message of Scripture is even clearer, but we do the same thing with it. The root of the problem is in the heart, and the fruit is an intellectual habit which will not allow us to enter sympathetically into the spirit of God's Word. We cannot handle the truth, so we misinterpret it. Rejecting the truth leads to moral corruption, which makes the truth even more unpalatable and foreign to us. This pattern becomes a vicious cycle until it is broken somehow by the Holy Spirit. "The god of the world has blinded the minds of the unbelieving, that they might not see the light of the gospel of the glory of Christ" (2 Cor. 4:4). None are so blind as those who will not see.

Does this lack of sympathy with the teaching of Scripture really keep us from any correct understanding of the Bible apart from the intervention of the Holy Spirit? Just think about the non-Christians you know. They have some possibility of understanding, but real spiritual understanding is beyond them. What is their understanding of the doctrine of justification by grace through faith alone, apart from works? The typical response is the question, "You mean that as long as you believe in Jesus you can do anything you want and still go to heaven? If I accept Christ I can go out tomorrow and commit murder and still be saved, but a good person who doesn't believe has to go to hell?" They then reject the gospel as absurd—and rightly so, based on their understanding.

It is hard to know where to begin explaining the problem with this version, so perversely close to the truth and yet so far away. No true believer takes the doctrines of grace and faith alone as a license to sin, though few could explain why. The usual answer is, "Well, I guess theoretically you could do that, but if you really had faith you would not want to." A more sophisticated theologian might point out that the error lies in neglecting the relationship between faith and regeneration; justification is not the only thing that happens as a result of faith. And he would be correct, but he would still be talking past the unbeliever. The real problem is not on a theoretical level at all. The unbeliever doesn't see what his eyes are blinded to—"the light of the knowledge of the glory of God in the face of Christ" (2 Cor. 4:6). His understanding of the gospel shows no real encounter with Jesus Christ, and hence no real love for Him. But the believer, whose eyes have been enlightened by the Holy Spirit to see precisely the glory of God in the face of Jesus, and who therefore is irresistibly drawn to Him and loves Him, knows at a deep level that salvation by grace alone could never be a license to sin. That is why, if you probe deeply enough, you will discover that the only people who really understand the gospel also believe it.

The Spirit's Answer to the Need

The work of the Holy Spirit in illumination begins with regeneration, and before that with conviction and calling. He changes the sinner's heart, softening it and enabling it to repent, to change its mind and believe. He gives it a new nature in place of the rebellious and sinful one which was the heart of the problem, the chief stumbling block in the way of a right and profitable understanding of the Word of God. We will deal with these things in more detail in their place. Illumination is not just a synonym for regeneration; it continues throughout the Christian's life, because the need for it continues. At regeneration, sinners are brought from death to life and given for the first time the possibility of understanding aright the Word of God. But they are not yet made perfect and sinless. The old nature is not immediately obliterated; old habits are not instantly stripped of all their influence; a basic change has been made at the root of their commitments, but this change has not yet worked its way out through the complex system of interlacing thoughts, impulses, and assumptions which form the branches and twigs of the human mind. Still the Holy Spirit must work to prune back these thickets in order to open up a clear view of biblical truth so that the branches may grow and bear wholesome fruit. This is illumination: letting the Sonlight in.

How Illumination Works

How then, in practical terms, does the Spirit's work of illumination proceed? It begins with the renewing of our mind, making it more susceptible to receiving God's truth, and goes on to positive teaching as the Spirit gives us insight into the meaning of Scripture and applies it to our hearts. Paul urged us, "Do not be conformed to this world, but be transformed by the renewing of your mind" (Rom. 12:2). Our minds are to be made new, recreated in the image of the mind of Christ (1 Cor. 2:16). The One who does this work of re-creation is the Holy Spirit—for "the thoughts of God no one knows except the Spirit of God" (1 Cor. 2:11). This is the same Spirit whose teaching the natural man will not receive, but who imparts it to those who are becoming spiritually minded (v. 14). Old prejudices are stripped of their power so that the will is enabled to repent and to receive the things of God. New attitudes, new ways of looking at things, new habits of thought, new assumptions, new commitments are implanted by the Spirit and begin to take root as the mind and heart become literally new. The new mind is capable of thinking thoughts it could never have entertained before. The Bible speaks of becoming a new person, of receiving a new nature; old things pass away, and all things become new. The renewing of the mind is thus an aspect of regeneration and its continuance in sanctification.

The Holy Spirit uses Scripture to create an increasing receptivity to the message of Scripture. The old mind shielded itself against the sharp two-edged sword which is the Word of God; but the Spirit wields this sword with power sufficient to cut through those defenses, and once it does it begins to create a new environment which is more and more hospitable for itself. The more of Scripture we understand and follow in the power of the Spirit, the more of it we become able to understand and follow. The more we get, the more we want and are able to take as our minds becomes increasingly renewed, more in harmony with the mind of Christ.

Not only does the Holy Spirit renew our minds, making them more receptive to the message of Scripture, but He also speaks to us directly through the words He inspired. The Bible has much to say about the Holy Spirit's role as a Teacher. When Pharaoh heard Joseph's interpretation of his dream, and even more his wise advice pursuant to it, his comment to his servants was, "Can we find a man like this, in whom is a divine spirit?" (Gen. 41:38). Pharaoh spoke with more theological accuracy than he knew; it was indeed the divine Spirit who had taught Joseph these things. I am not suggesting that illumination is of the same order as the prophetic inspiration which Joseph received. Yet Pharaoh's comment to Joseph is especially telling: "Since God has informed you of all this, there is no one so discerning and wise as you are" (v. 39). Wisdom and discernment are qualities imparted by the Spirit as He teaches us to understand and apply what God has told us. Joseph received the original revelation by prophetic inspiration; we receive it by reading the Bible. But in each case the wisdom, understanding, and discernment necessary to profit from that revelation come from the Spirit of God within us.

There is no doubt that the Holy Spirit is our Teacher when we study the Bible profitably. Nehemiah thanked God for giving "Thy good Spirit" to "instruct" the children of Israel in the exodus (Neh. 9:20). Jesus spoke of the Spirit's ministry in terms of "teaching," "reminding," "guiding," and "disclosing" (John

14:26; 16:13–14). It is hard to tell in each case whether the Lord was speaking of inspiration or illumination, but perhaps it does not really matter; both works are necessary if the job of revelation is to be carried out successfully. The point is that the Holy Spirit acts as our Teacher both by producing and by using the Word of God, and He does both as the Agent of Jesus Christ, who "opened" the disciples' "minds to understand the Scriptures" (Luke 24:45).

Recognizing Illumination

Isn't all this talk about illumination dangerously subjective? Anyone can claim to be led to a particular interpretation by the Spirit. Indeed, if we were to depend on such claims, we would soon conclude that the Holy Spirit is a very poor Teacher who leads different people to mutually contradictory conclusions. How do you know that you have been the recipient of illumination? The answer to this question comes from remembering the complementarity of illumination and inspiration. The Spirit inspired Scripture, not by ignoring or bypassing the personality, skills, interests, and education of the original authors, but by using them and working through them. So, too, He does not illumine the minds of the readers by striking them with the right interpretation, but by working through the normal processes of reason, study, and understanding. Just as the text is what He inspired, so the text is what He illuminates. No one is ever justified in claiming the Spirit's authority for any interpretation which cannot be successfully defended on lexical, grammatical, and contextual grounds. The check on the subjectivity of illumination is the doctrine of inspiration which we developed above.

The Holy Spirit's work of illumination then is no substitute for an alert mind, an honest heart, a sensitive ear, common sense, and a good concordance. These will not work without the Holy Spirit; neither does the Spirit normally work apart from them, but rather through them. The Bible is very practical about these things. It requires us to love the Lord our God with all our mind (Matt. 22:37); it commands us to use diligence in applying ourselves in the study of Scripture (2 Tim. 2:15); and it warns us that the greatest blessings of Bible study are reserved for those who sharpen their interpretive skills through practice! "Solid food is for the mature, who because of practice have their senses trained to discern good and evil" (Heb. 5:14). This of course involves more than just studying grammar and logic; the moral sensibility is what is primarily being discussed. But morally and intellectually the principle is that discernment is granted to those who submit themselves, under the Spirit's tutelage, to the discipline of practice. To claim spiritual authority while manifesting impatience with disciplined study is, according to the Bible, a sign of spiritual immaturity.

Practical Application

How then do we avail ourselves to the Spirit's work of illumination? We must first realize that He does such a work, and that illumination is essential to our spiritual growth. We must realize that He has been doing this work already without our even being aware of it, if indeed we are saved persons who understand and believe the gospel. What the Lord said to Peter after his great confession He could say to any of us: "Blessed are you, Simon Barjona, because flesh and blood did not reveal this to you, but My Father who is in heaven" (Matt. 16:17). And the Father and the Son did so through their Emissary, the Holy Spirit. So the first step in receiving illumination is to thank God for what He has already done and to pray in faith for more.

The second step is to avoid the false dichotomy between trusting in means alone without the Spirit and in trusting the Spirit alone without means. The results of the first approach are sterile; the results of the second are counterfeit. The Holy Spirit works through the means of study, comparison of Scripture with Scripture, logical thought, application, diligence, practice, and above all obedience.

Jesus said that "if any man is willing to do His will, he shall know of the teaching, whether it is of God" (John 7:17). The more we obey the Bible, the better we will understand it. The key is to use all the legitimate means at our disposal, but without trusting in them. We must use these things, not because we believe that we can by means of them wrest the true meaning away from the text ourselves, but because the Spirit has promised to bless them. We must be sure our methods are sound without thinking that this soundness alone will be sufficient. Rather we must use means in a spirit of humility, a posture of prayer, an attitude of dependence, and a sense of expectancy that the Holy Spirit will indeed work through the text He inspired. Then we should be prepared for Him to use the Bible in our lives in just the way we would expect the personal Agent and Representative of Jesus Christ to use it: for His glory.

> To this day whenever Moses is read, a veil lies over their heart; but whenever a man turns to the Lord, the veil is taken away. Now the Lord is the Spirit; and where the Spirit of the Lord is, there is liberty. But we all, with unveiled face beholding as in a mirror the glory of the Lord, are being transformed into the same image from glory to glory, just as from the Lord, the Spirit. (2 Cor. 3:15–18)

Questions for Further Study

1. What is the role of Jesus in illumination? How does the Spirit continue it for Him?

2. Can you carefully distinguish inspiration and illumination? How do they differ? How are they complementary?

3. Why do we need illumination if the Bible is perfect? What attributes of the natural man are relevant to this question?

4. How does illumination relate to regeneration and sanctification?

5. List some specific ways in which your approach to Bible study will change as a result of your understanding of illumination.

5

CONVICTION AND CALLING

Thus far we have been discussing the work of the Holy Spirit in revelation: How does He act as the personal Agent and Representative of Jesus Christ to glorify Christ by carrying out His work of making God known to us? He does it by inspiration, the production of Scripture, and illumination, the renewing of our minds to help us understand and receive it. It was necessary to deal with these matters first because Scripture is the primary and most basic means the Spirit uses in carrying out His work in the area of salvation. But salvation is the apex and crown of His work, for God supremely glorifies His Son Jesus Christ through the salvation of people. In that climactic moment just before facing the cross, Jesus prepared Himself by praying, "Father, the hour has come; glorify Thy Son, that the Son may glorify Thee" (John 17:1). In revelation, the Spirit makes God known *to* us; in salvation, He makes God known *in* and *through* us. Revelation proclaims and unveils Christ; salvation unites us to Christ by faith. If revelation is a love letter, salvation is the marriage to which that letter leads. And the work of the Holy Spirit is indispensable at each stage of the process.

Specifically, the work of the Holy Spirit in salvation is to apply and make real in our lives what Jesus has won for us on the cross. This includes such ministries as conviction of sin, calling to repentance, regeneration, sanctification, and glorification. In each case the Spirit is simply carrying out on behalf of the Lord Jesus Christ a work which Jesus began and which is essentially His own. We have already established these truths in earlier chapters, but we must be certain to remember them before we move ahead.

If it is true that the essence of the Spirit's work in salvation is the application to individuals of the atonement which Christ accomplished, then it follows that the doctrine of illumination becomes a key to much of what we are about to examine. Conviction, calling, and sanctification can be viewed as specific applications of the process of illumination we dealt with in Chapter 4. It is therefore important to be sure we have wrestled adequately with that material before we move on to study the Spirit's work in salvation. For that work in large measure consists of the Spirit's using the written Word to bring us into a saving relationship with the living Word, the Lord Jesus Christ. This begins with conviction and calling.

If people are going to be saved from sin, they must first be convinced that sin is their problem. That is what *conviction* is all about. It is a negative message, and having it brought home is a negative experience, as all those who have gone through it can testify. But it also has a positive side, for once we are convinced of the seriousness of the problem we need to be encouraged to avail ourselves of the solution—and that, in essence, is *calling*. As we will see, it takes no less a Person than the Holy Spirit to perform either ministry successfully.

Jesus in Conviction and Calling

The Lord Jesus carried out both functions powerfully during His earthly ministry. No sooner had He officially begun His public ministry than He began to preach repentance (Matt. 4:17). He was constantly making what seemed to the Jews of His day the most inflammatory statements as He analyzed their spiritual condition. "I say to you, that unless your righteousness surpasses that of the scribes and Pharisees, you shall not enter the kingdom of heaven" (Matt. 5:20). But for those who had the ears to hear, He was most eloquent in calling them to a better fate. He said to them, "Follow Me and I will make you fishers of men," and immediately they left everything to follow Him (Matt. 4:19–20). Jesus said,

> Come to Me, all who are weary and heavy-laden, and I will give you rest. Take My yoke upon you, and learn from Me, for I am gentle and humble in heart; and you shall find rest for your souls. For My yoke is easy, and My load is light. (Matt. 11:28–30)

As the Holy Spirit applies these words to people's hearts, they still answer the call and find rest in His yoke.

Since the day of Pentecost the Holy Spirit has indeed picked up the torch. The Lord promised that "when He comes, He will convict the world concerning sin, and righteousness, and judgment" (John 16:8). The apostle John revealed that it is both the Spirit and the bride who say, "Come!" (Rev. 22:17). Every believer who has answered that call today is living proof that this vital ministry of the Lord continues through the Spirit. Without it, no one could come to Christ.

The Need for Conviction and Calling

Why is it so difficult for people to come to Christ that it takes nothing less than a supernatural work of God to bring it about? The fact that it is so is beyond debate, for the Lord Himself said plainly that "No one can come to Me, unless the Father who sent Me draws him" (John 6:44). And the reasons are the same as those we saw when we looked at the need for illumination in Chapter 4, all of which can be reduced to one word: sin. Because of sin, "[The] natural man does not accept the things of the Spirit of God" (1 Cor. 2:14). In other words, it is not natural for sinners to accept Christ as the only answer to their dilemma.

The essence of sin is lawlessness, according to 1 John 3:4. This means that the sinner does not submit to any authority other than his or her own. Like Adam and Eve in the Garden and like Satan before them, the sinner wants to be like God, determining good and evil for himself and recognizing no law other than his own will and, grudgingly, the necessities of expediency. This is the heart of the commitment which was made for us by Adam in the Garden, a commitment which we have each ratified in our own lives again and again.

The essence of sin is not found in particular rebellious acts but in the orientation to rebellion rooted in the heart. These things being so, it is absolutely contrary to a sinner's nature to admit that he is a sinner, that he deserves eternal death, and to forsake his rebellion, lay down his arms, and petition the King for pardon on the basis of the blood of Christ. It goes against the grain for him to accept a pardon which comes entirely by grace, the unmerited favor of God. So, in order for him to do something utterly contrary to his own nature, he needs the Holy Spirit's ministry of conviction and calling, without which no sinner would ever be able to come to Christ.

Conviction of Sin

How exactly does conviction work? The Greek word used in John 16:8 when Jesus said the Spirit would convict the world of sin is *elegchein*. This was a technical term used to describe what a prosecuting attorney does in a courtroom in order to convict the accused of a crime. The attorney presents the incriminating evidence, argues the case, anticipates and refutes objections and rationalizations until there is no reasonable doubt of the prisoner's guilt. That is exactly what the Holy Spirit does in the courtroom of the sinner's mind before the jury of personal conscience: the Spirit acts as God's prosecuting attorney to convince the sinner of his own guilt and consequently his desperate need of Christ as Savior.

Most people feel some twinges of conscience whenever they do something which they know to be wrong. Even the Gentiles, says Paul, "who do not have the Law do instinctively the things of the Law," showing "the work of the Law written in their hearts, their conscience bearing witness" by either accusing or defending their behavior (Rom. 2:14–15). But most unbelievers find a way to live with the voice of conscience without confessing themselves to be sinners and seeking a savior. They might throw it a sop of a few good works (or maybe a lifetime of heroic service to mankind), or compare themselves to others who are worse than they. They take comfort in the fact that God is a God of love while ignoring His justice; they may even become seared to the point where conscience no longer speaks (1 Tim. 4:2). For most it remains a small, nagging voice telling them that all is not well between them and their Creator, but they find a way to coexist with it without really facing the issues it raises.

When the Holy Spirit begins a work of conviction, however, you can no longer avoid these issues. Somehow your sins keep coming back to your mind, forcing their way into your consciousness. The old rationalizations that once protected you from such things now seem hollow; the mind keeps seeing holes in them, and they no longer satisfy. Scriptures that speak of God's law, which you have violated, and the justice and holiness of God, whom you have offended, seem to scream at you, and you can't avoid them. It no longer helps to remember your good works or to think of people who have sinned more heinously than you. You begin to have the sinking feeling that you must deal with God. You begin to wonder if you aren't among the worst and more inexcusable of sinners in His eyes. You don't understand what is happening to you, because you've never been this way before. You can't shake it off, you can't get out from under it. This is because the Holy Spirit in His unseen and mysterious way has begun to act as God's special Prosecutor to bring you before the jury of your own conscience to convict you as a sinner, an inexcusable rebel before a just and holy God.

Conviction and the Christian Life

This experience varies in duration, intensity, and details according to the personality and history of the person involved, but something like it is necessary if sinners are to bow before Jesus as Lord with real understanding. He came to save us from sin, and I am firmly convinced that one great source of the spiritual anemia afflicting the church in our day is that we do not view the forgiveness of sin and cleansing from sin as the pivotal issue which the Christian life is all about. In interviewing candidates for church membership over the last decade I have noticed a disturbing trend. This is not a scientific survey, just a personal impression. I've found it borne out by the experience of others.

When you ask prospective members to give their testimony and explain what knowing the Lord means to them, increasingly they tend to talk of how their life was full of frustration and lacked meaning or direction, how they finally got to a place where they could no longer cope. Then they turned it over to Jesus and everything got better. Now, on this basis a person could be a Buddhist or a devotee of Krishna or a Muslim or even a devil-worshiper. They could all say the same thing with simply another name inserted in the slot. So you have to probe more deeply to find out if the person really is a true Christian.

You have to probe—and that is precisely the problem. Finally in desperation you ask, "Does the cross have anything to do with all of this?" "Oh yes," the candidate responds, "Jesus died on the cross to pay for our sins." They believe that and have accepted it, but it is not the first thing they think about when they describe their relationship with Christ. I hope and pray and believe they will be saved, but I would have a lot more confidence about it if they showed some evidence of knowing the conviction of sin. People who have been dealt with by the Holy Spirit in this way do not have to be prodded; they know that the cross stands at the center of the whole Christian faith, they know how to value the blood of Christ, and they know what it means to be motivated in Christian living and service by gratitude for His grace. People who have not known the conviction of sin in a profound way can never be more than spiritual infants. They simply cannot relate either to Paul's despair in Romans 7 or the triumph of Romans 8. They cannot understand what the fuss is all about. So it is no wonder that they never get beyond laxity in Christian living and shallowness in Christian worship.

So gracious is our God that we may hope that those who turn to Christ at any level of understanding will finally be saved. But while we must beware of stereotyping conversion experiences, the church would be much healthier and believers much more joyful and confident if we could return to a more biblical set of expectations for what may be considered a more or less "normative" conversion. Amidst all its diversity, certain elements are essential: one is the Holy Spirit's ministry of convicting the sinner of guilt and personal need in terms of sin. A spiritual church would be one in which there was an atmosphere of expectancy which encouraged seekers after God to expect and seek and be open to such conviction as they are encouraged to come to Christ. We would then have fewer conversions that do not "stick," fewer professing Christians who are hard to distinguish from the world, and more believers whose conversion experience fits the biblical pattern, which begins, "Depart from me, for I am a sinful man, O Lord!" and ends in the heartfelt praise of the grace of God who could redeem a chief of sinners. Nobody is really ready to receive Christ with full understanding and appreciation until experiencing conviction of sin.

Calling

The logical result of seeing yourself as a sinner before a God of absolute holiness is despair. You realize that no amount of future good works, no matter how noble or how many, could ever change the fact that you are a sinner, and that being a sinner there is no hope you could ever change anyway. You finally see your sin as God sees it, as an intolerable burden weighing you down to hell, a burden which no effort on your part could ever remove. The Holy Spirit has convicted you of your sin so effectively that you agree with the verdict and the sentence of eternal death, and almost wish God would go on and carry it out. And the Spirit has brought you so low, not because He is cruel, but because He is kind; for now you are ready to hear the words of Jesus, "Come to Me, all who are weary and heavy-laden, and I will give you rest" (Matt. 11:28).

Now the Holy Spirit opens the eyes of your heart to see Jesus Christ in all His loveliness as the only answer to the problem of sin. You see something of the perfection and majesty of the plan of salvation as the only thing in heaven or earth which is adequate to meet your need. Once you wondered why anyone would want to surrender his freedom to this frail looking character you had seen in Sunday School art. Now you see something of the strength of His character, the depth of His love, the beauty of His holiness, the perfection of His person, and the dynamism of His personality. The meaning of His sacrifice for your sin hits home, and He becomes the one thing altogether desirable in the whole universe. Your heart seems drawn irresistibly to Him, and though your will may still resist the idea, the only appropriate response to Him seems increasingly clear: to bow before Him, acknowledging His rightful lordship, confessing your rebellion and pleading with Him to receive you into His service and forgive your many sins against Him. Somehow, when you think of His cross, you know that, though you don't deserve any such favor, He will forgive you.

What is happening? How did you ever come to consider such a commitment, so diametrically opposed to your independent, wayward, and self-centered nature? The answer is that the Holy Spirit is calling you to faith in Christ. If you respond to His call, you will look back on it for the rest of your life as something almost irresistible which changed the course of your life forever. You will know that without the Spirit's work you would never have put your faith in Christ.

Paul described the whole process well (2 Cor. 4:3–6). The unbeliever's eyes are "blinded" by Satan to "the light of the gospel of the glory of Christ." But for the believer, "God, who said, 'Light shall shine out of darkness,' is the One who has shone in our hearts to give the light of the knowledge of the glory of God in the face of Christ." That is the essence of the Holy Spirit's work: to glorify Jesus Christ by making Him real to us.

How Conviction and Calling Work

How exactly does He do it? What are the means that He uses? How does He bring self-reliant and self-satisfied sinners to a point of needing and desiring an all-sufficient Savior and an all-encompassing Lord? First and foremost, He works through Scripture:

> For the word of God is living and active and sharper than any two-edged sword, and piercing as far as the division of soul and spirit, of both joints and marrow, and able to judge the thoughts and intentions of the heart. (Heb. 4:12)

Scripture was given that character by the Spirit when He inspired it, and it receives that power again as it is wielded by Him today. It is almost impossible to find a Christian with a clear testimony who will not tell you how God used some particular passage of Scripture to awaken him to his need and call him to the Savior. What is it about these words that can suddenly and unexpectedly grip you like a vice or pierce through all your defenses like a sword? It is the fact that the Holy Spirit is still active in convicting us of our sins and calling us to faith.

The second means the Spirit uses in conviction and calling is the witness of believers. Even when someone testifies that he was saved simply by reading the Gideon Bible in his hotel room, there was a faithful Christian who placed it there. And in most cases, unbelievers will not read the Bible at all unless they are brought into contact with it by believers who, through the force of visible spiritual reality in their own lives, gain a hearing for the Word of God which introduced them to the Savior that they might be transformed and continues to nourish them in their faith.

The New Testament has a great deal to say about the connection between the Holy Spirit and the witness of believers in calling people to faith in Christ. Just before His ascension the Lord commissioned His disciples with the task of proclaiming "repentance for forgiveness of sins. . . to all the nations" on the basis of the fact that He had been a suffering Messiah (Luke 24:46–47). Verse 49 intervenes between the giving of the commission and its execution: "And behold, I am sending forth the promise of My Father upon you; but you are to stay in the city until you are clothed with power from on high." The source of this power is identified in Acts 1:8. "You shall receive power when the Holy Spirit has come upon you; and you shall be My witnesses."

There is a connection between the Holy Spirit beginning His ministry and the disciples beginning theirs. We usually place that connection at the point of the Spirit's enabling, and rightly so, for power is the emphasis given by the texts. But we should remember that the ministry given to the disciples is a ministry of calling sinners to faith and repentance, a ministry which has already been established as the Spirit's own. The implication is that the disciples are the means the Spirit plans to use to carry out that ministry. They cannot carry it out apart from Him (this the text makes plain by ordering them to wait); He normally will not carry it out apart from them.

Jesus told the disciples not to worry about being arrested for their testimony (Matt. 10:18–20). This verse, (v. 19), has been abused by people looking for an excuse for lack of preparation for preaching or teaching, but it gives no support for such irresponsibility. The New American Standard Bible gives an accurate translation: "Do not become anxious about how or what you will speak." It gives a promise of supernatural aid which is specifically limited to a situation in which no opportunity for preparation has been possible. Don't worry then, said Jesus; "For it is not you who speak, but it is the Spirit of your Father who speaks in you" (v. 20). The point is that at least some of the speaking the Holy Spirit does to the hearts of people without Christ is done in the mouths of Christ's followers. Acts 6:10 shows one example of this promise being fulfilled: When Stephen was accosted by the Jews "they were unable to cope with the wisdom and the Spirit with which he was speaking." Unfortunately they closed their ears to the Spirit's call, but they were certainly susceptible to His conviction through Stephen, as the fury of their subsequent reaction showed. They were reacting to something more than the impromptu eloquence of the first martyr of the church.

Parallels with Inspiration and Illumination

What have we seen then? Without a supernatural act of conviction and calling on the part of God through the Holy Spirit, sinners would never come to Christ. With it, they can and some will: "whom He predestined, these He also called; and whom He called, these He also justified" (Rom. 8:30). This ministry of conviction and calling is parallel to the Spirit's work in inspiration and illumination which we have already examined.

The Spirit's work of inspiration parallels the work of illumination in the following ways. Inspiration is a supernatural work giving supernatural qualities of inerrancy and relevance and power to Scripture. It works through the natural channels of the minds and wills of the human authors. Illumination, likewise, is a supernatural work by which the Spirit gives understanding of spiritual things to human beings who have no natural aptitude for them. It works through the natural channels of study and practice. In each case, the truly supernatural works, not apart from or instead of, but in and through the natural. So, in conviction and calling, the Holy Spirit of God does a truly supernatural work, a work of which nature is not capable. The Spirit works through common and ordinary means: black ink on white paper and the words and lives of normal men and women like you and me.

Implications for Witness

A better understanding of conviction and calling should be a great encouragement to us in the task of evangelism. There is no task for which we feel more inadequate, no subject which can make us more quickly and inextricably tongue-tied, and for good reason. We are called to attempt something which no amount of effort or expertise on our part can possibly accomplish: bringing people who are spiritually dead to life (Eph. 2:1–5). We cannot do that, but the Holy Spirit can, and He will do it through us if we are open to being used.

Tremendous implications for our practice as Christian witness flow from this doctrine. The first of these implications for witnessing is the importance simply of doing it. A Christian trying to witness for Jesus Christ apart from constant and conscious reliance on the Holy Spirit to do the actual work is like a light bulb trying to shine without electricity. But it is just as frustrating to the way the light is designed to work to have the electricity turned on with no bulb screwed into the socket. The Holy Spirit cannot use a presentation of the gospel and an invitation to receive Christ which is never given. But the Word is quick and powerful and sharper than a double-edged sword, and once we take it out of the sheath, anything can happen.

Then, once we are plugged in to the Great Commission, there are ways of working with what the Spirit is trying to do, and ways of working against it. A clear understanding of the doctrine of the Spirit and His work will indicate what many of these ways are. The Spirit's work of conviction and calling is part of His ministry of bringing glory to Jesus Christ. He calls people to

Christ by exalting the person of Christ (John 12:32). It is by contrast with the purity and holiness of Christ that we realize what sinners we really are, and it is in response to the goodness and love of Christ that we are drawn to embrace Him as Savior and Lord. Therefore, if the Holy Spirit is to use our witness as the means of calling people to Christ, we must view the task of evangelism as primarily one of exalting and glorifying the Lord Jesus Christ Himself. Anything which would call attention away from Him and direct it to ourselves must be rigorously excluded.

We are not sent to show off our cleverness (though all our intelligence will be called for) nor our spirituality (though the utmost purity of devotion to Christ on our part will be required). We are not sent to discuss our philosophy or our opinions (though a well worked-out, biblical worldview is helpful). We are sent to unveil to people the wonderful person of our Lord Jesus Christ.

Because evangelism is simply one mode of our whole life-calling of giving glory to Jesus Christ, we should be sure to use the Bible in our witnessing. It is, after all, God's Word, not ours, which is quick and powerful and sharp as a sword, and which was inspired by the Spirit for the express purpose of glorifying the Lord Jesus. Our words are important for setting the context, for winning a hearing for the Bible, and sometimes for explaining and applying its language. However, if Christ is to be presented as Lord and Savior in such a way that people are drawn to Him in faith, it is ultimately the Bible which has to speak. The good seed which is sown in human hearts and produces fruit in receptive soil is, after all, the Word of God (Luke 8:11). Therefore, we will be effective instruments of the Holy Spirit in conviction and calling to the extent to which we bring people into contact with Jesus Christ as He is revealed in Scripture.

Too often our witnessing takes the form of a vague discussion of our religious ideas or of our religious experiences. These things are all well and good, but the power of the Holy Spirit to convict sinners and call them to faith is in large measure tied to Scripture. Is there then no place for our personal testimony? Of course there is. Unless the Christ of Scripture has produced in us the blessings which we tell others are to be found in Him, we will have a hard time winning a hearing for the Word of God at all. There must be a coherence between what the unbeliever hears from us and what he sees in us, a complementarity between the Christ revealed in Scripture and the Christlikeness of His messenger. If we present Christ as the Savior from guilt, sin, and death while our lives are morally compromised and trapped in the same pitfalls as the non-Christian, we will hardly be effective instruments for the Holy Spirit to use.

Conclusion

The ministry of the Holy Spirit is to glorify Jesus Christ, acting as His personal Representative, by making Him real to us. In conviction and calling, He makes Christ real to unbelievers through Scripture and believers; and His method of operation is to make Jesus real *to them* by making Him real *in us*. The "in us" will be our subject throughout most of the rest of the book. It begins with conviction and calling and proceeds to regeneration and sanctification.

Before going to the next chapter, please stop and ask yourself some questions.

Have I known the conviction of sin?

Am I willing to see sin as God sees it in me?

Do I see Jesus Christ as the only possible solution to the problem of sin?

Have I been moved to bow before Christ and give myself to Him without reservation, taking Him as my Savior and Lord? If not, will I do so now?

Am I the kind of instrument Christ can use to call others to the same joyous faith? Am I willing to be at any cost?

If the answers are yes, you are ready to go on to the wonders and delights of the Christian life.

Questions for Further Study

1. Can you accurately and concisely define conviction and calling in your own words? Look the words up in a good theological dictionary and see how your definition compares with what you find there.

2. Jesus said no one can come to Him unless drawn by the Father (John 6:44). Why is it so hard for people who need Him so badly to do this?

3. What were some things the Spirit used to overcome your natural resistance to the gospel (if you were converted at an old enough age to have been conscious of such things)? Ask some Christian friends the same question.

4. How do your answers to question 3 affect your strategy as a witness for Christ?

5. Is there anything in your life-style which would hinder the Spirit from using you as an instrument for calling men to Christ?

6

REGENERATION
AND CONVERSION

Since about 1975 Bible-believing evangelicals have been known as the "born-again" movement. Like all terms which are taken up as buzz words by the popular media, the phrase "born again" has suffered from semantic erosion, with most of its original meaning being lost in the process. This is unfortunate, for the term names something essential to the whole process of salvation. "Born again" is simply an Anglicization of the more Latinate word "regenerate," which in turn translates the Greek *palingenesis*—which means, of all things, "born again" or rebirth. Because of sin, humans are born spiritually dead (Eph. 2:1), and if we are to know God and live with Him forever we must have a spiritual birth in addition to our physical birth. Why is this so? What is it like? What role does the Holy Spirit play in it? How is it related to conversion and the rest of the work God does for our salvation in Christ? These are the questions to which we must now turn our attention.

Regeneration and Salvation

It may be helpful first to see how regeneration fits in to the whole context of what happens to us when we are saved. Salvation has both an objective side and a subjective side. Objectively, God does something concerning us or with respect to us when we receive Christ; subjectively, He does something in us and to us. The objective transaction is outward, official, and legal; the subjective work is inward, experiential, and personal. The one has to do with our position before God, the other with our possession of God. The one has to do with our standing, the other with our state. Both aspects are essential parts of one unified work, but the objective aspect is in a sense more crucial because it is logically prior and the subjective results from it.

Justification

One of the problems God has to overcome to save us is that of righteousness. Sinners are devoid of righteousness, but they have to have it if they are to have fellowship with God either now or in eternity. The death of Christ is the solution to the problem, and it is applied in two ways. Objectively, those who put their faith in Christ as Lord and Savior receive justification, the legal, official declaration that, because Christ bore the full penalty for sin for all believers, those who come to Him for pardon are pronounced innocent with respect to the demands of the Law (Rom. 3:20–28; 8:1).

Justification is an objective and forensic act which confers a legal standing of righteousness on the basis of which pardon is pronounced and fellowship with God is restored. Our sins are imputed to Christ (i.e., officially reckoned or counted as His) and His righteousness is imputed to us, for He stands before God as our Representative (Rom. 4:3). Only on this basis could we ever be saved at all, for if it were left to us to become actually righteous we would never make it. That is why justification is and can only be by grace, through faith, plus nothing, not of works lest any man should boast (Eph. 2:8-10; Rom 3:28). Anne Ross Cousin spoke of this in her hymn "The Sands of Time are Sinking" (1857):

I stand upon Christ's merit;
I know no other stand
Not e'en where glory dwelleth
in Emmanuel's land.

Only thus can sinners be restored to fellowship with God.

Sanctification

Once this objective and official standing before God has been granted, there is a subjective counterpart: sanctification, the process through which God begins to transform us so that we increasingly become actually righteous, as not only the guilt but also the power of sin in our lives is overcome. How is this done? It is by the communication of Christ's life to us through the mediation of the Holy Spirit. But how can the Holy Spirit indwell sinners who still lie under the condemnation of God? How can God communicate life to those who are estranged from Him, with whom He has no personal relationship? He cannot, and that is why we said that in salvation the subjective aspect flows from and depends on the objective. Justification is the key to sanctification and is logically prior to it; the subjective flows from the objective.

Every form of teaching which implies the necessity of works for salvation simply reverses the biblical order, making justification dependent on sanctification, as if you had to improve to a certain extent on your own to become worthy of justification. Even if you view God as helping you make the improvement, you have in effect overturned Paul's statement that salvation is the free gift of God (Rom. 6:23). Rather, a full and free pardon is granted immediately when a person receives Christ; then God's official declaration that, as far as He is concerned, this person represented before the throne by Christ is objectively righteous begins to work itself out subjectively in that person's daily experience.

Regeneration

The second difficulty to be overcome in salvation is the fact that, not only does the sinner stand condemned, he is actually spiritually dead because he has no relationship to the Source of life. Justification having made possible a relationship between God and the sinner, God then objectively decrees what that new relationship will be by adopting the believer as His child. Adoption is an objective fact, and it has its subjective effect in regeneration, as new spiritual life flows from God to His new child. These two aspects of salvation are linked in the prologue to John's Gospel. The Word was in the beginning and was God; He came into the world, and in Him was life; and though He was rejected by those who should have received Him, He gave to those who did receive Him "the right to become children of God" (John 1:12, cf. Gal. 4:1–7). That is adoption. But then these adopted children are immediately described as people who were "born not of blood, nor of the will of the flesh, nor of the will of man, but of God" (John 1:13). That is regeneration.

The Necessity of Regeneration

This impartation of new life—really, a new kind of life—is so necessary that there can be no salvation without it. Jesus said quite plainly, "Unless one is born again, he cannot see the kingdom of God" (John 3:3). Why is this so? The answer to that question will teach us a great deal about the whole plan of salvation.

In the first place, regeneration is absolutely necessary because spiritually dead people cannot inherit the kingdom of God. To talk about being spiritually dead and to talk about being a sinner by nature is to say the same thing in different words. Paul even combined the two ways of speaking when he said that before we met Christ we were "dead in trespasses and sins" (Eph. 2:1). The wages of sin is death (Rom. 6:23), and the essence of sin is death. Eternal life is defined by the Lord as knowing God (John 17:3), and sin is contrary to everything God stands for. The essence of sin is rebellion against God, and the essence of death is separation from God. So it is no wonder that Paul asked,

> Do you not know that the unrighteous shall not inherit the kingdom of God? Do not be deceived; neither fornicators, nor idolaters, nor adulterers, nor effeminate, nor homosexuals, nor thieves, not the covetous, nor

drunkards, nor revilers, nor swindlers, shall inherit the kingdom of God. And such were some of you. (1 Cor. 6:9–11)

We cannot be saved by forsaking these (and other) sins, but neither can we be saved without forsaking them, for they are absolutely incompatible with the life of Christ. These things have no place in the kingdom, but as sinners in Adam we are guilty of all of them in principle, and would no doubt continue to practice them if were not for the grace of God. There must, therefore, be a change as radical as the change which happens at birth, for spiritually dead people simply cannot inherit the kingdom of God.

This is not to deny human free will. I am simply highlighting one side of a profound mystery Scripture presents. All people are called to Christ and held accountable for their choices; hence, they must be able to respond. At the same time they are represented as spiritually dead (not mortally ill); therefore, any response they make must be attributed itself to the grace of God already at work in them, vivifying and enabling a response which is contrary to their very natures as fallen and sinful human beings. Thus on the one hand I present the gospel as if people can respond and pray the Spirit will enable them to. But on the other hand, once they have responded, I give all the glory for their salvation to God, not even claiming that their own good sense in believing the gospel was an unaided contribution of my own nature to the process. My allegiance to Scripture requires me to believe that both of these truths are spiritually important and true without contradiction. Explaining how they relate to each other is another matter.

In the third place, spiritually dead people cannot confess Christ as Lord. And that confession too is absolutely necessary for salvation. Romans 10:9 says that "if you confess with your mouth Jesus as Lord, and believe in your heart that God raised Him from the dead, you shall be saved." First Corinthians 12:3 says that "no one can say 'Jesus is Lord,' except by the Holy Spirit." Must people really confess Christ as Lord as well as Savior to be saved? Our resistance to the idea stems from a habit of bending over backward to avoid sounding like we are advocating salvation by works. And we must definitely not even come close to advocating that. We are saved by the grace of God in Jesus Christ, period. But who is this Jesus? The absolutely basic, rock-bottom confession of the first-century church was, "Jesus Christ is Lord." A Jesus who is not Lord is not the real Jesus by faith in whom we must be saved, but a figment of our imagination. So Paul was not only clear but correct when he said that salvation comes by confessing Jesus as Lord—and this no person dead in sin can do unless he is made alive by the Holy Spirit.

Finally, regeneration by the Holy Spirit is necessary for salvation because people who are spiritually dead cannot live forever. They will exist forever, but that is not necessarily the same thing as living. The best way to understand eternal death is by comparison with the biblical definition of eternal life the Lord gave us: it is to "know Thee, the only true God, and Jesus Christ whom Thou hast sent" (John 17:3). Life is knowing God, and having fellowship with Him; death is estrangement from Him. All that is wholesome, creative, and good comes from Him; all that is decaying, sterile, and evil has no part in Him. To be a sinner is to be estranged from Him and therefore from life.

God warned Adam in the Garden that on the very day he sinned he would die (Gen. 2:17). Physically, he continued to exist for almost a millennium; but on that very day his fellowship with God was broken, and he died spiritually. His physical death later was merely a symptom, or a sign, of the estrangement from the Source of all life and vitality which had already taken place. It has been well-said that all the other religions of the world are concerned to make bad people good, but Christianity alone is concerned to make dead people live. For that to happen, their connection with the Source of life must be restored. Because Christ by His death has opened the way by dealing with our guilt before God, the Holy Spirit as the liaison between Christ and His people can then reestablish that connection by coming as Christ's own Representative to live in our hearts, once again imparting spiritual life to our souls.

The Nature of Regeneration

What then is the exact nature of this thing which happens to us when we believe in Christ? The New Testament uses at least three sets of terms; these are just three ways of speaking about the same thing.

New Birth

The first is the familiar language of rebirth or new birth. John 1:12–13 says that those who receive Jesus as their personal Messiah receive also the privilege of adoption as children of God and a corresponding birth which is spiritual. It cannot be accounted for on the basis of biology ("not of blood, nor of the will of the flesh"—i.e., I take it, biological impulses) or psychology ("nor of the will of man"). In his conversation with Nicodemus by night, Jesus stressed the fact that "unless one is born again, he cannot see the kingdom of God" (John 3:3). The word used can be translated either born *again* or born *from above*, and both ideas are true. It is a new birth, subsequent to and different from the physical birth humanity shares, and it comes from God (John 1:13). Finally, lest we think this terminology is unique to John's Gospel, Paul also used it: "He saved us, not on the basis of deeds which we have done in righteousness, but according to His mercy, by the washing of regeneration and renewing by the Holy Spirit" (Titus 3:5). Regeneration is simply a synonym for *rebirth*.

New Self

That passage also introduces us to a second set of terminology, which speaks of the same event in terms of renewal or being made new. The classic passage which speaks this way is Ephesians 4:22–24. People who have truly "learned Christ" do not continue in the old life-style of futility, darkness, ignorance, sensuality, and greed (vv. 17–21). Rather, they have been taught that

> in reference to your former manner of life, you lay aside the old self, which is being corrupted in accordance with the lusts of deceit, and that you be renewed in the spirit of your mind, and put on the new self, which in the likeness of God has been created in righteousness and holiness of the truth.

Things are changing in their lives because of what has happened to them. This change began when they received Christ and continues to work itself out in their lives. They can be exhorted to go on with the change on the basis of the way they first learned Christ. This is so radical that it can be described as becoming a new person, for a new "self" comes into being.

New Creation

Again, this passage introduces the final set of terms: the new self has been *created* by God in them. "If any man is in Christ, he is a new creature (or creation); the old things passed away; behold, new things have come" (2 Cor. 5:17).

When Jesus Christ comes into a person's life, that person will never be the same again. He was condemned, but now he is justified; but also where before he was dead, totally impotent, sterile, and lifeless as far as spiritual things are concerned, now he is made alive to God once again. He is renewed, he becomes a new person; and so radical is this change that it can be described as a new birth, or as being created all over again. So regeneration is the creative act of the Holy Spirit whereby spiritual life is implanted where before there was only spiritual death.

This spiritual life is simply the life of Christ communicated to us by His personal Representative and Agent, the Holy Spirit. Paul summarized this spiritual life in Galatians 2:20. "I have been crucified with Christ; and it is no longer I who live, but Christ lives in me; and the life which I now live in the flesh I live by faith in the Son of God, who loved me, and delivered Himself up for me." One who has the Son has life, it is as simple as that. And he receives that life from the One who serves as His link with the Son until His return, the Holy Spirit.

Regeneration and the Spirit

It is highly appropriate that the Holy Spirit should be the member of the Godhead to actually communicate to us the new life won by Christ on the cross, for the Spirit was the One who imparted life to creation in the beginning. When the earth was yet unformed and empty, it was the Spirit of God who brooded over it like a dove (Gen. 1:2–3). Then when God actually brought man to life, He did it by breathing into the clay the breath of life. Interestingly, in Hebrew the same word means both "breath" and "spirit" (Gen. 2:7). "Thou dost send forth Thy Spirit, they are created; and Thou dost renew the face of the ground" (Ps. 104:30). The Holy Spirit is a spirit of life, and the One who implants physical life in all living things. Therefore, it is natural that He should be the One to bring to us the spiritual life we receive from the living God and His Son. Gerald Manley Hopkins put it in his poem "God's Grandeur":

> The world is charged with the grandeur of God.
> It will flame out like shining from shook foil;
> It gathers to a greatness like the ooze of oil
> Crushed. Why do men then now not wreck his rod?
> Generations have trod, have trod, have trod;
> And all is seared with trade; bleared, smeared with toil;
> And wears man's smudge and shares man's smell: the soil
> Is bare now, nor can foot feel, being shod.
>
> And for all this, nature is never spent;
> There lives the dearest freshness deep down things;
> And though the last lights off the black West went
> Oh, morning at the brown brink eastward springs—
> Because the Holy Ghost over the bent
> World broods with warm breast and with ah! bright wings.

The Spirit broods in conviction and calling; and then, where before there was only death, He creates new spiritual life. The old nature, the old self, the old fleshly life, are not immediately destroyed, but a new nature, a new self, a new principle of life has been introduced. From now on the spirit lusts against the flesh and the flesh against the spirit, and the new life must be nurtured until it grows strong and becomes the dominant force in the young but growing Christian. That is the process of sanctification which might be looked on as the extension and maintenance of regeneration through time. The new life becomes increasingly dominant until in heaven it will be the only life we have, and the new person the only person we are. But this discussion must await a later chapter.

Regeneration and Conversion

For now we must face the question of the relationship between regeneration and something else which happens simultaneously with it: conversion. The nature of that relationship according to the Bible is not what most of us most readily assume. But first, what is conversion?

Nature of Conversion

Three closely related words are used almost interchangeably in our English Bibles to translate a similar constellation of Greek words. The Greek words are *epistrepho*, to turn, and *metanoeo*, to repent or change one's mind. The English words are repentance, turning, and conversion. These words all describe something crucial which happens to people when they come to know the Lord. Paul, for example, heard in Macedonia and Achaia and in every place how the Thessalonians had "turned to God from idols to serve a living and true God" (1 Thess. 1:9). Peter, in the very first evangelistic sermon after the day of Pentecost, exhorted his hearers to "repent, and let each of you be baptized in the name of Jesus Christ for the forgiveness of your sins" (Acts 2:38). A little later Peter used both terms: "repent therefore and return, that your sins may be wiped away" (Acts 3:19). The inward change which takes place in regeneration has an outward manifestation in a change of direction, orientation, and allegiance.

To convert something is to change it into something else; to repent in Greek is literally to change one's mind; to turn is to face the opposite direction. The change these words describe must happen whenever a sinner receives Christ as Savior and Lord. He changes his mind about who he is, what he needs, and what his relationship to God must be. He turns from sin to God, and thus he is converted from a lost sinner to a sinner saved by grace, a saint by calling, on his way to saintly living.

Conversion and the Mind

Let us examine each of these facets of conversion more carefully. The change of mind which takes place when a sinner becomes a Christian is radical, though outwardly it may not seem so in a person raised in a Christian home who receives the Lord at an early age. Even then there is a basic change in orientation from being a person who wants his own way to being one who at least in principle has accepted God's way. For the average man or woman in our secular society, though, the change of mind which is necessary to accept Christ as Lord is far-reaching indeed. Such a person must say, "I no longer think that I'm OK and you're OK and everybody is OK. I've changed my mind about that. I now realize that I am a sinner before a righteous and holy God and that I deserve eternal death." The sinner must say again, "I no longer think that everybody will be accepted by God as long as they are sincere. I've changed my mind about that too, and I now acknowledge Christ as the only way to God." In reaching those conclusions he will have changed his mind about the existence of moral absolutes, the authority of Scripture, and any number of other points. If his thinking does not change in these areas, he can hardly be said to have believed the gospel at all.

Conversion and Repentance

When the sinner changes his mind on all these issues, he also makes a new commitment of his will to turn from sin to God, from self-reliance to trust in God's grace, and from self-will to acquiescence in the lordship of Christ. He is not saved by forsaking his sins nor by his new obedience, nor must he measure up to a certain standard of success in living out these commitments to be accepted. He is saved by the pure grace, the unmerited favor of God, apart from works, accepted as a free gift by faith alone. But he is saved by faith; and it can hardly be called sincere faith in Christ to accept His death as the payment for his sins with the full intention of continuing in them without a break. The new believer will fall, and may fall often and disastrously; but his new relationship with Jesus Christ necessarily entails a new relationship to sin and the old life of self-will as well. A break has been made with it, at least in principle, and the new life which has been implanted in his soul by the Holy Spirit will no longer let him continue in sin comfortably.

The principle of salvation by grace through faith apart from works lest any man should boast (Eph. 2:8—10) is not a license to sin with impunity as long as we have walked an aisle and repeated the right formula. It simply means that we are not in any way saved by our performance of our new principles; but if the principles themselves have not changed it is sheer hypocrisy to claim that we have saving faith. Paul made this point with clarity; "Are we to continue in sin that grace might increase? May it never be!" (Rom. 6:1–2). Those who continue in sin as if nothing has happened will not inherit the kingdom of God (1 Cor. 6:9). So although salvation is by grace alone, the acceptance of that grace in conversion to Christ necessarily involves repentance, a change of mind and heart in which sin is confessed and forsaken as Christ is embraced as Lord.

Conversion and the Spirit

What then is the Holy Spirit's role in conversion and repentance? To say that unless a person repents and is converted he cannot see the kingdom of God is really parallel with saying that unless he is born again or regenerated he cannot see the kingdom. Repentance and conversion are the initial outward manifestation of regeneration, the first visible stirring of the new life implanted by the Spirit. Yet this formulation radically reverses the way most of us normally think about these things. Regeneration is something the Holy Spirit does, and repentance is something we do. We normally think of regeneration as happening in response to our repentance, our decision to accept Christ. Which way of looking at it is biblical? It may be confusing at first, but the unavoidable answer is that both are!

There is a sense in which regeneration depends on conversion, for we are exhorted to repent in order that our sins may be wiped away (Acts 3:19). This is the more familiar perspective, and the one with which most of us are more comfortable. But we must not stop there, for there is also a sense in which conversion and repentance depend on regeneration. Paul urged Timothy to correct with gentleness those who opposed the gospel "if perhaps God may grant them repentance leading to the knowledge of the truth" (2 Tim. 2:25). We have already seen that the unsaved person is not capable of receiving the things of the Spirit of God (1 Cor. 2:14) and thus incapable of accepting Christ. It goes against his nature to do so. It follows that if he has done so, his nature must already have been changed.

When things get confusing, it is always wise to go back and confirm the facts we are sure of. Three such facts are plain: first, the Bible clearly presents both perspectives; second, the two perspectives seem to be contradictory; third, the two perspectives are not contradictory. Explaining how they are not is a difficult job, one which has not been perfectly performed by all the greatest theologians of the church after two millennia of reflection on the New Testament texts, and which may not be until we reach Heaven, if then. But a few helpful things can be said.

It may take us part of the way to realize that there is more than one kind of priority operating when we ask which comes first, regeneration or conversion. One kind of priority is *temporal priority*. Which comes first as our experience of redemption unfolds in time? Here the answer is neither. Regeneration and conversion are simultaneous. You can find no moment of time in which there exists a regenerate person who has not yet been converted or a person who is truly converted but not yet born again.

A second kind of priority is *logical priority*. Which is cause and which is effect? Here the biblical answer seems to be that regeneration comes first. If the unsaved do not have it in them to respond to Christ and if repentance itself must be granted by God (2 Tim. 2:23), then it seems clear that, while both God and the sinner perform a significant act in conversion, it is God's act which comes first. God takes the initiative.

Yet there may also be a third kind of priority, which we might call *existential priority*. Which aspect of this unified event of redemption must be the focus of our attention when we address, not the mind which analyzes, but the will which chooses? And here the answer is repentance. An evangelist exhorts a sinner to repent and believe. The sinner cannot do it unless God changes him, true; but he is still the one who repents and believes. He is dependent on the Holy Spirit, who enables him to do both.

In summary, when the Holy Spirit's work of conviction and calling culminates in conversion, several things happen immediately and simultaneously. In the heavenlies, there is *justification* as God pronounces the person innocent on the basis of Christ's sacrifice in payment for his sins, and *adoption* as the Father takes that person as His child. In the soul of that person there is *regeneration* as the Holy Spirit creates spiritual life where before there was only death. In the mind and heart of that person, and also in the outside world, there is *repentance* and faith as, enabled by the Holy Spirit's act of regeneration, the sinner turns from sin to God and confesses Christ as Lord before others. That sacred moment when the soul, in response to the preparatory and enabling work of conviction and calling, makes contact with the saving grace of God is a mystery which remains secret, hidden from our most penetrating glaces either of theology or psychology. However, we must cling to two facts: a person does truly act, but God's is the initiative. When people ask for God's grace, they find in the very act of asking that grace has already been there as the Holy Spirit brings Christ into their lives.

Practical Implications

As usual, there are profound practical implications of a correct understanding of the biblical teaching on the work of the Holy Spirit. The first is the urgency of repentance. You have not fully understood the role of the Holy Spirit in conversion and regeneration until you realize your absolute dependence on the Holy Spirit even for your ability to turn to Christ. It is like suddenly seeing the sheer precipice on which you have been standing. Suddenly empty space yawns right next to your feet. You gasp, "You mean I can't just get saved anytime I feel like it, whenever I'm ready?" No, you cannot! The whole emphasis of Scripture is that "now" is the acceptable time, now is the day of salvation (2 Cor. 6:2). Even more pertinently, "Today if you hear His voice, do not harden your hearts as when they provoked Me" (Heb. 3:7–8, quoting Ps. 95:7–8).

When God brings you to that time of crisis in which the call of Christ summons you to a decision about His claims, do not resist! The extension of that opportunity is in itself an act of incomprehensible grace. If you spurn it, God is under no obligation to extend it again; and though He may, you have no guarantees. Eventually, if you harden your heart in the face of the Spirit's conviction and calling, God will grant your wish and leave you to your own devices. This means leaving you with no further place for repentance, though you seek it with tears (Heb. 12:17). No, you may not assume the ability to repent and be saved at your own convenience; you must do it now, while God is working in your heart, while Christ is still calling you to Himself through His personal Emissary, the Holy Spirit.

A second implication of a biblical understanding of the Holy Spirit's work in regeneration and conversion is to realize that there is no hope of salvation in the "fire-insurance" religion which is so popular in American Christendom. God's work of redemption is one package which we cannot split up according to our own arbitrary desires. Every person whom God foreknew as a believer in Jesus Christ He predestined to be conformed to the image of His Son. These are the same people whom He called, justified, and will glorify (Rom. 8:28f). There is no justification apart from regeneration, no forgiveness without a changed life. Not that you must change your life, indeed your nature, to be justified. But salvation is a free gift received by grace alone through faith. Salvation is a gift which changes those who receive it. They have been prepared for it by conviction and calling, and when it comes it brings new life and a new nature in regeneration, all of which are supernatural works of the Holy Spirit.

We must be slow to judge: sometimes the first stirrings of the new life are too faint for anyone but God Himself to see. But neither should we encourage people who show no evidence of repentance from sin, a daily walk with the Lord, and commitment to a Bible-believing local church to think they are saved because they have walked an aisle, signed a decision card, or even repeated the correct formula! We are not saved by these things but by grace through faith in Jesus Christ, who sends His Holy Spirit to regenerate those who trust in Him.

Finally, we should glorify God for the greatness of the work of His Son in our salvation, which purchases for us not only forgiveness but also new life, not only a new standing with God but also a new relationship with His Son through the Holy Spirit. We should also glorify God for the totality of that work, not only providing the sacrifice but enabling us to receive its benefits through the work of the Spirit. That new relationship into which we are enabled by the Spirit to enter with the Son at conversion is called the Christian life, and the change in us which was inaugurated in regeneration continues in the process of sanctification. Sanctification is that aspect of the Holy Spirit's work with which we are most concerned in our daily lives as believers pursuing our walk with the Lord. About it much has been written, many questions raised, many controversies stirred up. You might wonder, after all we've seen that is done for the believer at conversion, why this ministry of the Spirit is even needed. The answers to such questions will occupy us for much of the remainder of our studies, for on them to a large extent the effectiveness or frustration of your Christian life depends.

Questions for Further Study

1. Carefully define the following terms in your own words; then check them in a good theological dictionary and compare the results.

    A. Salvation

    B. Justification

    C. Sanctification

    D. Regeneration

    E. Conversion

2. Look up the term *ordo salutis* in a theological dictionary and in the index of a couple of standard systematic theology texts (e.g., Hodge, Berkhof, Strong, Erikson, etc.). What does it mean? What difference does it make which order we adopt in our understanding?

3. Why is the Holy Spirit especially appropriate as the One who effects regeneration in believing sinners? How is this

work related to His general work as the personal Agent and Representative of Christ?

4. List some practical applications of biblical teaching on regeneration and conversion. Specifically, how can we preach the gospel in such a way that people simultaneously feel their hopelessness apart from the Spirit's work and freedom to respond to His enabling as they come to Christ?

7

SANCTIFICATION: SIN AND HOLINESS

In our discussion of regeneration we learned something about the important distinction between the objective and subjective aspects of God's work of salvation in our lives. We are given both a standing and a state, both position and a possession, both an objective and subjective work, and the subjective depends upon the objective. In dealing with our sin, God first objectively justifies us: He pronounces us innocent of sin on the basis of Christ's sacrifice in our behalf. In God's eyes it is as though I had never sinned, a popular and a good definition of justification. Only thus could we be saved, for we are given a standing and a position before God which we never could have earned through our own efforts to stop sinning. But there is a discrepancy now introduced between our standing and our state. The guilt of sin has been dealt with, but the corruption of sin and the tendency to sin still remain in our nature. Before we come to glory, these things must also be removed; not only that, but they constitute a hindrance to our spiritual lives as long as they remain.

God's solution to this problem is to give us, along with justification, a new nature in regeneration. He means for that new, holy, and spiritual nature to grow stronger and more dominant until, when we reach heaven, it will be the only nature we have. In the meantime, the process of nurturing that new life and putting to death the old is one of the main businesses of the Christian life. It is a process of becoming actually as well as officially holy. It is the work of the Holy Spirit, and we call it sanctification.

The Seriousness of Sin

Sanctification deals with the lingering effects and remnants of sin in the life of a person who has already been decisively redeemed from sin. Though sanctity is merely a synonym for holiness, we have to begin our study of sanctification by giving our attention to sin. The saints of old, both in biblical times and in church history, had a hatred for sin which is rare among professing Christians today, a hatred of sin which made sanctification a matter of great importance to them. Therefore, if we are to view the doctrine of sanctification biblically, we will have to recover something of the seriousness with which those old saints viewed their daily warfare against the world, the flesh, and the devil. Wasn't sin totally removed from our record by the blood of Christ? Doesn't the Bible teach that our justification is absolute? Why is a little continuing entanglement with sin in this life such a big deal, especially since we aren't saved by works anyway? The answer to that question lies in seeing what sin really is in itself and to God.

Current Weakness on the Doctrine of Sin

Of all the doctrines we say we believe as evangelical Christians but really find ourselves embarrassingly weak on, the doctrine of sin is one of the chief. Our very language betrays our weak view of what sin is, for it is the language of euphemism. Euphemism is the substitution of a softer, less threatening word for a more accurate word which we do not wish to face. People do not die any more; they "pass away." A schoolboy who is lazy "has difficulty concentrating"; if he is also a brat, he "has difficulty adjusting." These are euphemisms, and we habitually use a great many of them to soften the reality of what sin is. Thus, people do not commit crimes because they are wicked; they "make a mistake" because they are "victims of society." (For some reason, the people against whom the crime was committed seem to be the only ones who do not adopt such a position.) Likewise, instead of committing fornication or adultery it is now possible instead to have an "intimate relationship." If that intimate relationship happens to involve gross perversion, it becomes an "alternate life-style." While most believers do not indulge in such blatant euphemisms as these, they have been affected by the verbal environment they create to the point that they too have great difficulty speaking plainly about sin.

When I taught freshman English at the University of Georgia, I had a student who was a zealous member of a prominent parachurch organization. He was emboldened by the fact that he had a Christian professor to write a paper on evangelism which included a sample presentation of the gospel. The closest he got to suggesting that the gospel has anything to do with sin was advising that Christian witnesses suggest to potential converts that they "admit to God that you have tried to live independently of Him." The formula is true as far as it goes, but it does not go far enough. It is not just that we have tried to live apart from God and thereby missed out on a few spiritual goodies; we have transgressed His law and grievously offended His holy character. But my freshman friend's language was an example of the trend in Christian language against reckoning with the seriousness of what sin is. (We dealt with this phenomenon from another angle in our discussion of conviction.) Until we come to grips with the seriousness of sin, we will have only a shallow understanding of salvation and a shallow experience of sanctification.

Biblical Reactions to Sin

We might admit to being imperfect, but we sometimes feel as if God almost owes us salvation. We aren't really all that surprised that He loves us. The contrast between our language and the biblical language is nothing short of astounding. Job was by

God's own account a righteous and upright man; but when he met God, he reacted like this:

> I have declared that which I did not understand, things too wonderful for me, which I did not know. Hear now, and I will speak; I will ask Thee, and do Thou instruct me. I have heard of Thee by the hearing of the ear; but now my eye sees Thee; therefore I retract, and I repent in dust and ashes. (Job 42:3–6)

When Isaiah saw the Lord, he had a very similar reaction: "Woe is me, for I am ruined! Because I am a man of unclean lips, and I live among a people of unclean lips; for my eyes have seen the King, the Lord of hosts" (Isa. 6:5). When Peter caught a glimpse of who Jesus really was in the miraculous draft of fishes, he fell down at his feet crying, "Depart from me, for I am a sinful man, O Lord!" (Luke 5:8). Paul, when he thought of the remnants of sin and its power in his own post-conversion life and how it frustrated the joyful concurrence with the law of God in his inner being almost screamed, "Wretched man that I am! Who will set me free from the body of this death?" (Rom. 7:24). Such is the typical biblical response to the awareness of sin in one's life.

Are your modern sensibilities a bit offended with that kind of talk? Does it make you at least a little uncomfortable? If someone gave a fervent testimony in those terms in an evening service at your church, would it make you just a bit embarrassed? Do you find such language somewhat exaggerated and even theatrical? If so, yours is a typical modern response, and it demonstrates just how much our relativistic age has conditioned our own thinking about the seriousness of sin. At least one more question must be asked: do we really think we are any better than those ancient heroes of the faith?

The biblical writers we have quoted had one thing in common: they were all men who had met God. And a glimpse of God as He really is will do two things to your concept of sin. First, it will deepen your awareness of the extent of your sinfulness. As long as you compare yourself with other people, you can convince yourself that you are not so bad. But when you see yourself in the unspotted light of God's holiness, it is a different story. I once illustrated this point for my congregation by holding up a piece of paper and asking them to tell me what color it was. "White," they all replied. Then I held it up next to a sheet that was really white. The original sheet of paper suddenly turned a dingy yellow or tan. It doesn't matter how we look compared to other people. God is the Judge of all the earth, and the standard of His judgment is the unerring and incomprehensibly pure standard of His own burning holiness. *He is the One with whom we have to do.*

The second thing an encounter with God will do to your concept of sin is deepen your awareness of the evil of any sin. When you catch even a far-off glimpse of His immeasurable and incomprehensible goodness you realize in a new way what sin really is. It is not simply the transgression of an arbitrary set of rules; it is not some peccadillo to be sniffed at by a fastidious conscience. It is a wicked, despicable, ungrateful rebellion against our good and gracious King; it is a loathsome cancer eating away at the moral fabric of the universe He made and loves, for which He holds us responsible! It is shameful, offensive, and ugly. It is repulsive to God. And to the extent to which we love Him who first loved us, we will find sin's presence in our lives simply intolerable.

The Theology of Sin

There are many benefits to taking sin seriously, not the least of which is that it fosters good theology. This is particularly evident when we come to the doctrine of sanctification. It is an inviolable rule that a person's understanding of the holiness of God will be coordinated with the depth of his sense of sin. Isaiah is the perfect example of that principle at work. It was after his great vision of the Lord high and lifted up, with His train filling the temple and the seraphim calling out "Holy, Holy, Holy is the Lord of hosts, the whole earth is full of His glory," that Isaiah recognized his own sinfulness and was able to receive forgiveness and cleansing (Isa. 6:1–7).

It is impossible to even begin to comprehend the love and the grace of God until we reckon with the sinfulness of sin. The most profound verse in all the Bible may be Romans 5:8—"God demonstrates His own love toward us, in that while we were yet sinners, Christ died for us." He did not die simply to redeem people who are the victims of sin, but people who are the perpetrators of it, people who are in love with it and who consequently hate Him and all that He stands for. (If we do not think that sin involves hatred of God, it is because we are not thinking of the God who is there in all His holiness and justice, with His implacable demands for our ultimate allegiance. We might as sinners be in love with the comfortable and unimposing Grandfather in Heaven who exists only in our own self-serving imaginations; but the living God is another story.) A love so sacrificial for creatures who were ultimately unlovable—a love strong enough to overcome the force of His righteous wrath against all sin and evil, including us—such is the love of God. You will never plumb the depths of it until you are willing to face the true blackness of sin.

In every aspect of the theology of salvation, a healthy view of the seriousness of sin points us in the right direction. All cheap views of the atonement, all shallow views of the application of the atonement have in common an inadequate appreciation of the seriousness of sin. When you see sin for what it is you will also see the necessity of the vicarious, substitutionary atonement through the death of Christ and the hopeless superficiality of all views which make the attainment of salvation in any way dependent on human works. It is either all of God or not at all. Trivializing the seriousness of sin inevitably leads to compromise of the principles of grace alone and faith alone, and ultimately the loss of the gospel.

Sin and Sanctification

In the area of sanctification, a right view of sin immediately shows us both the importance of the doctrine and the rationale for the Holy Spirit's involvement in the work. When sin becomes as intolerable to us as it is to God, we will want to be rid of every vestige of it, and we will no longer be able to deny its presence. It is peculiarly the work of the Holy Spirit to aid us in that quest: for the essence of His work is to glorify the Lord Jesus Christ by making Him real in our lives. The essence of sin is that it detracts from the glory of God in us (Rom. 3:23). It blurs the portrait of Christ which the Spirit is painting in us as we become conformed to His image (Rom. 8:29).

Christ is glorified in our justification as the love and the justice of God are blazoned forth on the cross for all the universe to see: God's justice demanding the death penalty for sin, and His love taking that penalty on Himself to spare us. In our sanctification, Christ is glorified by the progressive defeat of sin in its remaining effects and power and by the Christlike lives which that defeat releases into the world. Hence sanctification is essential to the Spirit's mission of glorifying Jesus Christ.

In Romans 8:28, God predestined those He called and justified to be conformed to the image of His Son and eventually glorified (the culmination of sanctification in heaven when the defeat of sin is rendered final and permanent, when we see Christ face to face and know Him as we are known). What God predestines must of necessity come to pass, so there is no prospect of anyone's being justified and not sanctified. Sanctification becomes then, not the basis of justification, but certainly evidence of it. The Holy Spirit cannot be expected to convict and call and regenerate people and then leave His task half done by neglecting their sanctification. Sanctification is not an optional "graduate level" course for gung-ho Christians, but an absolute requirement for all. Its progress may be slow or rapid. The believer may cooperate with it or hinder it, but if he is truly saved, he is going to have to deal with it. You simply cannot be indwelt by a Spirit who is holy and escape the issue.

A proper sense of the sinfulness of sin will also keep us from depending on our own strength. It will keep us mindful of our dependence on the Holy Spirit for anything of spiritual good that will ever be in us. This consciousness of sin may thus be the key to the whole doctrine (and experience) of sanctification, and may therefore explain why it is often the holiest people who, like Paul, think of themselves as the chief of sinners (1 Tim. 1:15). May we all come to think—and live—as Paul did, to the glory of Jesus Christ.

Questions for Further Study

1. What is the difference between justification and sanctification? What does each contribute to the whole process of salvation? Which is the ground of the other? Why?

2. Why does sin continue to have an influence on the lives of redeemed people?

3. Contrast the reactions of biblical figures (Job, David, Isaiah, Peter, Paul, etc.) to the realization of sin in their lives with typical modern responses to the same realization. What do you think accounts for the difference?

4. Develop a biblical response to the following statement: "Because all sin, past, present, and future, is covered by the blood of Christ, and because salvation is in no way dependent on my works or performance, there is therefore no need to be concerned about the continuing presence of sin in my life." (Hints: In what way is it a misapplication of important biblical truths? In what passages does the apostle Paul respond to similar reasoning?)

8

SANCTIFICATION:
THE NATURE OF HOLINESS

In the last chapter we saw something of the urgency with which we should pursue our study of the doctrine of sanctification. At the time of our conversion we are justified in heaven, but we are not yet glorified. Although sin is erased from our record in justification, sin is not yet eradicated from our experience nor from our natures, and that fact distresses us. We need the continuing work of the Holy Spirit in our lives as believers after conviction, calling, and regeneration to make us increasingly what we already are officially—sinless. That work we call sanctification.

Because sanctification deals with the daily ins and outs of the Christian walk, and because its successful pursuit directly affects the quality and intimacy of our fellowship with God, it has been of great interest to God's true people, especially in times of great spiritual awakening. Hence a host of different perspectives have arisen in church history as people have come to different answers to the questions raised by the experience of living the Christian life. Whole theological systems have been generated and many movements spawned as people have sought help in this area. Many have been helped, but unfortunately a great deal of confusion has also resulted. Sanctification deals not just with outward behavior but also (and, perhaps more basically) with the inward state of the heart, where subjectivism becomes an ever-present danger. It is easy in moments of intense religious fervor to confuse the smoke of emotional experience with the fire of real advance in godliness. And while it may be true that where there is smoke there is fire, all who are skilled in woodcraft know that if there is any hard and fast relationship between the thickness of the smoke and the heat or clarity of the flames, it is that sometimes the hottest fires give off hardly any smoke at all. Often they do—but it is seldom a thick, black fume which calls attention to itself.

A great many questions have been raised about sanctification. We will try to give some biblical answers to some of the most significant. What is the definition of sanctification, or, what is the nature of holiness? How perfectly can it be achieved in this life? What, if any, role does a second crisis experience of grace (sometimes called the "second blessing") have to play? How does sanctification relate to the baptism with or fullness of the Holy Spirit? Are there means the Spirit uses to promote sanctification in our lives? What are they and how do we avail ourselves of them? Is the believer essentially active or passive in their application? If we can answer these questions biblically we will have a good start in understanding the doctrine of sanctification and the Spirit's work in it. In this chapter we will deal with the first: What is the real nature of sanctification and holiness?

Holiness: Definitions

The word translated "sanctify" in the New Testament is the Greek *hagiazo*. The adjective form is *hagios*, "holy." So *hagiazo* means to make holy or to consecrate. The idea comes from the Old Testament ceremony for consecrating the altar and the various implements used in the tabernacle (Ex. 40:9). When the anointing oil was applied to them they became holy, that is, set apart from common use and for the Lord's service. So the most basic meaning of sanctification is being made holy, and the root meaning of holiness is set aside or separated, set apart for a special purpose. God is holy, that is, transcendently separate from the world and its corruption. The temple vessels were holy, that is, set apart, separated from the world for the service of God. God's Spirit is particularly designated as the Holy Spirit. So, too, believers whom He regenerates and indwells must become holy—set apart from the world for the service of God. This involves being set apart in a practical sense, from the world considered as a system (*cosmos*) of things which is fallen, trying to exist in terms of its own principles apart from the sovereignty of God. So sanctification involves a willingness to become different in practical terms from the rebellious world around us: its patterns of thought, its priorities, its orientation to selfish gratification, its assumptions, its ways.

Holiness and Sanctification

Most people think of sanctification as moral purity or victory over sin and the flesh. Such definitions are really the connotation of the word, but they are legitimately derived from its denotation which is simply "separation." To be "separate" from the world in this sense is not simply to be aloof from it, must less isolated from it: it rather involves being set apart from the world unto God for His service in the world. We have been designated for the service of a God who is absolutely good, whose character is the foundation and source for the objective moral law built into the universe He created, and whose program for that universe involves the defeat of sin. Therefore, that very separation entails a consequent demand of moral purity on our part. The root meaning of holiness is separation and that involves a moving away from all that is evil and out of harmony with the character and will of God who has redeemed us. So the popular definition, though incomplete, is not at all inaccurate: the denotation and connotation form logical parts of one rich and unified concept.

The New Testament has much to say about Christians being consecrated, set apart from the world to the service of God. In

Acts 26:18, Paul described his mission as one of opening people's eyes so that they might "turn from darkness to light and from the dominion of Satan to God, in order that they may receive forgiveness of sins and an inheritance among those who have been sanctified by faith" in Christ. So faith in Christ not only saves but it also sanctifies, or sets the believer apart. Specifically, the believer is removed from darkness to light and from Satan's kingdom to God's. Without such a separation, or transfer, from one realm, one set of loyalties, one way of life, to another, there is no conversion. That is why Paul frequently uses the word *saint* ("holy one" or "sanctified one") as a synonym for believer or Christian (1 Cor. 1:2; 2 Cor. 1:1; Eph. 1:1).

There is a definite break with sin in principle when a person becomes a Christian. Theologians call that break *definitive sanctification,* and it explains why the New Testament calls all believers saints irrespective of their level of spiritual maturity. There still remains the task of working out the implications of that definitive break in the details of personality, thoughts, motive, and behavior. The "inner man" of the truly regenerate "concurs with the law of God," but another law in the members of the body still works to thwart the full implementation of that original commitment (Rom. 7:22–23). Therefore the inner man needs to be "strengthened with power through His Spirit" (Eph. 3:16) so that the outworking of that commitment may go forward. That process of outworking and strengthening is the work of the Holy Spirit, and it is the aspect of sanctification which is usually considered in the discussions; we might call it *progressive sanctification* to distinguish it from definitive sanctification.

Definitive sanctification is related to repentance, conversion, and justification; it is God's declaration of His ownership and the believer's consequent new identity. Progressive sanctification is the continuing and increasing actualization of that declaration and destiny in our experience. In justification we are forgiven for sin, and its guilt is remitted; in sanctification we are empowered to conquer sin, and its effects are defeated. In repentance we turn our backs on sin; in sanctification we are helped to live by that commitment. In adoption we are given a new identity; in sanctification we are enabled to live up to it. In regeneration we are given a new nature and a new life; in sanctification we are strengthened to live according to that nature and simply to live that life. It involves the daily process of crucifying the self, dying to sin, living to Christ, and producing the fruit of the Spirit for the glory of the One who sent Him to indwell us.

The Necessity of Sanctification

We are to become actually as well as declaratively holy, and that involves moral purity. The emphasis in the New Testament on the necessity of moral purity in the lives of believers and its connection with sanctification is astounding for those who have never surveyed it. "God has not called us for the purpose of impurity, but in sanctification," said Paul, adding that those who reject this principle have rejected the God who gives the Holy Spirit (1 Thess. 4:7–8). Those who show no evidence of sanctification at all are presumed to be false brethren with no inheritance in the kingdom (1 Cor. 6:9–11).

Because God promises to be a father to those who turn to Him, we should "cleanse ourselves from all defilement of flesh and spirit, perfecting holiness [sanctification] in the fear of God" (2 Cor. 7:1). The whole point of reconciliation is so that God can "present you before Him holy and blameless and beyond reproach" (Col. 1:22). Shall we continue in sin simply because we are saved by grace and not works, accepting as it were justification alone without sanctification? Paul found this thought inconceivable: "May it never be!" (Rom. 6:2).

Especially significant is Romans 8:29–30, the so-called "golden chain" of salvation. Christians disagree on whether God predestines specific individuals to salvation or merely foreknows who will believe, but there can be no debate that "whom He foreknew, He also predestined to become conformed to the image of His Son." What goes for predestination goes also for election: "He chose us in Him before the foundation of the world, that we should be holy and blameless before Him" (Eph. 1:4).

In other words, our usual concept of the plan of salvation is backward. God did not plan to save us from the guilt and penalty of sin and then, as an afterthought, decide to throw in sanctification as a kind of supplement to justification in order to deal with the pesky aspects of sin left over in this life. Rather, God's purpose was that we should be holy and blameless before Him in love. This could only happen as a result of the Holy Spirit's presence in our lives, and that could only happen if our relationship with God was restored. Our restoration made necessary a substitute to bear our guilt and represent us before the Father. Thus justification is not an end in itself. Together with sanctification it forms one unified package to accomplish God's purpose: a complete restoration of His fallen creatures to the image of Christ. As their Redeemer through His blood and Sanctifier through His personal Representative, the Holy Spirit, He would receive all the glory.

Holiness

Sanctification then is the process of becoming holy, separated unto God, and consequently morally pure. Ultimately, holiness is conformity to the character of Jesus Christ. "He is the radiance of His glory and the exact representation of His nature" (Heb. 1:3). He is the only begotten Son of the Father (John 3:16) who came into the world as light to declare to us the God whom no one can see (John 1:9,14,18). Therefore, it is no accident that the purpose of salvation is defined in terms of predestination to conformity to Jesus Christ (Rom. 8:29). In Him we see perfect obedience to the will of God. He did only what He saw the Father doing (John 5:19). Jesus said that His very meat and drink was to do the will of the Father (John 4:34), even if it meant death on a cross (Luke 22:42). Jesus stressed the necessity of inward as well as outward obedience in his most well-known discourse—lust is tantamount to adultery, hatred to murder (Matt. 5:22,28). When asked to define the greatest commandment, he quoted Deuteronomy 6:5: "You shall love the Lord your God with all your heart, and with all your soul, and with all your mind" (Matt. 22:37). Jesus added that Leviticus 19:18 was only second to it: "You shall love your neighbor as yourself" (Matt. 22:39).

What is holiness? What is the character of Jesus Christ? It is too rich a concept to be summarized easily, and so the Bible gives us many summaries: the Ten Commandments, the Two

Commandments, the Sermon on the Mount, the Fruit of the Spirit. It is the Old Testament viewed through the lens of the life and teaching of Christ as revealed in the Gospels. It takes nothing less than the whole of Scripture to do it justice. It is perfect obedience to the law of God flowing from a heart purely motivated by love of God and zeal for His glory first, and then love for one's neighbor as His creature. What is the standard and the goal? It is perfection in these things. "You shall be holy, for I the Lord your God am holy" (Lev. 19:2). "Therefore you are to be perfect, as your heavenly Father is perfect" (Matt. 5:48).

Perfection is the goal of sanctification. This is what the older theologians used to call "gospel holiness." It is God's will for every Christian; in heaven it is the destiny of every Christian; and it ought to be the burning desire of every Christian in this life. It is complete and perfect conformity to the character of God as revealed in Jesus Christ. It is perfect obedience to His law, flowing from perfect submission to His will, which flows from perfect love of His person. It is an absolute and constant purity of thought, word, and deed, of action, intent, and motive. It is a life which does not fall short of the glory of God, consciously or unconsciously, intentionally or unintentionally. This is holiness. There have been many debates concerning whether holiness can be entirely achieved in this life or not, and that is a question we must deal with in our next chapter. However, we must understand that holiness is the goal. Whether or not we can attain it perfectly before we reach glory, we are unbiblical if we are prepared to be satisfied with anything less.

This is gospel holiness, and it is not optional, for while sanctification does not save, it is nonetheless true that being saved sanctifies. Theology is unfaithful to its calling if it ever allows itself to degenerate into a merely academic discussion, and so I must not close this chapter without asking you: have you attained to a measure of such holiness? Are you content with the level you have? If you are, I fear for your soul! Are you hungry for more? If not, I can give you no assurance that you are saved and have any hope of heaven, for, whatever formula you may recite, you show no evidence of spiritual life, no evidence of being indwelt by the Holy Spirit, of being chosen before the foundation of the world that you might be holy and blameless in Him. Your state is a very serious one indeed, and you need to reexamine the ground you stand on carefully. You need to repent and receive Jesus Christ as your Lord and Savior from sin in true and living faith. If you do trust in Him, does your love for Him make you hungry for more of His holiness in your life? Then rejoice, for "by His doing you are in Christ Jesus, who became to us wisdom from God, and righteousness, and sanctification, and redemption" (1 Cor. 1:30). What you seek is found in Jesus Christ, who imparts it through His Agent the Holy Spirit.

Questions for Further Study

1. Give some biblical definitions for sin and holiness. How do they contrast?

2. What do justification and regeneration contribute to salvation? What do they leave undone? How does sanctification relate to them?

3. What are some of the questions about the process of sanctification which have been raised in the history of the church?

4. What is the difference between "definitive" and "progressive" sanctification?

5. Why is the doctrine of sin (hamartiology) an important part of the context for the discussion of sanctification?

6. What is the goal of salvation? Of sanctification in that context?

7. "We must neither confuse justification with sanctification nor separate them." Is this statement true? Why or why not? What are the consequences of "confusing" or of "separating" the two?

9

SANCTIFICATION: HOW FAR IN THIS LIFE?

We have seen so far that the work of the Holy Spirit is to glorify Jesus Christ by communicating to believers the blessings which He won for them on the Cross; in other words, to make Jesus real in our lives. We have seen that in sanctification the Holy Spirit makes real in our practical experience the *righteousness* of Jesus Christ which was legally reckoned as ours at conversion in justification—holiness. And we have seen that holiness is *separation* from the world and all evil, being *set apart* from the world for the service of God, a particular kind of separation which has as a necessary consequence an absolute demand of moral purity. Holiness is nothing less than perfect conformity to the character of Jesus Christ.

Traditional View

Well, how do you pursue it? The Protestant Reformers emphasized what they called "the means of grace." The idea was God has instituted certain practices and ordinances which are designed to help us grow, and the Holy Spirit works through these things to nurture the new spiritual life implanted within us at regeneration. They include Bible reading, preaching, prayer, public worship, baptism, the Lord's Supper, and Christian fellowship. God has commanded these practices and promised to bless them, so the Spirit works through them when they are used in faith. The result is "Christ is formed in you" (Gal. 4:19). The process was expected to be lifelong; there might be setbacks and dramatic advances, but overall gradual improvement was looked for. The warfare of flesh and spirit would continue throughout this life with no *final* victory until the next life; nonetheless a measure of victory could be expected and experienced through faith.

The view we have just outlined is from a historical perspective which might be called the "standard" view of sanctification; something like it, in different words, is what most evangelicals outside a very consciously Wesleyan tradition have been taught. "You have two dogs inside you constantly fighting: The flesh and the spirit. Which one will win? The one you feed the most." The emphasis is on an unending warfare which is won (though never finally in this life) through a *process* of *nurture*. And surely the main outlines of it are biblical. Few evangelical Christians of any denomination would dissent from it as far as it goes, but there have been some who have questioned whether it goes far enough. The most famous and important such questioner was John Wesley.

Wesley's Contributions

In the midst of the religious fervor of the eighteenth century revivals, John Wesley felt the standard view was *not* enough. He argued that what God commands He must grant by faith, and, therefore, a state of "entire sanctification" or "Christian perfection" was indeed possible for the saints in this life. His doctrine of entire sanctification was highly controversial then, and it remains so today. Like Calvin, Wesley has been misunderstood and misrepresented by both his opponents and his adherents. In his own day he had to contend with followers whose claims were less sober and more extravagant than his own (though his

97

own words were considered inflammatory at the time). His teaching survives in the Wesleyan Holiness tradition and has had an influence on other forms of "deeper life" teaching. For those reasons alone it would be important for us to wrestle with Wesley's views. An even better reason lies in what following that intense seeker after holiness on his quest can teach even those of us who cannot assent to all he taught. *Can* Christians be entirely sanctified in this life? And what did Wesley mean by that phrase in the first place?

Wesley had always had a deep interest in holiness. He was a leader of the famous Holy Club at Oxford even before his evangelical experience at Aldersgate. He pursued his goal with rigorous self-discipline. The very name of his movement is indicative of his temperament: A "methodist" was originally someone who adopted a methodical approach to religion. But something more was needed, nothing less than a supernatural work of God.

The germ of the insight from which Wesley's doctrine of sanctification was worked out was radical. It affected him as the recovery of the gospel did Luther. It was that sanctification was not the result of self-mortification and self-effort; since God had commanded it, He must grant it *by faith*. Sanctification was then to be received by faith just as justification was. This was an important and liberating realization. It has been made by many saints in many ways, and perhaps most who have really known a close walk with the Lord would agree it is at least part of the truth. But Wesley's development of it had features which were hard for many to accept.

Sanctification was by faith and could, therefore, be received by faith just like justification—and not necessarily at the same time. Though theoretically you could be justified and sanctified at once, most believers would need a *second* crisis experience of grace—subsequent to conversion—when they would receive sanctification or "heart-cleansing" by faith. As some contemporary Wesleyans express it, "Conversion takes the Christian out of the world; sanctification takes the world out of the Christian." This "second blessing" would produce a state of heart in which there was an absence of any conscious or deliberate sin and in which love for God and others was the supreme ruling motive for action. This was "entire sanctification" or "Christian perfection," and there was no reason for any believer not to enter into it. Actually, all are *commanded* to enter into it. There *could* be a *complete* and potentially permanent victory over sin in this life, and the traditional teaching which denied such a possibility was simply defeatist, producing stunted Christian lives lacking in faith.

Wesley's Arguments

Such claims were startling, to say the least, and took some supporting. Wesley argued simply that God commands perfection and nothing less. He went back to texts such as Matthew 5:48, with its command to be perfect as God is perfect and 1 Peter 1:16 with its command to be holy as God is holy. He cited 2 Corinthians 7:1, which exhorts us to cleanse ourselves, "perfecting holiness in the fear of God." And he noted Paul's prayer in 1 Thessalonians 5:23 that God might "sanctify you entirely." Wesley then proceeded to argue in a very commonsense fashion that God, as a reasonable being, would not command the impossible; so since He obviously commands perfection, He must, therefore, also provide it through faith.

The reaction against the new doctrine was strong. People were horrified at what seemed to be the downgrading of conversion and faith in Christ implied in the need for a further experience and at the seemingly blasphemous claims to sinlessness implied by the testimonies of those who claimed that experience. In fairness to Wesley, it should be noted the emotional strength of the reaction produced a polarization in which it was easy to misrepresent Wesley's actual teaching. Some of his followers have compounded the problem by making more extravagant claims than he himself would have been comfortable with. He did speak of "Christian perfection," that is, the perfection proper to a Christian, but he did not like to use the phrase "sinless perfection." Wesley also viewed the state of entire sanctification, not as a plateau for believers who had now spiritually "arrived," but as a state within which there was room for and the need for further growth. His own followers have not always remembered these things, but *we* should as we evaluate his teaching biblically.

Evaluation of Wesley's View

What then are we to say of Wesley's doctrine of sanctification? Two features of it need close scrutiny: His view of the extent to which complete victory over sin is achievable in this life and his view of the means by which this victory is achieved. Is it biblically appropriate to speak of "entire sanctification," and what are we to make of the "second blessing" experience? We will address the first question in this chapter and turn to the second in the next chapter.

It must be said first of all that Wesley and his followers certainly take the Christian life and the problem of indwelling sin seriously. They are not easily satisfied with the mediocre commitment and the lukewarm spirituality which have become all too common in the average evangelical church of today. The intense desire for "more," even when it becomes misguided, is certainly preferable to the dead orthodoxy and the blasé attitude toward spiritual things which are too often the only alternatives people have been exposed to. For this the Wesleyan holiness tradition is to be commended. Also, it has done a great deal of good in that, by making holiness seem possible, it has encouraged many people to seek it actively. Wesleyan theology has fostered a deep and vital godliness in the lives of many of its adherents. If others of them have too easily confused godliness with a certain type of emotional experience (the besetting danger of that kind of approach to spirituality), Calvinism could be equally embarrassed were it to be judged by the lives of some Calvinists.

Moreover, the state of heart which Wesley describes—in which, at least for a while, all conscious and deliberate sin is banished and love for God and others holds sway—is certainly possible for believers in this life, and should be the condition that they aspire to be in. The key words are *conscious* and *deliberate*. As for love, it is difficult to be objective in evaluating the purity of our motives. But the alternative, unconfessed sin and a lack of love, should not be tolerated or accepted as inevitable by believers at all.

Having said all this, I would suggest that it is nonetheless a serious mistake for us to call this desirable and attainable state "entire sanctification" or perfection in any sense. Wesley bent over backward to deny that he was claiming that sinlessness was attainable in this life or that entire sanctification was a static state of perfection which required no further advance. Nevertheless, his very teaching required him to be making such denials constantly and they are not always convincing. When reading his works, one often gets the impression that his language is inconsistent, that in fact he is trying to have it both ways. If sanctification is really *entire*, how can further growth be possible? If we have reached a state of perfection in any sense, how can sin still be present at all? These inconsistencies signal us that there may be logical and biblical problems with Wesley's approach which lie beneath the surface.

A Dubious Assumption

I would suggest that the Wesleyan doctrine of sanctification (and many of its mutated descendants) suffers from at least three weaknesses. In the first place, its argumentation rests on an unproved assumption which may suggest more of eighteenth century rationalism than biblical theology: the assumption that God would not command the impossible. Why can't God command the impossible, at least in some sense? Where in the Bible is this principle revealed? Nowhere. It is true that God is a rational Being; therefore, He never is guilty of a true contradiction. It is not true that He is bound by logic; rather, His very character in its truthfulness is the source of logic. But many things which look illogical at first glance do not turn out to be so at all.

It is true, for example, that God will never command the logically impossible. He will never command anyone to draw a square circle or to do something and not do it at the same time. But holiness, sinlessness, is not logically impossible in this sense. It is not nonsense. It is a state which can exist, and which has existed—in Adam before the fall, and in Christ since. If we have made ourselves morally and existentially incapable of sinlessness through sin, if it has become practically impossible for us in that sense, why should God lower His standards to accommodate us? He commands perfect obedience of the unbeliever as well, but it is impossible for him. God could supernaturally grant the ability to perform what He commands perfectly, and confirm us in that gift with no possibility of falling. And He will in the next life. But to argue that He must in this life does not follow.

We ourselves often ask the impossible of ourselves. At least I do; every time I preach I aim higher than I can hit in terms of effectiveness and power. So it is perfectly reasonable for God to do the same. It proves nothing to say that because God commands perfection He therefore must grant it. We must see what the Bible *says* about whether and when it will be granted. That we will enjoy it in this life is simply not proved by the argument. It rests on assumption, not biblical teaching.

An Inadequate Definition of Sin

A second fallacy which besets Wesley's doctrine of sanctification lies in his definition of sin. We have frequently used the phrase "deliberate and conscious sin" in speaking of Wesley's teaching. This is because Wesley defined sin as "the voluntary transgression of a known law." And again, this is a good, reasonable, commonsense definition; but it is not the biblical definition. Biblically, sin is transgression of the law of God. But does the transgression have to be voluntary, conscious, and knowledgeable to be sinful? The answer is found in Leviticus 5:17–19.

> Now if a person sins and does any of the things which the Lord has commanded not to be done, though he was unaware, still he is guilty, and he shall bear his punishment. He is then to bring to the priest a ram without defect from the flock, according to your valuation, for a guilt offering. So the priest shall make atonement for him concerning his error in which he sinned unintentionally and did not know it, and it shall be forgiven him. It is a guilt offering; he was certainly guilty before the Lord.

The only way to claim that sin has been completely defeated in this life is to underestimate the subtlety of sin by limiting it to the "voluntary transgression of a known law." If you did not know it was wrong, you are not responsible; you might have made a mistake but were not guilty of sin, and therefore your level of spirituality is unaffected. But the biblical perspective is quite different: The sin of ignorance incurs guilt, needs atonement, and demands repentance and prayer for forgiveness. If it incurs guilt and needs atonement, then it also affects one's relationship with God and one's state of sanctification whether or not one is aware of these things.

Even in human law, the maxim is *ignorantia legis non excusat*: ignorance of the law is no excuse. In the higher standards of divine law the same principle holds. Sin is not the voluntary transgression of a known law; it is any deviation whatsoever from the character of God revealed in Jesus Christ. It is falling short of the glory of God (Rom. 3:23). If this seems unfair, it is probably because we are confusing a lessening of responsibility and guilt with an exoneration from these things. Imagine a concrete example of a sin of ignorance. Suppose a missionary goes to a tribe with a highly promiscuous culture and wins a convert. This convert commits fornication several times as usual, then finds out that this "normal" practice of his people is wrong. What is his position? He has done something which displeases God. He did it in ignorance, but he has done it. He is guilty of fornication. This knowledge grieves him, and he must confess his sin, forsake it, and ask (and receive) forgiveness. Now if he does it again, the guilt which goes with the act in itself is compounded by the additional sin of defiance. We have become so spiritually jaded that we can no longer recognize sin and guilt for what they are unless the compounding guilt of defiance is also present. But God, not our jaded consciences, is Judge.

The obvious conclusion is that the absence of conscious sin is no safe index of the entirety of our sanctification. Sin is too subtle and our hearts too deceitful and prone to rationalization for us ever to advance the claim that we have been "cleansed" from all remnants of indwelling corruption. This is not a counsel of despair but of realism about what the present life is like. Sanctification is like cleaning a large and complicated house with many rooms: Every time you think the job is done, you find another closet full of dust. Is this defeatism? No. Just because the job is bigger than you thought is no reason to wallow in the mud.

Eschatological Anachronism

The most serious objection against the conclusion we are reaching is that it limits the power of God, making sin ultimately stronger than the Holy Spirit. Yet the question is not whether God can finally remove all the effects of sin from our lives, but when He plans to do so. Why leave us in this world at all after we are saved?—To struggle against the enemy, who is within as well as without. That struggle is part of God's plan for this age of the world, and the final overthrow of the enemy is not yet. So the final reason not to encourage people to look for complete and total victory in this life is that such an expectation is eschatologically anachronistic. It misunderstands our position in the history of the great war in the heavenlies which still rages around us and within us.

When does Scripture say that this kind of final victory will take place? It has already taken place on the cross in one sense. It was as a result of Christ's victory there that God "raised Him from the dead, and seated Him at His right hand in the heavenly places," where He "put all things in subjection under His feet" (Eph. 1:20–22). But when will this victory be made manifest and experienced in its fullness? The burden of proof would be on anyone who suggested some time other than the return of Christ in judgment. For our position as believers in this age is that we live still in a creation which "groans and suffers the pains of childbirth" in its longing for redemption from the futility to which it is subjected. "And not only this, but also we ourselves, having the first fruits of the Spirit, even we ourselves groan within ourselves, waiting eagerly for our adoption as sons, the redemption of our body" (Rom. 8:22–23).

It is instructive to note that this description of our present situation is found in the supposedly "victorious" Romans chapter 8, not in the supposedly "defeated" chapter 7. So this is what the "victorious Christian life" actually feels like: frustration, pain, longing—and joy immeasurable and victory too. But the victory in our experience is obviously not as complete and full as it will be when Christ returns, a day we anxiously await. There is victory, there is joy, but it is not yet complete. We already have the first fruits of the Spirit, but not the final harvest. The same perspective is found in Ephesians 1:13-14, where we are sealed with the Holy Spirit who is given as a pledge or down payment of our inheritance. The wonderful thing about the Christian life is that we already have a foretaste of heaven because the Holy Spirit has come to indwell us and sanctify us. The word translated "pledge" in Ephesians 1:14 means a first payment in kind which closes the deal and obligates the parties to conclude the bargain. We have in the ministry of the Holy Spirit received a foretaste, a down payment, a deposit, an earnest of greater joys to come. But we will not be in heaven in terms of our experience until we get there. This earthly life is still designed to be a time of testing and trial and warfare even for believers who are in Christ already seated in the heavens. He represents us there; His presence there is the pledge that we will go there. In the meantime we represent Him here in a vale of tears from whose hardships and struggles we are not exempt.

We are made holy by our union with Jesus Christ. We are joined to Him already through the Liaison He has sent, the Holy Spirit. As He makes Jesus real to us, we become more like Him in character, thus fulfilling the Spirit's ministry of glorifying Jesus' name. But though we are truly united to Christ already, our union with Him is not as complete and full as it will be when He returns. "For now we see in a mirror dimly, but then face to face; now I know in part, but then I shall know fully, just as I also have been fully known" (1 Cor. 13:12). That vision, and nothing less than that, is the only thing that can bring about our entire sanctification. Such is the beauty and glory of His face, that to see it, to look fully upon it, will banish all thought of sin and all susceptibility to sin forever from those who love Him. Even the foretaste of it, as He is brought into our hearts by His Representative, the Holy Spirit, is enough to break the hold that sin has on us so that we already begin to be sanctified even now. When the dim glass is taken away and we know Him as we are known, then and only then will its hold be broken completely, finally, and forever. Until then, like Paul, I am "confident of this very thing, that He who began a good work in you will"—the tense used in Greek suggests we should translate—"continually perfect it until the day of Christ Jesus" (Phil. 1:6). We are still under construction, and the job will not be finished until that day.

Practical Implications

What are the practical conclusions we should draw from this discussion? One certainly is that we should be very careful both how we use and how we interpret our language when we speak of these things. It is easy to give the opposite impression from what you meant to say. I can remember preaching a sermon in which I was trying to make the point that preachers are human, that they have the same struggles in the Christian life as anyone else. A person came up to me afterward and said, "I'm sorry you think it's all right for Christians to sin." Needless to say, I was totally flabbergasted. I had not intended to convey any such thing, but that is what she heard: Christians sin all the time; even the preacher sins; it is to be expected. We are all going to be totally defeated until we get to heaven, so we might as well give up and resign ourselves to being poor, sinning Christians until then—sinning that grace might abound!

It should hardly need be said that the above description is a false picture of people who have been regenerated and are being indwelt by the Holy Spirit—people who already have foretastes of heaven and who are being progressively sanctified through the inward work of that same Spirit as He makes Jesus increasingly real in their lives. But it *does* need to be said, loud and clear and over and over again, such is our perverse tendency to misunderstand one another.

On the other hand, I am continually amazed by the picture of the Christian life which is painted by certain kinds of testimony. Often there is a tendency in public testimonies to make claims which in private conversation die the death of a thousand qualifications. Such a discrepancy between public and private reality serves only to discredit the Christian message in the eyes of a critical world. This is ultimately the problem with the Wesleyan view of the Christian life: It is guilty of false advertising. If traditional evangelicals have a tendency to complacency, to settle for less than what God can accomplish in their lives, movements which seek for "more" often end up only with inflated rhetoric and a tendency to confuse emotional intensity with real godliness.

There are many such movements. I have simply chosen the Wesleyan holiness tradition as the most credible and theologically developed example. We will meet some of the others before these studies are over. In dealing with all of them, great sensitivity is needed to what they are actually saying and what it means; for nothing has been more harmful to our ability to learn from one another than the polarization which results from hasty reactions to unfamiliar language. There can be no doubt in reading about Wesley's life that he was on to something *real*, something which many Christians have not yet attained. But his experience was not what he thought it was. It was neither entire nor perfect, and the unbiblical claims made for it and the unbiblical assumptions behind the exposition of it have perhaps made it even harder for Christians to experience it to the extent to which it can be known even now. Thus polarization works to weaken the whole church, as one side is led by wrong doctrine to dissipate their spiritual energy in exaggerated claims while the other throws out the experiential baby along with the doctrinally questionable bath water.

A second lesson is that the Christian life is a life of continual repentance. We never outgrow the need to pray "Forgive us our debts, as we also have forgiven our debtors" (Matt. 6:12). Our Lord's inclusion of this request in the model prayer indicates our continual need of praying it. It is, praise God, always abundantly answered by His grace (1 John 1:9). But we ought never to give the impression that we have left behind our need to pray it. This is not a stance of defeatism, but of humility before a God of holiness and grace. And with it the words of all the saints agree.

Wesley himself said in 1765, "I have told all the world I am not perfect. I have not attained the character I draw." If only all those he influenced were as honest and realistic about themselves! Then they, like Wesley, would be following the Lord's command: "So you too, when you do all the things which are commanded you, say, 'We are unworthy slaves; we have done only that which we ought to have done'" (Luke 17:10). And they would be following the example of the apostle Paul, whose testimony strikes the true biblical balance:

> Not that I have already obtained it, or have already become perfect, but I press on in order that I may lay hold of that for which also I was laid hold of by Christ Jesus. Brethren, I do not regard myself as having laid hold of it yet; but one thing I do: forgetting what lies behind and reaching forward to what lies ahead, I press on toward the goal for the prize of the upward call of God in Christ Jesus. (Phil. 3:12–14)

"Let us therefore," he continues, "as many as are perfect, have this attitude" (Phil. 3:15). What attitude? The attitude which constitutes Christian perfection for Paul is one which confesses that it is not perfect—yet.

Paul's testimony also leads us to the third lesson which this discussion ought to bring home to us: That, while the Christian life is not to be lived in a spirit of naive and premature triumphalism, neither is it to be a life of defeat and complacency. We press on. There are only two reasons why any believer would become complacent about the remaining influence of sin in his life: Either he thinks "God can't change me," or he thinks "God doesn't need to." As a result of the polarization which has taken place, many believers have unthinkingly begun operating on one of those two assumptions, though they would be reluctant to admit it even to themselves. But for people who really love Jesus Christ neither of these assumptions will satisfy for long. Those who have come to love Jesus instinctively know better than either, and they say with Paul, "One thing I do . . . I press on!" That is the testimony of a person who manifests in his life the work of the Holy Spirit, who came to glorify Christ as His personal Representative and Agent in our lives—by making us like Him—by making us holy.

Questions for Further Study

1. Summarize the "standard" view of how sanctification works.

2. What are the distinctives of Wesley's doctrine of sanctification? How did he support them?

3. What are some positive features of Wesley's teaching?

4. What are the three main weaknesses of his approach to "entire sanctification"?

5. What are some practical steps we can take to avoid falling into the traps either of defeatism or triumphalism?

10

SANCTIFICATION: WHAT ABOUT A SECOND BLESSING?

The Holy Spirit's mission is to glorify Jesus Christ by communicating to His people the blessings won by Christ for them on the cross. This involves making us Christlike as Christ Himself is brought into our lives and made real there through the Spirit. This also involves making us holy. It involves the process of sanctification. How this actually takes place in the depths of our souls is one of the great mysteries. We see what the fruit of the Spirit is, but it is much harder to see how it grows. This process of growth is never to be looked on as complete in this life, for the piety modeled by the New Testament saints is a piety of humility, though not a piety of defeatism. Now we must look more closely at the mechanics of the process, if you can call them that. Once again we find that the Wesleyan Holiness tradition is helpful in raising the questions, though we cannot completely agree with the way it answers them.

A Second Crisis Experience?

Wesley, as we have seen, argued that sanctification is to be received by faith in the same way as justification, but not necessarily at the same time. For most believers it would come at a special time of fresh dealing with God subsequent to conversion. So the question we must look into now is this: Does the Bible teach a definitive second crisis experience of grace as a or the primary way that a believer becomes sanctified?

Each word in that phrase is a technical term which needs to be precisely understood if we are to catch the full meaning of what is intended. We are speaking of a definitive experience, that is, a definite, clearly defined experience which can be identified and labeled. It is a second experience, subsequent to and distinguished from conversion. It is a crisis experience, occurring at a point in time and usually involving great emotional intensity. It is an experience; you know when you have had it—it is something you can feel. And it is an experience of grace; God is at work through His Spirit imparting the blessing in response to faith, not works.

Arguments for the Second Experience

The argument for the definitive and normative character of this experience is really quite simple, and has two strands. One depends on the assumption that what God commands He must grant, which we examined above. The emphasis on granting leads to an emphasis on receiving, with the implication that what is received is a package that one either has or has not opened. The other strand is the exhortation based on Acts 1:4 to tarry or wait until one is empowered by the Holy Spirit, with the assumption that what happened at Pentecost (or something like it) is intended as a pattern for subsequent generations of believers. Much debate usually ensues on whether the conversions recorded later in Acts reflect the Pentecostal pattern: whether the experience recorded was really a second or a first, and whether there was a special reason for the second experience if it is admitted.

The Central Issue

Unfortunately, people have sometimes not understood what the real debate is about. (The rise of the Pentecostal and the charismatic movements have confused the issue even further, but we will leave those matters until later.) Wesleyans do not deny that gradual growth occurs both before and after the second experience, and traditional evangelicals do not deny that there can be a fresh work of the Spirit after conversion which gives a great boost to the process of sanctification for many believers. So the issue is not whether second blessing(s) occur or whether they are real, but rather what their significance is and where the emphasis should be placed in our exhortation and instruction in the Christian life. Wider recognition of that fact would go a long way toward easing the polarization which has occurred between the two groups over the years.

Waiting?

As we evaluate that question, several facts are to be noted. The first is that the instruction to "wait" for a second work of the Holy Spirit is given once, in Acts 1:4, before Pentecost—and it is never repeated. There are incidents which proponents of a definitive second work claim as examples of it, but not one instance of a convert being exhorted to wait in those terms ever again. Now this fact is highly curious and demands explanation. The one which comes most readily to hand is what happened at Pentecost was in fact a unique occurrence which was not intended to be repeated. The command to wait was given because the Holy Spirit had not yet been poured out on the church. He had not yet begun His distinctive New Testament ministry. Therefore, the carrying out of the Great Commission, which depended on the Spirit's ministry, could not begin until the Spirit came. Does every believer need a personal Pentecost, or did the church as a whole rather need one Pentecost? The total absence of Pentecostal exhortation after the church got what it needed is a strong argument for the latter. It is not that fresh movements of the Spirit resulting in personal or corporate revival are not to be expected, but the evidence for making one of them a normative experience of grace parallel to conversion is lacking.

When you look at the New Testament in terms of its exhortations for people to go on in the Christian life, the preponderance of emphasis on using the means of grace to nurture a process of growth is striking. It is true that we are exhorted to be filled with the Holy Spirit (Eph. 5:18), but the verb tense used implies a continual process of filling rather than a one-time crisis. We are not exhorted to wait for such a crisis. Rather, we are urged to attend church (Heb. 10:25), to read our Bibles (1 Pet. 2:2; 2 Tim. 3:15), to pray (1 Tim. 2:1–2, Eph. 6:18), to resist the devil and draw near to God (Jas. 4:7–8), to exercise our spiritual gift(s) (1 Tim. 4:14), to set our minds on things above (Col. 3:2), to rejoice in the Lord (Phil. 4:4), to work out our salvation in fear and trembling (Phil. 2:12) as God works in us, to love the brethren (Phil. 1:9), to use discernment (Rom. 12:2, Phil. 1:10), to submit to the Lord and trust in Him (1 Pet. 5:6), to add to our faith virtue and knowledge (2 Pet. 1:5–7). In other words, we are to walk with the Lord, not to wait for some extra experience or blessing after conversion to make the Christian life work, but simply to get on with it.

Definitive or Progressive?

A second salient fact is that when sanctification is spoken of in the New Testament as something which happened at a definite point of time in the past, the context suggests that it is all believers who are being described. In 1 Corinthians 1:2, for example, Paul equated the church of Corinth with "those who have been sanctified." These same Corinthians used to be fornicators, idolaters, and thieves, but they ceased from such practices when they were washed, sanctified, and justified (1 Cor. 6:9–11). Yet these same people are described as carnal (3:2–3). Clearly carnality and entire sanctification are incompatible. The only way to reconcile such statements is to view the sanctification mentioned here as definitive sanctification, which, as we have seen, occurs at conversion.

It is an extremely romantic and unrealistic view of the New Testament church to assume that they had all been entirely sanctified by a second experience subsequent to conversion; yet such naiveté is required to make the statements about a past and completed sanctification square with a Wesleyan framework. The Corinthians, carnal as they were, had been set apart from the world by their repentance and faith in Christ. They had seen impressive supernatural manifestations of the Spirit, but they were not sanctified entirely by any means. They had had their second experience, but it is not what Paul mentioned when he referred to their sanctification, and it certainly had not done for them what the Wesleyan tradition would lead us to expect from it.

Progressive Sanctification

A third fact is that, while sanctification, apart from the definitive setting-apart which is entailed by repentance and conversion, is never clearly spoken of as a sudden occurrence, it is often clearly spoken of as a continuous, lifelong process. Second Corinthians 3:18 says, "We all, with unveiled face beholding . . . the glory of the Lord, are being transformed into the same image." Even in Wesley's proof text, 2 Corinthians 7:1, the commandment to cleanse ourselves from all defilement is explained by a present participle which implies a continuous process of "perfecting holiness in the fear of God." The goal of the ministry of spiritual gifts is that we should "grow up in all aspects into Him, who is the head, even Christ" (Eph. 4:15). Peter put an emphasis on qualities which should be ours and increasing (2 Pet. 1:8).

So What Was Pentecost?

Surely in the light of these facts, our emphasis in Christian growth should not be placed on the repetition of an event which was by its very nature unique but on the means of growth and nurture which the New Testament itself continually emphasizes. Pentecost was the point at which the Spirit began the distinctive ministry of indwelling and empowering for which He was unleashed by the resurrection and ascension of Christ. The first time for anything is always a unique and unrepeatable experience: Your first date, your first solo in the family car, your first sight of the ocean—none of these experiences is repeatable. In like manner, the Holy Spirit could only be poured out on the New Testament church for the first time once. That there were to be and have been fresh movements, fresh outpourings of the Spirit in power is not to be denied. But to take the disciples' experience before Pentecost, who were in the unique position of needing to wait for the Spirit to empower for witness, and make it paradigmatic for the experience of later generations of believers whose position in redemptive history was quite different, is neither warranted nor even reasonable, given that the rest of the New Testament does not exhort or teach in those terms.

What then did happen at Pentecost? Clearly it was not the beginning of the Spirit's ministry *per se*; if He had not been active in conviction, calling, and regeneration in some sense the disciples could not have followed the Lord at all, nor could there have been anyone saved throughout the Old Testament period. Humanity was just as fallen during those times, and their need for and dependence on those ministries of the Spirit which we have already examined were just as absolute as they are in this age. But Christ had not yet come, the veil of the temple was not yet torn, the sacrifice not yet made, nor was our human nature exalted to the right hand of the throne in the person of our resurrected and triumphant Mediator.

With all these things a new stage in God's program of bringing glory to Himself through His Son had been reached, and therefore the Spirit's ministry of glorifying Jesus Christ could be kicked into a higher gear. It is not now the promised Messiah but the risen Lord which the Spirit makes real in our lives, which allows for a corresponding increase in the depth and power of the Spirit's work. Jeremiah had prophesied it:

> "Behold, days are coming," declares the Lord, "when I will make a new covenant with the house of Israel. . . . This is the covenant which I will make. . . . I will put My law within them, and on their heart I will write it; and I will be their God, and they shall be My People. And they shall not teach again, each man his neighbor and each man his brother, saying, 'Know the Lord,' for they shall all know Me, from the least of them to the greatest of them," declares the Lord, "for I will forgive their iniquity, and their sin I will remember no more." (Jer. 31:31–34)

Surely the Old Testament saints knew the Law, had a relationship with God, and experienced the forgiveness of sin; but once Christ had come, those blessings would become known more fully as we move from a provisional, promissory age to one of fulfillment. And that is precisely what happens in the New Testament: A deeper, more thorough internalization of the law of God, a more intimate fellowship with the Father through the Son, and a surer rejoicing in the forgiveness of sin is possible once the mission of Christ is completed.

Thus the Spirit's ministry of applying these things to the hearts of God's people enters into a deeper, more intense mode. Its purpose is to empower the church for its task of glorifying Christ through its witness to Him, as the Great Commission can now be undertaken in a way which never came to fruition in the Old Testament; Pentecost was the day it officially began, with great fanfare and fireworks. The first coming of Christ released the power of the Spirit in a new way, as already the powers of the age to come can be experienced. The final fruition of His work awaits the Second Coming, when we will be glorified by that same Spirit.

Summary

The instruction to "wait" for a special post-conversion experience with the Spirit is never repeated after Pentecost. Sanctification, when referred to as an attainment gained at a point of time, refers to the whole church, not just to a few selected believers. While there are no exhortations to wait for another "experience," there are plenty of exhortations to grow in grace. Although sanctification is never clearly identified with a crisis experience other than conversion, it is frequently spoken of as a continuous process. Pentecost simply ushers in a new phase in the Spirit's work which corresponds to the new situation introduced by the death, resurrection, ascension, and enthronement of Christ at the right hand of the Father, a phase in which the blessings enjoyed by the Old Testament saints are made available in a deeper way because now the Messiah they looked for has come and received glory.

Therefore, while subsequent crises in which the Holy Spirit furthers His work of glorifying Jesus through the sanctification of His people are by no means precluded, the Bible gives us no reason to identify a particular, definitive subsequent crisis experience with the work of sanctification. Rather, the emphasis is on a process of growth through the nurture of the spiritual life implanted in believers by the Spirit at regeneration.

Implications: The Unity of the Spirit's Work

Our theology of the Holy Spirit should reflect the unity and continuity of His work. Conviction, calling, illumination, regeneration, and sanctification are all aspects of the same work analyzed from different perspectives according to their aims and effects. Conviction and calling prepare the sinner for the introduction of spiritual life; regeneration is the implantation of that life; sanctification is the nurture and growth of that life from a moral and volitional standpoint, and illumination is the same work from a cognitive or intellectual point of view. It is misleading to say that Christ saves and the Spirit sanctifies; rather, it is all Christ's work from beginning to end, accomplished by Christ and applied by His personal Agent in our lives, the Holy Spirit.

The Necessity of Sanctification

Sanctification, gospel holiness, separated living, the Christian life, or whatever you want to call it, is not an optional graduate-level course for especially spiritual Christians. It is a required course, not an elective. It is not a second experience which you may or may not have, but it is implicit in and demanded by the original experience of conversion to Christ. Why then do so many professing Christians today show little evidence of sanctification? There are at least two reasons. First, not all professing Christians are in fact saved. We are saved by faith in Christ, not by an unthinking outward profession of the religion of our parents or our peer group. Unless a profession of faith in Christ produces some evidence of commitment to Christ, there is no reason to believe that it is genuine saving faith. The second reason is a lack of sound teaching and an abundance of false teaching concerning both salvation and the Christian life. Too many inquirers are encouraged to believe that they can accept Christ as Savior now and worry about His lordship over their lives later.

It is impossible to produce an example of such evangelism in the New Testament. The Philippian jailer was told simply to believe, but he was to believe on the Lord Jesus in order to be saved. Our efforts to bend over backward to avoid implying works for salvation are well-intended but theologically misconceived, for we cannot preserve an orthodox soteriology by compromising our Christology. Faith in a Jesus who is not *Lord* is faith in a false Christ who simply does not exist except in the deluded imaginations of people. We are saved by faith alone; but unless it leads to a confession of the lordship of Christ it is not what the New Testament means by faith (Rom. 10:9). Such a diluted gospel has two effects: It encourages people who are not Christians at all to think that they are, and it freezes some who are truly saved in a state of permanent spiritual infancy. The cure for this malady is for the church to recover and proclaim a unified and biblical view of the work of the Holy Spirit in the totality of redemption once again.

The Centrality and Sufficiency of Christ

To see the centrality of the Holy Spirit in the whole work of redemption is to see the centrality of Jesus Christ in the whole of that work, for the Spirit acts for Him as His Representative and Agent in that work. In sanctification, holiness is conformity to Jesus Christ which flows from the unity with Him which the Holy Spirit effects as the Liaison between us and Jesus Christ until Christ returns. Therefore, the person who truly has Jesus Christ has everything needed to live the Christian life. There is nothing "extra" which he needs to wait for or seek. It is all there from the beginning; you simply need to work the implications of it out ever more fully in your life (Phil. 2:12–13).

Paul made this point in his letter to Philemon. He prayed for Philemon that "the fellowship of your faith may become effective through the knowledge of every good thing which is in you for Christ's sake" (v. 6). How are Christians to grow? Not by seeking some extra blessing beyond the knowledge of Christ but by becoming aware of all that is already there because Christ is there.

In Ephesians 1:3 Paul blessed the God who has blessed believers with *every* spiritual blessing in the heavenly places in Christ. Beyond all argument, it is impossible to have more than every spiritual blessing. But while it is not possible to have more *than* every spiritual blessing, it is possible to have more *of* every spiritual blessing. That is why Paul went on to pray for these same people that they might be enlightened to know the hope of their calling, the riches of the glory of their inheritance, the surpassing greatness of God's power, the strength which the Spirit gives in the inner man, the incomprehensible love of Christ, and the very fullness of God (Eph. 1:17–19; 3:14–19). Those who are in Christ have every spiritual blessing, but they need to know more about what is in them, not just intellectually but experientially and practically. What they have to learn is something endless and inexhaustible: It is the person of Jesus Christ, slain and risen for them and brought into their lives by the Holy Spirit.

Evaluating Our Experiences

What then of the many believers who can give convincing testimony to a second crisis experience of grace when their heart was cleansed and they received power for service in a new way from the Holy Spirit? Are these experiences counterfeit? Not necessarily. If spiritual growth is anything like physical growth, it may not proceed in a smooth upward curve; there can be fits and starts, setbacks, and sudden growth spurts. My children have not grown physically in a steady fashion: They may stay much the same size for months, and then suddenly almost overnight they are two inches taller and their clothes no longer fit.

So there are at least three logical possibilities in our interpretation of such testimonies. Some are indeed counterfeit, especially when there is a discrepancy between what is claimed and what is lived. In the second place, many people who have been raised in a Christian home and unthinkingly adopted their parents' religion may not have yet had a real experience with the Lord. Then perhaps the personal nature of the gospel comes home to them and they really make a personal commitment of their lives to Christ. Yet, thinking themselves already to be Christians, they may misinterpret their first true experience of grace as a second. Many others, finally, have simply had a spiritual growth spurt. Every true believer has them. If he has been taught to look for a definitive second experience he will naturally pick one of those spurts and attach that label to it, calling it "sanctification." He may thus mistake a part of the process for the whole and have unrealistic notions as to its significance. Still, what he is mistaken about is something *real* nonetheless.

What then should be our approach to the Christian life? We should neither discount nor denigrate crisis experiences with God; indeed, we may hope to have many of them. But neither should we expect to be entirely sanctified by any one of them. Sanctification is a lifelong process of growth in grace nurtured by the Word, prayer, public worship, good and faithful expository preaching, and Christian fellowship and service. The standard exhortation of the New Testament is not to seek a second experience but to live in accordance with the reality of the first one. Subsequent experiences may be used by God to further that process, but the best way to ensure that they will be of God and have their intended effect is by concentrating, not on a desired experience, but on your walk with the Lord.

We need now to look at the means which the Holy Spirit uses to foster spiritual growth and sanctification in our lives. But first, we must clear up another area of confusion created by certain movements in the church. What is the baptism and/or fullness of the Holy Spirit, and how do they relate to sanctification? We will take up that question in the next chapter. In the meantime, let us walk in a manner worthy of our calling (Eph. 4:1), to the glory of Jesus Christ.

Questions for Further Study

1. Carefully define each word in the phrase, "definitive second crisis experience of grace."

2. What are the arguments for viewing such an experience as a normative part of sanctification?

3. What are the arguments against the normative and definitive character of such experiences?

4. How should we evaluate the significance of intense religious experiences subsequent to conversion?

5. Explain how a correct understanding of biblical teaching on this issue brings into focus the unity and the Christocentric character of the Spirit's work.

11

SANCTIFICATION: BAPTISM AND FULLNESS

So far we have been developing the doctrine of the Christian life with reference to issues raised by the Wesleyan holiness tradition, which frequently asks fruitful questions even if we cannot always agree wholly with the answers it gives. Since Wesley's day, even more controversial movements have arisen in the church, and the issues they raise also need to be addressed with care. Chief among these is Pentecostalism, with its more popular offspring, the charismatic movement. These movements focus our attention on the meaning of the terms "baptism of/with the Spirit" and "the fullness of the Spirit" for sanctification and the Christian life.

Pentecostalism and the Charismatic Movement

The two movements are closely related, but also need to be carefully distinguished. Pentecostalism properly refers to the denominations and theology which came out of the Azusa Street revival of 1906. Starting with a basically Wesleyan understanding of sanctification, it moved beyond Wesley by equating the second blessing with the experience of the disciples at Pentecost in the Book of Acts. Taking the Pentecostal experience as a pattern, it stressed the importance of an experience subsequent to conversion when the believer is "filled" with the Spirit and manifests this fullness by speaking in tongues, which is seen as the necessary and definitive sign that the filling has taken place. The early Pentecostals were by and large evangelical, Bible-believing people who thought they had recovered New Testament Christianity in all its fullness. They were somewhat separatistic in outlook, and although they could not be called an intellectual movement, they did place a high value on doctrine and had a well-developed doctrinal understanding of the fundamentals of the faith and of their own distinctive.

The charismatic movement arose when Pentecostal experience began to spill over from the classic Pentecostal denominations into mainline churches. It tends to be non-separatist, and, more importantly, less doctrinally oriented than Pentecostalism. Pentecostals tend to be orthodox in soteriology and share a common basic doctrinal understanding of Spirit baptism and the gifts. While many, perhaps most charismatics share that same theology, many do not—you can make no assumptions about what a charismatic believes. The basic attitude seems to be that "doctrine divides, but experience unites." Many charismatics accept anyone who speaks in tongues as a fellow believer, even if he belongs to the Roman Catholic Church and is committed to a denial of the Reformation doctrine of justification by faith—the very heart of the gospel. This general lack of concern for doctrine makes the movement difficult to discuss. Therefore, in this study we will deal with the views of Spirit baptism, fullness, and tongues as commonly held by classical Pentecostalism. This may or may not be the way your charismatic friends interpret the same experiences.

Spirit Baptism: The Traditional View

Biblical language certainly makes some connection between baptism, the Holy Spirit, and the church. John the Baptist baptized in water but looked for a greater One who would baptize in the Holy Spirit (Luke 3:16). Jesus before His ascension told the disciples to expect to receive that baptism "not many days from now" (Acts 1:5); and Paul said that by one Spirit we are all baptized into one body (1 Cor. 12:13). Probably the most common assumption among traditional, non-Pentecostal evangelicals is that these two baptisms with which the Spirit is connected refer to the same event and that it is the coming of the Spirit to indwell the believer at the time of conversion. The Spirit unites us to Christ and, by doing so, unites us to the church of which Christ is the Head. Such a view would make good sense of all the relevant passages of Scripture and would be consistent with all the considerations we saw in the last chapter against viewing sanctification as occurring at a second crisis experience subsequent to conversion and regeneration. Besides, Romans 8:9 clearly states that anyone who has not received the Holy Spirit does not belong to Christ at all.

Pentecostal Teaching

Nevertheless, Pentecostalism does reject that common viewpoint, and the nature of that rejection has frequently been misunderstood. While you can hear these Christian brothers carelessly speak of "receiving the Holy Spirit" subsequent to conversion, their actual theology does not deny His indwelling presence in the believer prior to the Pentecostal experience. What they actually claim to receive at that point is not the Spirit Himself but the *baptism* of the Spirit, which ushers in a new stage in the Christian life in which His presence and power are felt in their fullness. So, contrary to many polemics, standard Pentecostal teaching does not explicitly deny the truth of Romans 8:9.

Pentecostal theology distinguishes between being baptized into the church by the Holy Spirit which happens to all believers at conversion, and being baptized with the Holy Spirit by Jesus which happens only to some, usually after conversion. Speaking in tongues is viewed as the evidence that this second baptism has taken place. (Some fringe groups hold that tongues speaking is necessary for salvation, but their thinking is not representative.) We will examine the question of tongues when we come to the discussion of spiritual gifts. In this chapter we will try to see if the basic distinction between the two baptisms holds up in the light of Scripture. What does the New Testament teach about the baptism and fullness of the Holy Spirit, and how do these works fit into His ministry of bringing glory to Jesus Christ?

John the Baptist

The idea of a baptism in/by/with the Spirit administered by Jesus goes back ultimately to John the Baptist, who contrasted the baptism in the Spirit which Jesus would perform with his own baptism in water. In Luke 3:16 (Matt. 3:11) John said to people who were wondering whether he might be the Christ,

> As for me, I baptize you with water; but One is coming who is mightier than I, and I am not fit to untie the thong of His sandals; He will baptize you with [Greek *en*, which can be translated in, with, or by] the Holy Spirit and fire.

This verse is echoed by Jesus in Acts 1:5, making it clear that what happened at Pentecost was the very baptism John had prophesied. Consequently, we should expect John's words to give us some important clues as to how we should understand what took place there—and in fact, they do.

"The Holy Spirit and Fire"

Most Pentecostal interpreters of Luke 3:16–17 rightly stress the connection between the Spirit baptism mentioned there and the Pentecostal experience of Acts 2, but few have recognized the real implications of that connection. One of the key terms in understanding that relationship is the word *fire*, usually identified with the tongues of flame which stood above the heads of the disciples in the upper room. This baptism of fire is then assumed to be synonymous with the baptism of the Holy Spirit, and it has the effect of calling up associations with tongues, warmth, zeal, and revival fires. But this interpretation is almost certainly incorrect, as it totally ignores the use of the word *fire* in the immediate context in John's statement, the implications of which are of paramount significance to our discussion.

In verse 17, John said that this One who is coming to baptize with the Holy Spirit and fire also has a winnowing fork in His hand to clean out His threshing floor; He will gather the wheat into His barn, but the chaff He will burn up with "unquenchable fire." Clearly the reference is to the fact that the coming of Messiah will be an eschatological event which brings judgment as well as salvation and calls for decision. Those who receive the Messiah are the wheat gathered into the barn, and those who reject Him are the chaff. The fire in verse 17 is the fire of judgment, indeed of eternal punishment. Consequently, we must also take the fire of verse 16 as a reference to judgment. To use the same word in two radically different senses in two consecutive sentences without giving any clues to the change of meaning would be incredibly inept; I cannot bring myself to believe that either John, Matthew, or Luke in editing his speech, or the Holy Spirit in inspiring the text were such poor communicators as that. Therefore, the baptism of fire in verse 16 is not parallel with the baptism of the Holy Spirit, but is its opposite.

Implications of John the Baptist's Teachings

What John is saying then is that the coming of Jesus brings history to a crossroads: We must all now face either the baptism of the Holy Spirit or the baptism of fire. No other alternative is given; no intermediate class of people other than wheat or chaff is mentioned. Note carefully what this means: The contrast is not between spiritual and carnal believers but between the saved and the unsaved. The issue which Spirit baptism addresses is not spirituality but salvation. It is simply impossible to envision John as thinking of baptism in the Holy Spirit as an event which could happen subsequent to conversion and regeneration. The whole idea of a person's being saved apart from that baptism would have been inconceivable to John once the eschatological age had been ushered in by Messiah's ministry. It would seem that John's language only makes sense if we take the baptism of the Spirit as a way of speaking about His coming to indwell the believer at the time of regeneration and conversion.

The larger context of John's preaching also supports this view. The contrast between John's baptizing ministry and that of Jesus is one of promise and fulfillment, symbol and reality. When Jesus baptizes you with the Holy Spirit you will receive the reality which John's baptism in water symbolizes. And what was the baptism of John? A baptism of repentance for the remission of sins! The very use of baptismal language to refer to the Spirit's coming ties in explicitly with regeneration and conversion and makes it the common possession of all who have sincerely made the baptismal confession of faith in Christ for the forgiveness of sin. This understanding does not rule out the possibility or the validity of post-conversion crisis experiences in which the reality of what God has done for us in Christ hits home in a new and fresh way; but it does suggest that referring to such experiences as the baptism of the Holy Spirit is not in accord with the biblical usage of that language, at least in its initial use by John the Baptist.

When we receive Jesus as our Messiah, He sends His Spirit to regenerate us and indwell us as His Representative in our lives. The Spirit's presence is essential to our being gathered into the barn with the wheat and escaping the fire of judgment reserved for the chaff. (We'll see more of this truth when we consider the doctrine of sealing.) And the fact that the New Testament refers to the Spirit's coming into our lives as a "baptism" suggests that faith in these truths is part of what we symbolize when we confess Christ in the ordinance of water baptism, through which we formally identify ourselves with Christ and with His body, the church.

Spirit Baptism in the Book of Acts

The implications of John's language seem clear. But when we move from the prophecy as given by John the Baptist to its fulfillment in the book of Acts, a host of questions arises. Jesus in Acts 1:8 seems to connect the baptism in the Holy Spirit coming "not many days from now" (1:5) not with regeneration but with power for service, particularly enablement in witnessing. Certainly for the apostles at Pentecost, and arguably for several other converts later in the Acts narrative, the coming of the

Spirit in power did not coincide with conversion. What are we to make of these facts? A closer reading of the Acts account itself in the context of the larger New Testament should lead us to some answers.

Pentecost

What exactly did happen at Pentecost? Clearly it was not the beginning of the Holy Spirit's ministry. We have already established that apart from His ministry of conviction, calling, and regeneration, there could never have been any salvation at all. People in the Old Testament period were no less incapable of receiving spiritual things than they were in the New, or than they are now. So in the Old Testament the Spirit must have convicted, called, and regenerated sinners. Also, the Spirit is frequently recorded in the Old Testament as having "come upon" men to empower or equip them for a special task (Ex. 31:2–3; Judg. 6:34, 2 Chron. 15:1). There is then a continuity with what we see Him doing in the New Testament, but also a difference.

His New Testament ministry seems to be more personal, more permanent, and more powerful. The Old Testament saints knew the forgiveness of sins, fellowship with God, and power for service, but the New Testament saints know all these things more fully and more surely because now the long-awaited Messiah has come. The ministry of the Holy Spirit is kicked into a higher gear in accordance with the move from the era of promise to that of fulfillment. For the first time, the believing community is powerful enough to take the gospel to the ends of the earth. It is essentially the same ministry, but now it is no longer the anticipated Messiah but the crucified and risen Lord that the Spirit makes real in the lives of His people. There is an added dynamic in that the power of the resurrection has now been unleashed, which is why this new phase of the Holy Spirit's work could not begin until after Jesus had been "glorified" (John 7:39).

It was thus no accident that the Old Testament had associated special manifestations of the Spirit's ministry with the dawn of the Messianic age, as in the passage from the prophet Joel (2:28–32) quoted by Peter in his Pentecost sermon. Though some of Joel's language seems to fit better with the second coming of

Christ, that would have been no problem, for the resurrection had inaugurated the final age of history of which the return of Christ would be the climactic event. In the meantime we are His witnesses, and "every one who calls on the name of the Lord shall be saved" (Acts 2:21). By representing the risen and now ascended Lord in the lives of His people, the Holy Spirit provides the dynamic which will allow the gospel to be taken to the uttermost parts of the earth before the end finally comes.

It is possible then to view Pentecost as the moment at which this post-resurrection phase of the ministry of the Holy Spirit was officially inaugurated. His whole unified ministry was intensified with the result that we can see John the Baptist's emphasis on its association with regeneration and conversion and the Lord's emphasis on power for service and witness as equally relevant. Conversion makes one a witness. The Spirit comes to the church at Pentecost and to the individual at conversion. If He is subsequently grieved or quenched and the individual later finds a renewed submission and fullness of the Spirit, that is no reason to call that subsequent filling the baptism of the Spirit, contradicting John's equation of Spirit baptism with salvation. A person who receives Jesus also receives the Holy Spirit in the wholeness of His ministry, which cannot be divided because Jesus cannot be divided. The phrase "baptism of the Holy Spirit" then most logically refers to that moment when the preparatory work of conviction and calling results in regeneration, new life, and union with Christ, in whom dwells all the fullness of the Godhead bodily.

Peter confirmed this interpretation in his Pentecost sermon (Acts 2). Verse 33 makes the identification between Pentecost and both John's prophecy of Luke 3:16 and Jesus' of John 7:38–39. God has raised this Jesus from the dead and exalted Him to the right hand of the Father: "And having received from the Father the promise of the Holy Spirit, He has poured forth this which you both see and hear." Then he comes to the crux in verse 38. What shall we do in response? "Repent, and let each of you be baptized in the name of Jesus Christ for the forgiveness of your sins; and you shall receive the gift of the Holy Spirit." What could be more clear? Repentance, forgiveness, baptism in

Jesus' name, and the gift of the Holy Spirit are tied together in the most intimate association. Peter does not say, "Repent and receive forgiveness and justification, and then later wait for the baptism of the Holy Spirit and fire."

Surely the coming of the Spirit into the life of the believer is called a "baptism" because of its close association with water baptism, which seems in the early church to have followed immediately upon one's initial confession of Jesus as Lord, if it did not in fact constitute that confession. The language of baptism is the language of initiation, and never does the New Testament speak normatively of a twofold or two-stage initiation into the life of Christ.

The apostles are of course an exception to this general rule because they lived in a transitional period so that they were converted before the resurrection. Of necessity then for them, Pentecost was a separate event from conversion. They are an exception to the general pattern in their experience, but never in their teaching. Peter, Paul, and John the Baptist were all in complete harmony in their theology of the Spirit. But what of the many other conversions recorded in Acts in which conversion and being baptized with the Holy Spirit seem to be distinct? The Pentecostal case depends heavily on those examples, but when they are examined carefully, they tend to militate against the Pentecostal interpretation rather than for it.

The Samaritan Converts

One such passage occurs in Acts 8:14–17. Having heard that a group of Samaritans had "received the word of God," the apostles in Jerusalem sent Peter and John to pray for them that they might receive the Holy Spirit. "For He had not yet fallen upon any of them; they had simply been baptized in the name of the Lord Jesus" (v. 16). The Samaritans received the Holy Spirit when the apostles laid hands on them.

On the surface this passage certainly fits the Pentecostal pattern of conversion followed by an indefinite period of "waiting," followed finally by "praying through" to receive the baptism of the Holy Spirit. But one does not have to probe very deeply to discover that the text undercuts any such interpretation, both here and elsewhere in Acts. The words fatal to the Pentecostal view are the seemingly innocent explanatory parenthesis in verse 16: You see, the Spirit hadn't fallen on them yet—they had just been baptized in the name of Jesus. The very fact that Luke felt the necessity of inserting such a parenthesis proves that he found the Samaritan incident in need of explanation. It was not the way things were supposed to happen; it did not fit with either the theology or the experience of the circles in the early church of which Luke was a part—nor that of the Jerusalem apostles either, apparently, since they felt an apostolic delegation necessary to deal with the problem.

We do not know why the reception of the Spirit by these Samaritans had been delayed after what seemed a genuine conversion to Christ and baptism in His name. It is possible that the "word of God" they had received was too vague, incomplete, or distorted, and they did not actually become Christians until the arrival of Peter and John (we will see a clear case like that later). Some have suggested that the baptism of the Spirit was deliberately delayed until apostolic witnesses were present in each case where the gospel penetrated a new people—Samaritans here, Gentiles later. The Jewish Christians were still too chauvinistic to have accepted anyone else as full members of the Christian community without a confirmatory repetition of the precise Pentecostal pattern as they had experienced it in Acts chapter 2. This theory may be true, but it is difficult to prove, as the text does not explain any of the incidents explicitly in such terms. What is certain is that Acts 8:14–17 is presented as an anomalous incident, one which called for special explanation; therefore, it cannot be used as a normative pattern. In fact, it rather tends to disprove the idea that New Testament Christians held to a two-stage view of conversion to Christ.

It is sometimes objected that, while Spirit baptism might be ideally coincidental with conversion, and usually occurs simultaneously with it in a healthy church, lack of faith and a theology which denies the currency of spiritual gifts inhibit it in post-apostolic ages so that it occurs later in many Christians and not at all in others today. New Testament writers assumed that all believers would be Spirit baptized because they lived in a

THE PERSON AND WORK OF THE HOLY SPIRIT

healthy church, but that assumption no longer applies to our age of unbelief. But aside from the hopelessly romantic view of first century Christianity which this argument presupposes, it sounds suspiciously like special pleading. The words of Peter (Acts 2:3) and John the Baptist (Luke 3:16–17) remain unaffected by it, and they still teach a unified view of the Spirit's work which gives no ground for viewing baptism in the Spirit as an optional, post-conversion experience. We are not to seek a second baptism but to live in awareness of and in accordance with the realities we confessed and received by faith when we identified ourselves with Jesus Christ in His death, burial, and resurrection.

The Conversion of Cornelius

The next major passage in which the reception of the Holy Spirit is mentioned is the conversion of Cornelius in Acts 10. Several things are interesting about this passage. The word "baptism" of the Spirit does not occur—it is stated that the Spirit "fell" on the Gentiles (v. 44), that the "gift" of the Spirit was "poured out" on them, and that they "received" Him just as the Jews had (v. 45, 47). They showed they had received the gift by speaking in tongues and exalting God, which astonished the circumcised and led Peter to administer water baptism in the name of Jesus.

Quite clearly, the "gift" of the Spirit was viewed by the Jews present as the same gift they had received at Pentecost, which we have already identified as the baptism of the Holy Spirit. And undeniably, Cornelius and his friends experienced that baptism at the very moment of their conversion to Christ. Their Spirit baptism is taken as justification for the administration of water baptism, a step which definitely needed justification for the Jews present. The important thing for our purposes, however, is the connection between the two. This passage alone certainly could not prove the identification of baptism in the Spirit with His coming to indwell the believer at conversion and regeneration; but what weight it has is definitely on the side of that view.

The Ephesian Disciples

The final passage sometimes urged as an example of Spirit baptism taking place subsequent to conversion is that of the Ephesian disciples of Acts 19. However, this passage weighs heavily against a Pentecostal interpretation. Although the spiritual status of the Samaritans prior to the coming of the Spirit on them was ambiguous, that of the Ephesians is perfectly clear. They had not even heard of the Holy Spirit, and apparently, they were unclear about the relationship between Jesus and John the Baptist (Acts 19:2–4). These people were not even Trinitarians (if we can use that word somewhat anachronistically at this early stage of doctrinal definition—at least we can say that the theology of the early believers was such that Nicene Trinitarianism would be its natural and logical development; that of these Ephesian "disciples" was not). It was not until they were baptized in the name of Jesus (v. 5) that they were really His disciples rather than merely John's. Immediately upon their conversion they received the Holy Spirit.

It is often argued that the tenses of the verbs in verse 2 prove a separation between faith and the coming of the Spirit in power. According to this view, the New American Standard Bible rendering of Paul's question, "Did you receive the Holy Spirit when you believed?" would be more accurately translated, "Have you received the Holy Spirit *since* you believed?" It is true that the word translated "receive" in Greek is in the imperfect tense, and that the word for "believe" is an aorist participle, the action of which is normally thought of as taking place prior to that of the main verb. On that basis, the translation "since you believed" is perfectly legitimate.

Two things, however, need to be said in response to this line of argument. First, the time values of the Greek participle are highly relative, and several examples can be found in the Greek New Testament of aorist participles which refer to the same time as the main verb (see the treatment of the aorist participle in any standard Greek grammar). Second, there is more than one kind of priority. If manifestations of the Spirit's presence are looked on as evidence of conversion—as they clearly were in several of these passages—then there is a sense in which conversion is logically prior to the evidence for it though it may be not be temporally prior. Water baptism is an expression of faith; therefore, faith is logically prior to it. But, as in the case of Cornelius, when the expression follows immediately upon the faith, how would you speak of it later? To ask, "Were you baptized when you believed?" or "Have you been baptized since you believed?" would be equally possible, but for Cornelius the first version of the question would seem more natural. No firm conclusions about the temporal separation of the two events could be drawn from the grammar of either question.

The same principle applies to the Ephesian disciples. Paul apparently asked about their experience with the Holy Spirit not because he thought true believers might not have received Spirit baptism, but because he wondered whether these people had really been saved. Fortunately, his diagnostic question worked, and he was able to lead those disciples to the Lord—whereupon they immediately received the baptism of the Holy Spirit.

Summary

The accounts of Spirit baptism in Acts then give us no firm grounds for departing from the basic theology of the baptism of the Holy Spirit taught by John the Baptist. This baptism is administered by Jesus; it distinguishes, not the spiritual Christian from the carnal Christian, but the saved from the lost. It is the spiritual reality which corresponds to the symbol of water baptism; therefore, it is a biblical way of speaking about the coming of the Spirit to indwell the believer at the time of conversion and regeneration. It marks the transition from the preparatory work of conviction and calling to the moment of actual union with Christ. Christ comes to us in the person of His personal Agent and Representative, the Holy Spirit. Consequently, to distinguish the coming of Christ into a person's life and the baptism of the Holy Spirit as even theoretically and potentially separable events goes contrary to the tenor of what the Bible has taught us thus far about the Holy Spirit's role and the fundamental character of His work. It is Christ in us through the Holy Spirit which is the hope of glory (Col. 1:27). Even when it is initiated with powerful external manifestations, as is sometimes the case, that is a relationship which takes some growing into. There may indeed be dramatic breakthroughs in that growth subsequent to conversion, but biblical usage connects the language of Spirit baptism with the initiation of the process quite clearly.

Perhaps one of the best summaries of this relationship between Jesus' pouring out of the Holy Spirit and the rest of the Christian life is found in Titus 3:5–7.

> He saved us, not on the basis of deeds which we have done in righteousness, but according to His mercy, by the washing of regeneration and renewing by the Holy Spirit, whom He poured out upon us richly through Jesus Christ our Savior, that being justified by His grace we might be made heirs according to the hope of eternal life.

Jesus pours out the Spirit in order that we might be *justified* and inherit eternal life. The primitive theology of John the Baptist has survived intact through the first turbulent decades of the apostolic age; if only it could have survived as well the first two millennia! Much needless confusion could have been avoided if we were content to interpret our experience in the light of biblical teaching rather than vice versa.

The standard Pentecostal distinction between the baptism in the Holy Spirit by Jesus and the baptism into the church by the Holy Spirit then breaks down in the light of the biblical data. Being baptized into the church is then simply one aspect of being baptized with the Spirit; being united to Christ's body is one effect of being united to Christ Himself by His Spirit (1 Cor. 12:13). There is really no debate over when baptism into the church takes place—at conversion. The unity of the body of Christ no less than the unity of the work of Christ then both hinge on a correct understanding of the ministry of the Holy Spirit, the ultimate Ambassador of Christ.

The Fullness of the Spirit

What then of the fullness of the Holy Spirit? Pentecostalism equates it, or at least closely associates it, with the baptism of the Holy Spirit, but that association falls apart very quickly in the light of a few basic biblical facts. John the Baptist, for example, never experienced the baptism of the Spirit; he prophesies it as something Jesus would do in the future, a future he never lived to see. The fulfillment of his prophecy took place at Pentecost after the ascension of Jesus when John the Baptist was dead; yet we are told that John was filled with the Spirit from his mother's womb (Luke 1:15). His father Zacharias (Luke 1:67) and a host of Old Testament saints are spoken of as having been filled with the Spirit at one time or another. It is then possible to be filled with the Spirit even without being baptized in the Spirit (at least in the full New Testament sense), and if the carnality of the Corinthians is any indication, it is equally possible to be baptized in the Spirit without being filled. Before we try to figure out how the two ideas are related, we need a clear notion of what the fullness of the Spirit is. The most helpful passage for finding that is Ephesians 5:18.

Ephesians 5:18

In Ephesians 5:18, Paul exhorted us, "Do not get drunk with wine, for that is dissipation, but be filled with the Spirit." This passage helps us to define the fullness of the Spirit by contrast with the fullness of wine. The two types of "fullness" are opposite in their effects but parallel conceptually, which gives Paul's comparison its point. The person who is drunk is "filled" with wine; if we catch him trying to drive on our modern highways, we say he is "under the influence." His behavior is influenced or controlled by that with which he is filled. To be filled with the Holy Spirit then is simply to be under His influence, to be totally yielded to, directed by, and controlled by Him. The result of being under the influence of wine is dissipation; the results of being under the Spirit's control are worship, praise, thanksgiving, and mutual submission. Seen in this light, the fullness of the Spirit is not some strange, mystical concept but an extremely practical one. The language is parallel with that of Romans 6:13: "Do not go on presenting the members of your body to sin as instruments of unrighteousness; but present yourselves to God as those alive from the dead, and your members as instruments of righteousness to God."

Several important points about Ephesians 5:18 should be noted here. First, we must be careful that our interpretation of the verse clearly distinguishes the ways in which the two kinds of filling are alike and unlike if we are to understand Paul's point correctly. Nothing in the verse suggests that the states of being Spirit filled and being drunk are subjectively similar from an experiential standpoint. It gives no sanction to orgies of irresponsible emotionalism. That is part of the contrast. Such dissipation is the effect of wine, not of the Spirit. After all, self-control is listed as part of the fruit of the Spirit (Gal. 5:23). It is ironic that subjective conditions which, from a biblical standpoint, are *prima facie* evidence of the Spirit's absence have frequently been taken as almost infallible signs of His presence! By definition, people who are filled with the Spirit are simultaneously people who are controlled by the Spirit and who are manifesting self-control; that is, their total yieldedness to His will and purposes is a conscious decision and commitment of their own wills which continue, moment by moment, to participate fully in the process.

The principle we saw in inspiration, illumination, and conversion applies to sanctification as well: The Spirit works through the normal human faculties of intellect, will, and personality, using them and not bypassing them, to achieve His purpose of bringing glory to Jesus Christ in the lives of His disciples. Surely people who are filled with the Spirit manifest the fruit of the Spirit; therefore, by definition, Spirit-filled believers are in control of themselves; therefore, the conditions of being filled with the Spirit and being "slain" in the Spirit are actually mutually exclusive. Not all who emphasize the fullness of the Spirit show any biblical signs of it any more than all who say, "Lord, Lord" will end up in the kingdom of heaven (Matt. 7:21).

Second, we should note that the language of "fullness" is obviously relative language. A cup can be full or empty or any stage in between and even spawn heated debates over whether it is half full or half empty. A drinker can be slightly elevated, mildly tipsy, or in the throes of *delirium tremens*. By the same token, we may doubt whether the question "Have you been filled with the Spirit?" can always be given a simple yes or no answer. No truly saved person is ever quite "empty" of the Spirit, for if he could be he would cease to belong to Christ (Rom. 8:9). Yet can he ever be so full—so completely and perfectly in harmony with the character of Christ which the Spirit works to form in us—that there is no need or room for further growth? I doubt it; even Paul felt the need to "press on" to higher things (Phil. 3:12–14). Perhaps then what is needed is not so much a concern for some mythical and static condition of having been filled as a recognition that any Christian at any moment is more or less filled with the Spirit and should seek to be more full than he is now.

Third, the verb "to be filled" is an imperative verb, a command, expressed in the Greek continuous present tense. It could accurately be translated "be continuously being filled." It clearly describes not a one-time crisis experience but a way of life which is a conscious choice. This fact fits right in with the relative nature of the language noted above. The fullness of the Holy Spirit is an expanding experience which we grow into throughout a lifetime of walking with the Lord and getting to know Him better. Walking in the Spirit, living by the power of the Spirit, and entering into the fullness of all that these things mean, is how we walk with Jesus. And that is what the Christian life is all about.

We are then commanded to grow in the Christian life, continually being filled with the Holy Spirit, more consistently and more fully manifesting in our thoughts, our feelings, our intentions, and our actions the influence of this heavenly Guest sent to represent Jesus in and to and through us. How do we go about obeying that commandment? Our next chapter will be devoted to that all-important question. But first it might be well to pause for some summary conclusions about Pentecostal teaching in general, for Pentecostal influence continues to grow outside of traditional Pentecostal circles.

General Conclusions

Some Pentecostal "experiences" with the Holy Spirit are definitely from God; many of them may be; but many also that are claimed to be are not. Some experiences obviously contradict biblical descriptions of the nature and quality of the Spirit's work and its effects; many others are, by virtue of their inherently subjective character, impossible to evaluate. But the standard Pentecostal explanation of these experiences and their significance—even the valid ones—is simply not biblical. An inductive study of the relevant passages in their whole New Testament context does not produce any evidence for a distinction between Spirit baptism and regeneration or between being baptized with the Spirit by Jesus and being baptized into the church by the Spirit. The text not only does not support these distinctions, but also plainly contradicts them. The conclusion is inescapable that traditional Pentecostal teaching on these points (as well as on the significance attributed to tongues, which we will address later) results from a determination to find in the text a rationale and justification for a certain type of religious experience which is assumed to be self-authenticating. The experience itself thereby becomes the standard by which all is judged, rather than letting Scripture be the final interpreter and evaluator of our experience.

It is this mentality which fosters and justifies a subjective approach to Scripture—rather than any particular aberration of doctrine or interpretation—which is in reality the most dangerous and problematic aspect of the whole movement. Subjective experience rather than the text of Scripture becomes in effect the final criterion of truth. The same mentality is shared by both Pentecostals and charismatics, manifesting itself in the hermeneutical gymnastics of the one to justify its doctrine and in the disdain for doctrine often found in the other. It manifests itself in the tendency to accept as one's fellow believer anyone who shares his experience (or claims to) regardless of doctrinal affirmations. It manifests itself in a frequently appalling lack of spiritual discernment, in a "leading" of the Spirit often contrary to the clear teaching of Scripture. I once counseled a woman who was "led" to divorce her husband because he was "unspiritual," that is, he did not speak in tongues. She was unmoved by the fact that, according to biblical teachings, she was forbidden by Christ Himself to do this.

I am not suggesting that all Pentecostals and charismatics are guilty of such things—far from it. But I am saying that both movements foster a mentality which makes it natural to be guilty of such things, encourages it, and even sometimes justifies it. And perhaps the most disturbing sign of spiritual ill health in the church today is the fact that essentially the same mentality increasingly can be found in traditional evangelical believers who would not be caught dead speaking in tongues. They too operate on the basis of what makes them feel good rather than what Scripture teaches. They too cannot tell the difference between emotional manipulation and worship in Spirit and in truth. They too, in less blatant but no less disastrous ways, have let the authority of Scripture slip through their fingers even as they continue to affirm it with their lips.

I do not mean to be unduly harsh and critical; I have written these things because I am convinced that they desperately need to be said. Martin Luther rightly held that the doctrine of justification by faith was the watershed of a standing or falling church, and we need to realize that the other great Reformation principles of *Sola Scriptura*—Scripture alone has ultimate authority in our lives—is equally crucial and foundational. It is time for us to stop apologizing for our "biblicism" and "rationalism" and forthrightly call the church back to its foundations: not subjective feelings but the apostles and prophets, Jesus Christ being the chief cornerstone.

You see, it is ultimately the supremacy of Jesus Christ which is lost by this deadly mentality of subjectivism which allows alleged experience of the Spirit to overthrow the authority of the Spirit in the text of Scripture which He inspired on behalf of the Lord Jesus Christ. The Holy Spirit is Christ's Representative, and speaks for Him; so the same wedge which is driven by this approach between the Spirit and the text is also driven between the Spirit and the Lord. That is why the basic Pentecostal teaching on the baptism of the Spirit goes contrary not only to the teaching of the relevant texts but also to the whole theology of the Spirit's work we have been seeing in Scripture. The very unity and integrity of that work is compromised. It is as if Jesus saves, but the Spirit sanctifies and empowers; the Christocentric emphasis of Scripture is lost. In actuality it is Jesus who does it all, and who communicates it all to us through the Spirit. Every spiritual blessing—election, conversion, regeneration, justification, adoption, sanctification, power for service, and on to glorification—is in Christ (Eph. 1:3). To receive Him is to receive the Spirit and all the rest. We need to grow into it and learn to live in the light of it to be sure; but to suggest that a person who has received Jesus Christ needs anything else to be complete is to detract from His glory. To suggest that the "something extra" which is needed is the baptism of the Holy Spirit is ultimately to divorce the perfect unity of the one seamless work they perform together for us. This obscures the fact that Jesus does it all for us through the Spirit and the Spirit does it all in us for Jesus. This detracts from the glory which rightly belongs to Jesus Christ, and whatever does that must surely grieve the Holy Spirit.

Questions for Further Study

1. Summarize the main points of the classic Pentecostal view of the baptism and fullness of the Holy Spirit.

2. John the Baptist introduced the concept of a baptism in the Holy Spirit in Scripture. What does he seem to have meant by it? Can he be read as separating it from conversion? What are the chief interpretive clues in the text which determine the answer?

3. The Pentecostal case for distinguishing baptism into the church by the Spirit and baptism into the Spirit by Jesus depends heavily on the Book of Acts. Does Acts really support this theology? Why or why not?

4. Make a chart of all the conversions in Acts, listing under each one faith, water baptism, Spirit baptism/coming/ fullness, and tongues: Which ones are mentioned and in what order? Does any normative pattern emerge?

5. We have suggested that Pentecostal hermeneutics tends to read its experience into Scripture. Suppose someone countered, "You are just reading your own lack of experience into Scripture." How would you respond to this charge?

12

SANCTIFICATION: THE MEANS OF GROWTH

So far in our discussion of the Christian life we have concluded that, while God may use a second crisis experience subsequent to conversion to give a boost to the process of sanctification, it is not biblical to identify such an experience with sanctification or to make it a normative part of growth in grace. We have suggested that as we seek to grow in our walk with the Lord, we should put our emphasis where the preponderance of prescriptive New Testament passages seem to put it: Not on waiting for some extra, stereotyped "experience," but on getting on with the pilgrimage in faith and in dependence on the Lord's enabling presence through His personal Representative, the Holy Spirit.

The "Deeper" Christian Life?

Yet in spite of that preponderance of sane apostolic counsel, a multitude of "something extra" or "deeper life" teachings abound. They strike a responsive chord in the hearts of many sincere believers who are frustrated with the dryness and shallowness of the conventional Christianity which surrounds them. Frequently, this teaching has been for them a catalyst which produces real Christian growth. Yet one often has the feeling that the growth is not related to the teaching in the simple way that is usually assumed.

I cut my spiritual teeth on the form of deeper life teaching known as the Keswick theology, after the English conference grounds where it was originally propounded. Keswick focused on Galatians 2:20—we are crucified with Christ so that it is no longer we who live but Christ who lives in us. You fail to live the victorious Christian life, it said, because you can't live it; but Christ can live it through you. You must stop trying to live it in your own strength and simply let Him do that: You must, in other words, simply "let go and let God" by becoming "totally yielded" to the Holy Spirit who was given to indwell you as God's provision for victorious living.

I have no real problem with these formulations when rightly understood. Certainly we cannot live the Christian life in our own strength apart from the power of the Holy Spirit, and certainly we ought to be totally yielded to Him. Keswick theology is often accused of an unbiblical passivity in its approach, and some of its spokespersons do give an unbalanced impression in that area, but I do not think it is necessary to understand Keswick that way. Christ is said to live through us, not instead of us: Our own wills are not bypassed in the process, but we deliberately yield them to the Holy Spirit moment by moment. I found, however, the teaching becoming fuzzy and unhelpful on the crucial question of how we get to be totally yielded. In the language of Romans 12:1, the notorious problem with living sacrifices is that they keep climbing back down off of the altar! Many of us went through a series of crises of consecration, commitment, and rededication which never seemed to produce any lasting results.

The Key

How do you get to be totally yielded? Through a second crisis experience? That seemed to work for some people, but not for others. Then I noticed something which turned out to be the key to the answer. Without exception, the people for whom it seemed to work were people who had formed good, consistent habits in the spiritual disciplines of Bible study, prayer, and involvement in a healthy, Bible-believing local church. And I also noticed that people who formed and maintained such habits tended to make progress whether or not they claimed a second experience, unless they pursued those habits in a proud and legalistic spirit. Maybe that was the answer: You can't become totally yielded to the Holy Spirit by wanting to be, deciding to be, trying to be, or even asking to be. Maybe it has to be by learning to be. And indeed it was the answer. The key to spiritual growth is a combination of the spirit of yieldedness and dependence on the Holy Spirit fostered by the Keswick type of teaching with a commitment to the right kind of nurture, exercise, and training, along with the realization that such growth is an endless process in this life—absolute totality of "yieldedness" will not be ours until we see the Lord face to face. In the meantime, though, there is much ground to be conquered, many victories to be won, and much joy to be experienced.

This combination is not the answer because I found that it works, but because the Bible teaches it—which is why it works. It is not we who live, but Christ who lives in us. Apart from Him we can do nothing. We can do all things through Christ who strengthens us. In the meantime, we are to study to show ourselves approved, pray without ceasing, and not forsake the assembling of ourselves together. We are to work out our salvation in fear and trembling because it is God who works in us both to will and to do. And of course the specific member of the Trinity who is in us is the Holy Spirit.

The same principle of His working which we saw in our discussion of inspiration, illumination, and calling, we also find operating here: The Spirit works, not apart from, but through our own individual personalities, including intellect, will, and emotions. They are the means He uses to accomplish His purposes. To depend on the means themselves apart from the Spirit is to doom ourselves to sterility and futility; to depend on the Spirit apart from the use of means is to deny Him the very opportunity to work. That is why "Let go and let God" by itself leaves you in a vacuum, while the use of spiritual disciplines by themselves leaves you merely frustrated and defeated.

When the two sides of the coin are held together—each supporting and being supported by the other, each nourishing and being nourished by the other—then real and lasting Christian growth occurs. Bible study pursued in the right spirit fosters that sense of dependence on the Holy Spirit which makes you want to study the Bible that the Spirit inspired even more. The cycle continues, spiralling ever upward toward glory. The same can be said for all the other disciplines as well.

The Means of Growth

The practical question then becomes this: What are the specific means which the Holy Spirit uses to help us grow? The New Testament is full of the answer. God has instituted a number of definite practices which He commands us to use, promising that if we use them diligently and consistently by faith and in dependence on Him, we will grow because the Holy Spirit is committed to work through these things to bring the grace of Christ into our lives. For this reason they were traditionally called the "means of grace." Since that phrase seems to some people to connote a sacramental and mechanical concept of grace, we will not insist on the term, but use the less controversial (and perhaps more accurate) phrase "means of growth." They are the key to growth because God has commanded them and has promised that the Holy Spirit will bless them and use them in our lives when we use them in faith. They do not "automatically" cause anything to happen in and of themselves, but they are the divinely appointed means of growth through which the Spirit has promised to work in response to our faith.

Traditionally, the phrase "means of grace" refers to the Word and sacraments, or the Word, sacraments, and prayer. These must remain central. But since the biblical basis of the concept lies simply in the fact that God has commanded us to do certain things for our spiritual health, we will speak of the means of growth somewhat more broadly, believing that whatever God has commanded for our good He intends to bless through His

Spirit. When a person becomes regenerate, then, he or she receives a new principle of spiritual life which needs to grow and develop. What does it need in order to do so properly? A newborn human needs basically four things to develop properly, and God's provision for the new spiritual baby seems to fit essentially the same pattern.

Needs of Growing Children

First and most basic is *food*: Its total absence will lead to death, and insufficient or inappropriate nourishment can lead to ill health or retarded growth. Equally important if not as obvious is the need for *fellowship*. A baby who is fed well but never fondled, held, talked to, and fussed over will also grow weak and sickly and quite possibly even die. These needs are absolutely essential for survival. But they are not all that is required for health. Unless the growing child receives the right kind of *exercise*, he will fail to grow strong in the various competencies demanded for an active and successful life. And finally he needs *direction* and guidance; he will not automatically refrain from ingesting poison or playing in the traffic, nor will he be able to drive a car or balance a checkbook if left to his own devices. Without food, fellowship, exercise, and direction, a newborn baby will simply not be able to survive, and if even one of these needs is not met or met inadequately he will find it extremely difficult if not impossible to grow and reach his potential. And just as God's plan is to provide these things for the physical baby primarily through the family, so He provides the same kind of support for the new spiritual babe in Christ through the Bible, the family, and the church.

Spiritual Nourishment

First is the need for nourishment. That is why 1 Peter 2:2 tells us that, just like newborn babies, we should "long for the pure milk of the word, that by it you may grow in respect to salvation." And after what we have seen already about the centrality of the Spirit's work in inspiration and illumination to His whole ministry of glorifying Jesus Christ, we ought not to be surprised to find that the Bible has a (if not the) central role in Christian growth. It is also our primary source of direction, guidance, and instruction, as we shall consider in a few pages; but that is not the point Peter made in this passage. At a deeper level than the cognitive and cerebral places where we deal with what Scripture says to us (though never in conflict with or apart from that dealing), our souls are fed, nourished by the Word of God. It will cause us to grow in respect to salvation. Literally, Peter said it will make us grow "into salvation." He is not denying the important Pauline truth that salvation is a free gift received by faith, but simply stressing the progressive nature of our experience of that gift. We do receive it once for all when we receive Christ, but it is a vast inheritance including every spiritual blessing and the complete transformation of our lives. In that sense, it is definitely something which takes some "growing into." And the thing which nourishes us in that growth is the sincere milk of the Word.

Bible Reading

The Christian life is essentially walking with Jesus, and growth in it is essentially growth in our relationship with Him. That fact is pictured by the Lord in John 10:4. Describing Himself as the Good Shepherd, Jesus noted the fact that a shepherd's sheep know him and follow him because "they know his voice." How do they know it? Because they have been listening to it constantly. They recognize it instinctively, not by careful analysis but simply by the sound. The Lord summarizes this teaching on Christian sheephood in the beautiful language of verse 27: "My sheep hear My voice, and I know them, and they follow Me." The obvious implication for our study at this point is that there is no way we can grow to have this kind of intimate relationship with Jesus without listening to His voice in Scripture. It is an absolute prerequisite to Christian growth that we be people who live with the words of the Bible, day in and day out, meditating on them and engraving them upon our minds and our hearts. The result of such deep drinking of the sincere milk of the Word is to grow, just like "a tree firmly planted by streams of water," with all the resulting effects which Psalm 1 enumerates.

Growth: Scripture teaches us, but it also does more. It reproves, corrects, and ultimately makes us adequate for every good work (2 Tim. 3:17). I believe that something more than learning is required to become adequate for every good work. In a way that includes but also transcends teaching, the right kind of exposure to the Bible does something to us: It feeds us, nourishes us, and makes us grow spiritually, bringing us to the kind of maturity implied by adequacy. Why? Because the Spirit who inspired it works through it. One wants to avoid magical views or language which implies them, but it is almost as if the words of Scripture are a conduit through which the Holy Spirit flows more fully into our lives. At least part of being full of the Holy Spirit is being full of the Bible.

But someone will say, "Bible knowledge alone doesn't make you spiritual." No, it doesn't—not necessarily. That is why Jesus said in Luke 11:28, "Blessed are those who hear the word of God, and observe it"—in context, more blessed than the virgin Mary. That is why he said, "If you abide in My word, then you are truly disciples of Mine; and you shall know the truth, and the truth shall make you free (John 8:31-32). As long as we are speaking of the Bible as *nourishment*, we might as well quote Puritan writer Richard Sibbes: "The whole conversation of a Christian consisteth of nothing else but knowledge digested into will, affection, and practice." The digestive juice which causes Scripture to become part of us and make us grow is saving faith, the kind of faith which takes the Lord Jesus seriously enough to produce obedience. It is not the hearers but the doers of the Word who grow, and faith—really believing it—is the key to doing it. In short, a believer who is not consistently in the Word will never grow; one who is may; if he reads it only for knowledge he will become puffed up, proud, and ugly (1 Cor. 8:1b); if he reads it with faith (which will be shown if he does what it says), he will grow and be fruitful: Some thirty, some sixty, some a hundredfold (Matt. 13:23).

Preaching and Teaching

Scripture is the most basic food we need, but God also wants to feed us on the right kind of preaching and teaching. Our Protestant emphasis on *Sola Scriptura*, and the universal priesthood of believers, so right in itself, can sometimes blind us to this second source of nourishment: If we're reading the Bible, what else do we need? But the fact is that God—not human beings—ordained the office of the pastor-teacher in the church to apply Scripture to our lives because reading it by ourselves is not enough to bring us to the full measure of maturity God designs (Eph. 4:11–16). While he is by no means an evangelical pope, the perspectives of a mature, wise, and trained expositor can open up to us things in the Scriptures which we would never have seen for ourselves. Could not the Holy Spirit have revealed them to us Himself? Of course, He could. However, He has chosen to do so through the ministry of the pastor, who in subjection to the Word ministers the Word, not infallibly, but—if the Spirit is in it—effectively. God has ordained the office of elder/pastor/teacher and commanded us to be subject to it (1 Thess. 5:12; 1 Tim. 5:17; Heb. 13:17). This implies that, wherever a godly pastor faithfully proclaims the Word to obedient hearers, the Spirit will be in it and growth will occur.

Since the proclamation of the Word is of central importance not only for evangelism but also for the health and proper growth of believers, we ought to examine carefully what the Bible says such preaching is. Not all verbiage which comes from a pulpit—even if it has proof texts—is the ministry which God has ordained and promises to bless. Ephesians 4:11–16 and 1 Timothy 1:5 both deal with it profitably, but perhaps the most succinct summary is found in Colossians 1:28: "We proclaim Him, admonishing every man and teaching every man with all wisdom, that we may present every man complete in Christ." In the first place good preaching is proclamation: The preacher is not primarily a pop philosopher, a storyteller, a social critic, or an orator, though he may be all these things as well. The preacher is primarily a herald, bringing a message which ultimately derives its authority from Another. In the second place, his proclamation must be Christocentric: He proclaims Jesus Christ. Though his message eventually touches the whole counsel of God and every area of life, it is all from the perspective of the glory of God in the face of Jesus Christ.

In addition, biblical preaching is more than mere teaching, but never less. It involves both admonishing and teaching. It is neither an academic lecture nor a pep talk: Exhortation is based on content that leads to exhortation because of the high stakes involved: the glory of God and the health of His church. It is to be done with all wisdom: It is thoughtful, not off the cuff or shallow, and rooted in "the fear of the Lord" (Prov. 1:7) which leads to godly living. The ultimate goal and effect of biblical preaching is to present every person complete—that is, *teleios*, which can be translated perfect, complete, or mature—in Christ. It is difficult to see how it can be all these things unless it is expository, submitted to the discipline of the systematic unfolding of the text of the Word of God—after all, its whole essence is to be a ministry of the Word.

Such is the preaching ministry of the pastor-teacher which God has ordained and which the Holy Spirit will bless. Consequently, for pastors to attempt anything less is for them to quench the Spirit. No one is adequate for these things, of course; but to aspire to anything less is to betray our calling and to rob the church of an essential part of its nourishment. That is what it means to say that preaching is a divinely appointed means of growth. To neglect it or to provide the frothy substitutes which abound even in "Bible-believing" churches is to ensure the onset of acute spiritual anemia. It is, in large measure, the explanation of the large and bloated but spiritually weak and morally decadent condition of so much of evangelical Christendom today. We are outwardly prosperous but inwardly—spiritually—malnourished.

The Ordinances

Nor do we fare much better in the third form of nourishment which God has ordained for our spiritual sustenance: the ordinances of *baptism* and the *Lord's Supper*. In an overreaction against Roman Catholic errors such as transubstantiation or baptismal regeneration, most conservative Protestants put far too little emphasis on the ordinances. Some churches only celebrate communion quarterly, and few provide any systematic teaching as to what it is all about. Yet it is undeniable that baptism and communion were instituted by the Lord Jesus Christ Himself for our spiritual good. Consequently, to relegate them to the periphery of our spiritual lives is tantamount to suggesting that the Lord did not know what He was doing. If Christ instituted these practices, then surely we can expect the Holy Spirit to work through them.

Baptism

We have already seen the strong connection between the Holy Spirit and baptism in a previous chapter. The initial coming of the Spirit to indwell the believer and unite him to Christ and His church at the time of conversion is called a "baptism," so it is appropriate that water baptism is the ceremony which celebrates symbolically our initiation into the Christian life and the fellowship of the saints.

The waters of baptism are a rich and powerful symbol with many facets of meaning in Scripture, but I would suggest that a central one is identification. Jesus, by submitting to a baptism "of repentance for the forgiveness of sins" (Mark 1:4) which He in His sinlessness did not need, identified Himself with us in our need, thus formally declaring that His messianic ministry would be one of sin-bearing. When we in turn "follow the Lord in baptism," we identify with Him, in His death, burial, and resurrection, and with His church.

Baptism is a public declaration, a public ratification of a covenant made between the baptized and his Savior. By submitting to the ordinance one says, in effect, "I hereby declare before God, men, and angels that I am henceforth to be identified as a disciple of Jesus Christ." (That is why baptism is attached to the Great Commission to "make disciples," Matt. 28:19). "I do this in specific terms dictated by Scripture. I identify myself as a sinner in repentance as in the baptism of John. But more than that, in Christian baptism (in terms of Rom. 6) I identify myself with the death, burial, and resurrection of my Lord as the sure ground of the remission and acceptance and justification John's baptism could only promise. I confess that Jesus' death should have been mine, and I confess my faith that God counts it as mine, and that is my only hope of forgiveness. I confess that the resurrection of

Jesus is the only reason I have of hoping to enjoy eternal life. I identify myself with Jesus and also, consequently, with His people, the church. I do this publicly because I belong to Him and to them and I want you to know it, which is why I am standing up here having all this attention called to these things in this dramatic way."

John baptized with water, but Jesus does it with the Holy Spirit, who as the Agent of Jesus brings conversion and regeneration and spiritual life into the soul. In other words, Spirit baptism does what water baptism says. And we have already seen that Scripture identifies this baptism as taking place at the moment of conversion. The Holy Spirit, applying to the heart the finished work of Christ, accomplishes what John's baptism had promised: remission of sins and all the spiritual blessings which flow from it. You might think that this fulfillment would render the water no longer necessary; but the Lord instructed that the outward baptism of water should continue in the church so that, the Spirit having done what the water says, the church through the water might now say what the Spirit does. For this reason, God also speaks in baptism, confirming through the ordinance that He has given His promise of the Spirit. In my baptism I identify myself with Christ, and the Father responds to me as He did to Christ in His baptism: "I accept your faith in my Son and I accept you for His sake; because you are identified with Him, I say to you what I said to Him: You—in Christ—are my beloved son (or daughter) in whom I am well-pleased." That too, if we understand it properly, is what baptism says.

In other words, if we watch and listen with understanding and with the ears of faith, baptism is an ordinance in which the Holy Spirit ministers Christ to us. Not that the water of baptism saves—only grace does that, through faith. Those who have faith without water are saved, and those who have water without faith are lost. But the water expresses, dramatizes, declares publicly, and hence reinforces that faith. When it is administered with faith and understanding, then the Holy Spirit uses it to feed and build our faith. He works through it to cement and strengthen the bond between us and the Savior. He uses it to make Jesus real to us—which is, as we have seen, the heart and soul of His ministry. It is so both when I undergo baptism myself and also when, as part of the church, I celebrate the baptism of others. Their baptism becomes an opportunity for me to remember, renew, and reconfirm the dealing between myself and my heavenly Father which was signified to me in my own. In that moment the whole church draws together in its identification with its crucified and risen Lord. And so Christ is glorified.

The Lord's Supper

We have dwelled on baptism at length because it illustrates the way in which the Holy Spirit uses the ordinances to nourish us spiritually. The Lord's Supper works in much the same way, except that, unlike baptism, it is repeatable. The older theological language called both ordinances "signs and seals of the covenant of grace" (Westminster Confession XXVII). They signify something (in Paul's words, the Lord's Supper "proclaims the Lord's death until He comes," 1 Cor. 11:26), and they seal it, visibly marking out the recipients as partakers of what is signified. And what they sign and seal is the "covenant of grace"—God's gracious covenant, His commitment to accept Jesus' blood as the price of our disobedience and to accept us for Jesus' sake when we put our faith in Him. Jesus spoke of the Lord's Supper in precisely such terms even as He instituted it, calling the cup "the new covenant in My blood" (Luke 22:20).

The Supper is many things. It is a visual preaching of the gospel which speaks of the incarnation and death of the Son of God (1 Cor. 11:26). It is a memorial of Christ's passion and triumph: We do it "in remembrance" of Him (Luke 22:19). But it is most centrally a ratification of the new covenant. When God through the person of His minister offers us the bread and the wine, He says to us, "My offer of grace in the new covenant is still in effect. My promise to accept the death of Christ as full payment of your sins and make you My child on the simple condition of faith in Him still holds good. You are Mine; the gift of salvation is yours; *here it is* in a form you can taste and feel, reminding you of the body and blood of your Savior which is its essence. Take it!"

By receiving these symbols and eating them and making them part of us, we say in return symbolically, "Yes! I do take it. I still believe that Jesus died for me and rose from the dead, and I still confess Him as my Lord and Savior. I still rest in the sole sufficiency of His shed blood as my only hope of heaven. I still love Him and worship Him, and I hereby express my continuing desire that He may increasingly become as intimately part of my life spiritually as this bread and wine will be physically when they are digested into tissue, energy, and life. I worship and thank and praise Him for all the riches of the glory of His grace as it is symbolized for me by these things."

The Lord's Supper then is an opportunity for us to draw near to God as He draws near to us. In it we remember, renew, and reconfirm the commitment we have to each other in terms of the new covenant. It is important not to miss the significance of the fact that the Holy Spirit works through these divinely instituted means to strengthen our Christian lives. It means that the ordinances do not work magically but personally. Water, bread, and grape juice can do nothing of themselves. It is our obedient faith in response to God's promises which allows the Holy Spirit to work through the ordinances to feed us on the rich banquet of the grace of God in Jesus Christ our Lord. God Himself in Christ has appointed them as one of the chief means used by the Spirit to bring Christ into our lives and make Him real to us.

As far as the spiritual nourishment we need to grow in grace is concerned, God has prepared us a lavish three-course dinner consisting of Bible reading, preaching, and the ordinances. The Bible is the main course; the other two dishes are in a sense applications of the Bible and derive their authority from it. The Bible remains the final court of appeal. But God has prepared the whole meal in such a way that the Bible will not have its full wholesome effect on us apart from the other two dishes—indeed, to neglect them is to be disobedient to (and hence contemptuous of) the Bible itself.

Spiritual Fellowship

Nourishment is the first and most basic need of the spiritual baby, but it is not the only one. Just as with physical infants, spiritual infants can grow properly only in the context of community. We were created to need relationships in order to be fulfilled. God Himself said it was "not good for the man to be alone" (Gen. 2:18). Consequently, we must have not only spiritual food but also spiritual fellowship if we are to grow in grace as we should.

Fellowship with God

The evangelical cliché which describes the essence of the Christian faith as "a personal relationship with Jesus Christ" is instinctively right on target. Jesus Himself defined eternal life as knowing God intimately (John 17:3). So our fellowship in the first place is with the Father and His Son as they are brought into our lives by the indwelling Spirit. The way we most consciously and directly carry on that fellowship is prayer. Much could be said about prayer, but we will confine ourselves here to the role which the Holy Spirit plays in the most recommended and least resorted to, the most praised and least practiced of spiritual disciplines. It is the role we have seen Him play at every point. He is the personal Liaison between us and the Lord Jesus Christ.

How is it that human beings can have fellowship with God? How can finite and sinful persons ever dare to approach the awesome throne of the infinite and holy One who dwells in unapproachable light? Quite simply, the answer is that there is one God and also one Mediator between man and God, the man Christ Jesus (1 Tim. 2:5), who, combining in His own person both perfect humanity and perfect divinity, bridges the gap between our natures, and who by His atoning sacrifice on the cross bridges the gap of morality and justice caused by our sin. He has entered into the holy of holies in heaven itself bearing His own blood to make atonement once and for all; and since we are "in Him" by faith, we too have been brought in behind the veil, whose earthly symbol in the temple was split in two at the time of the crucifixion in recognition of that fact. The Letter to the Hebrews summarizes the significance of this mediatorial ministry for prayer powerfully: It gives us "confidence to enter the holy place by the blood of Jesus;" therefore, since we have such a great and perfect high priest we should "draw near with a sincere heart in full assurance of faith" (Heb. 10:19–22). The work of Christ gives us a standing invitation into the throne room of God. The work of the Holy Spirit is to apply that work of Christ to our hearts and lives in our practical experience.

Paul indeed explicitly connects the ministry of Christ and that of the Spirit in this respect, "Through Him [Christ] we both [Jews and Gentiles] have our access in one Spirit to the Father" (Eph. 2:18). He also gives us some insight into the specific contribution made by the Spirit in the application of that work. Twice Paul connected the Holy Spirit with the cry, "Abba! Father!" (Gal. 4:6; Rom 8:15). In Galatians the Spirit Himself cries in us to the Father; in Romans the Spirit enables us to utter the same cry. We also find in Romans 8:26 that the Spirit helps us when we do not know how to pray, interceding for Himself with "groanings too deep for words."

The Spirit makes Jesus real to us by giving us the confidence to act on the objective facts of the gospel. It is the Spirit working within us when we find ourselves not just nodding our heads in assent to the doctrine of Christ's mediatorial work and the privileges it gives us but also actually crying out to the Father in that radical language of Jesus Himself which could almost be translated, "Daddy!" "Abba, Father!" That amazing blend of reverence and familiarity with which the child of God makes contact with his heavenly Father and knows with a knowledge too deep for words that he is heard and understood and accepted and loved is absolutely dependent on the work of Christ and the Holy Spirit. It is not a psychological illusion, for it does not come naturally even for the most devout believer. The gift of faith which makes it possible is due to the supernatural work of the Holy Spirit, making Jesus and the Father real to us.

Our fellowship is with the Father and His Son, through the enabling ministry of the Holy Spirit. Therefore, we should pray more often, more regularly, more deeply, and more intensely than most of us do. Such prayer will not inevitably feel like what I described in the paragraph above. That shouldn't be surprising; not every moment I spend with my wife achieves the same intensity of intimacy either. We remain human, and the Spirit remains a Person, not a button we can push to get a prescribed "blessing" or experience. But the moments when we do attain to such freedom in prayer are among the most precious foretastes of heaven vouchsafed to us in this life. Nothing is more effective to deepen and strengthen and build our relationship with God and our Christian walk. The way to receive more of this inestimable blessing is simply to put ourselves more regularly in the place where it is to be found: on our knees. For all of it that we receive we have our loving Savior and His personal Representative to thank.

Fellowship with Other Believers

Fellowship with God is not just the most important aspect of the Christian life—it is the Christian life. But just because it is, fellowship with other believers is extremely important too. When one receives adoption into the family of God, when one is granted the privilege in Christ of calling God his Father, one of logical necessity also comes into a new relationship with a rather motley crew of new brothers and sisters.

I have only two children, not millions, but I can tell you that it is difficult for either of them to be in harmony with me when they are fighting each other! Nor is it possible for either of them to be related to me without being also involved with each other. One of the surest ways for them to please me is for them to love one another. So it should not be surprising that God has ordained that our spiritual growth best takes place, not in isolation, but in fellowship with other believers.

The Bible in fact explicitly connects the two forms of fellowship in just this way. We saw Ephesians 2:18 speak of our access through Christ in one Spirit to the Father, establishing our fellowship with God. The very next verse makes an interesting application: "So then you are no longer strangers and aliens, but you are fellow citizens with the saints, and are of God's household" (Eph. 2:19). Paul went on to say that we as such are being built together into a "holy temple," a "dwelling of God in the Spirit" (Eph. 2:20–22). The Holy Spirit who indwells each of us binds us together like mortar binds bricks in a building (or, in 4:16, like the ligaments bind the joints of a body). We are the body of Christ together; together we are a holy temple dedicated to the glory of Jesus Christ. The biblical metaphors tempt us to elaboration: If Jesus is the cornerstone and we are the bricks, the Spirit is the mortar. If we are one body because we have one Head, it is also because the body is animated by one Spirit which joins us to that Head. The elaborations may be fanciful, but of this we can be sure: The Holy Spirit has a crucial role to play in making possible, not only our fellowship with the Father, but also the fellowship of the saints, and this ministry is central to God's ultimate purpose for His children.

The implications are clear. We can only be rightly related to God if we are also rightly related to the church and growing in Christian life. We saw one reason why that is so in our discussion of nourishment: God's divinely appointed way of feeding us on the Bible is in the context of the ministry of the church in the Word and the ordinances. We will see further elaboration of that principle when we take up the topic of spiritual gifts a little later. However, to allow pride or an unforgiving spirit or anything else to come between us and the body of Christ is to miss a major part of God's purpose in our redemption, to grieve the Father, and to quench the Spirit. To actually seek to destroy that body through careless gossip (yes, I'm afraid that is what it does) is to rip open the wounds of Christ anew and crucify Him afresh.

We need each other. We serve an infinite God, and none of us alone is adequate to receive everything He wants to give us. So He has ordained to give us many things through each other. We alone are inadequate to manifest His glory to the world. That is why He brings us together, for only when the world sees Jew and Gentile, bond and free, white and black, inexplicably loving each other will it begin to understand (John 17:23). We serve in a hostile world which not only rejects our message but constantly bombards us with stimuli which subtly undercut that message even in our own minds. So we need to encourage one another, stand together, and stir one another up to love and good deeds—all of which, no doubt, is why we are commanded "not forsaking our own assembling together, as is the habit of some" (Heb. 10:24–25). To disobey this commandment is to quench the

Spirit by taking out of His hands one of the chief means He uses to bring us to maturity in Christ.

Spiritual Exercise

The growing child needs the right kind of food, and he needs to establish the right kind of relationships with his parents and his peers if he is to grow and develop properly. He also needs the right kind of exercise to develop his muscles and reflexes. Otherwise, the only thing all the food and fellowship he gets will grow is fat. With spiritual muscle as with physical, the unbreakable rule is "use it or lose it." That is why the Bible is full of exhortations for us to get on with it, and why nowhere in all of Scripture can you find a saint who was a spiritual couch potato.

There is of course no prospect whatsoever of working up sanctification in our own strength, any more than salvation itself. Our own efforts help us grow only because God has graciously promised to bless obedience. The biblical balance is expressed in a verse which also gives us the key to the role of the Holy Spirit in spiritual exercise. "Work out your salvation with fear and trembling; for it is God who is at work in you, both to will and to work for His good pleasure" (Phil. 2:12–13). We are commanded to work *because* God is at work in us. It is all of grace: Apart from Him we could not even will, much less do. But with Him we will and do. What would be futile in and of itself is effectual only because out of pure grace God condescends to make it so. The pattern is inscribed on every page of the New Testament. Paul planted, Apollos watered, but God gave the increase (1 Cor. 3:6). In myself I can do nothing, but I can do all things through Christ. Without the Spirit's work of conviction, calling, and regeneration, planting and watering are futile. Yet, He normally does not bring the increase unless we plant and water. Planting and watering are not passive but active. And the same principle applies to the Spirit's work in our sanctification.

It is the same doctrine of "means" in relation to the work of the Spirit that we have seen since the first page of this study: In God's economy both are required. This is the perspective which allowed the same Paul who wrote Galatians 2:20 ("It is no longer I who live, but Christ lives in me") also to write the following without one hint of contradiction: "Be diligent to present yourself approved to God as a workman who does not need to be ashamed, handling accurately the word of truth" (2 Tim. 2:15). "Everyone who competes in the games exercises self-control. . . . Therefore I run in such a way, as not without aim; I box in such a way, as not beating the air; but I buffet my body and make it my slave" (1 Cor. 9:25–27). "Not that I have already obtained it, or have already become perfect, but I press on in order that I may lay hold of that for which also I was laid hold of by Christ Jesus" (Phil. 3:12). "Discipline yourself for the purpose of godliness" (1 Tim. 4:7). Each side of the apostle's emphasis must constantly be read in the light of the other.

In one sense we are simply reiterating a principle we learned above: It is the doers of the Word, not just the hearers, who are blessed. But there is more to it than that. Perhaps the most interesting verse on this whole topic is Hebrews 5:14: "Solid food is for the mature, who because of practice have their senses trained to discern good and evil." Applied here to Bible study, the ability to handle "solid food" is a principle which has applications to the whole range of spiritual life. Do you want to be a better student of the Bible? A better witness for the Lord? A better resister of temptation? A better pray-er? A more effective user of your spiritual gifts for the edification of the body? The answer is not some esoteric, mystical, spiritual "secret." It is as simple, as mundane, and as practical as this: practice! In the context of nurture, fellowship, and the right kind of guidance from the more mature, just do it! Fall on your face, and then get up and try again. And again. And again.

It is important to remember that spiritual exercise is part of a whole unified and integrated program of development prescribed by Scripture and that it is dangerous to try it in isolation from the rest of the program. You must first be sure that you are saved, that you are indwelt by the Spirit of God. Otherwise your job will be as futile as trying to train a corpse for the Olympics. Then you must eat right, get plenty of rest (it's no good to get burned out by an overdose of church work and activity), remember that the Christian life is a team sport, and follow the advice of a good coach. If you tried to take up an equally strenuous physical activity like marathon running or weight lifting without following the corresponding physical cautions, you would stand a good chance of seriously injuring yourself and doing yourself more harm than good. I suspect that many Christians with more zeal than wisdom have wrecked their spiritual lives in much the same way. (I can think of some well-meaning but misguided churches which seem scientifically designed to encourage just this mistake). To recognize the pitfalls is not the same thing as to deny the benefits—or the necessity—of spiritual exercise. We are, after all, talking about biblical commands.

We are then to get the right kind of balanced spiritual diet, to seek out the right kind of spiritual fellowship, and to practice doing what the Bible says. We learn by doing, which is to say that we work out our own salvation because it is God—in the Person of the Holy Spirit—who is at work in us. We are not saved by works, but we are saved for works (Eph. 2:8–10), and even those works are the fruit of grace. Apart from the sanctifying work of the Holy Spirit, we could not even will them, much less do them. With the Spirit we can do all things because He is the personal Representative of our all-sufficient Christ.

Spiritual Direction

We have then food, fellowship, and exercise, but we also need direction. A newborn baby needs a tremendous amount of instruction and guidance from parents, teachers, and a host of others to survive, much less grow up to be a healthy and productive citizen. Holding a fork, tying a shoe, buttoning a shirt, reading a book, writing a letter, driving a car, balancing a checkbook—none of these or a thousand other basic competencies evolves spontaneously from the consciousness of the untutored child. And with them the need for guidance and instruction has only begun as we try to find our way through the real issues of life. Why am I here? What is my purpose? How do I distinguish good from evil? The greater from the lesser good? Some of these questions we each must answer for ourselves, but it is almost impossible to answer them by ourselves. We need the wisdom and the skill of those who have gone before. The spiritual baby is no different.

Scripture

It would be needlessly tedious to cite a host of texts to prove that the Bible is there to provide just such instruction, direction, and guidance. Most of you are thinking of 2 Timothy 3:15–17 already, and it is sufficient to make the point. The God-breathed character of Scripture makes it profitable for teaching, reproof, correction, and training in righteousness so we can be adequate for every good work. What needs emphasis at this point is the sufficiency of Scripture. It is there to make us adequate for every good work. There is nothing we need to know in order to be saved, to please God, or to serve Him which is not either expressly taught in its pages or able to be deduced "by due and necessary consequence" from them. What exactly does this mean?

It does not mean that everything we need to know is in the Bible. As C. S. Lewis put it, the Bible, in telling us to feed the hungry, does not give us lessons in cookery. The Bible gives us a view of who we are and what life is and a completely adequate set of principles by which to live. In order to successfully apply those principles, we also have to study the world in which we live in the light of those principles. It is not a matter of Christian learning versus secular learning but a matter of getting as much of both as you can, remembering that the Bible must be in control of the outlook, the perspective by which all is seen and evaluated. It does mean that there is no moral or spiritual problem we can ever encounter to which the Bible does not ultimately contain the answer. Sometimes we find it directly, sometimes we only find the principles which are the key to an answer we must work out for ourselves, but we find that the answers which matter are there. There is no good work God requires of you which the Bible cannot teach you about and instruct you in.

Other Sources

It does not mean that the Bible is the only guide we need—otherwise the teaching ministry of the church would never have been ordained by God. The Bible is a big book and a complicated book, big and complicated enough to be able to guide us in the whole spectrum of life. So while even a child can understand its basic message, no person understands it all and no person understands it perfectly. Ministers, counselors, and Christian friends can help us, but their counsel must be judged by Scripture as the final court of appeal. They are not infallible like Scripture. When they truly open up to us the words of Scripture, the Holy Spirit speaks through them for our instruction. We are intended to learn from them. That is why the Christian life is so often spoken of in terms of discipleship, why Timothy was commanded to entrust the things he had learned from Paul to other faithful men who would be able to teach others also (2 Tim. 2:2). Two thousand years later the process still continues, and no one grows in the faith as he should without it.

This book is hopefully a part of the process. As your fellow believer, I stand with you under the Scriptures which govern and judge us both. As a minister of the gospel I have the office of a teacher of the church, a responsibility which makes me shudder and which I could not begin to carry out were it not for my confidence in the Holy Spirit whose inspiration of the Book—of which this book is but a humble and imperfect servant—guarantees the Bible's adequacy as a light unto our path and a lamp unto our feet. Only as it helps you understand and apply the message of that Book, can this book be a part of that process which the Holy Spirit uses to edify the church and bring it to maturity. Only as you search the Scriptures daily to see whether these things are so (Acts 17:11) and commit yourself to live in the light of them where they are, only if you do so with an attitude of humble dependence on the Spirit's enabling and eagerness to give all the glory to God, only then will the power of the Spirit begin to be unleashed in your life. And then will Jesus' words be fulfilled: "He shall glorify Me; for He shall take of Mine, and shall disclose it to you" (John 16:14).

Conclusion

Do you want Jesus to be glorified in you? Do you want to experience the ministry of the Holy Spirit in your life? The two questions are one and the same, and a third is like unto them: Do you want to grow in your walk with the Lord? Only the Holy Spirit can make this happen, and He has declared His intention of normally working through certain channels to do it. You need to feed your faith on the Bible, good expository preaching in a Bible-believing church, and the ordinances; you need to share it and deepen it in fellowship through prayer and good Christian friends; you need to exercise it by practicing what you preach; you need to educate and instruct it through the Bible, sound teaching, and the counsel of mature and experienced believers. If you do these things humbly, quietly, patiently, and consistently, you will eventually find yourself growing and being transformed in ways these things in themselves alone could hardly account for—because through them the Holy Spirit Himself works to glorify Jesus Christ. They are for that reason the means of growth.

Questions for Further Study

1. Summarize Keswick theology. What are its strengths and weaknesses?

2. What are the four major needs children have in order to grow? How well do you think the analogy of these needs to spiritual growth holds up?

3. What is the relationship between dependence on the Holy Spirit and the use of "means"? What is the biblical basis for this relationship? Can you explain how it applies to each of the means of growth?

4. The "sufficiency" of Scripture is a biblical and important concept, but it is also more complex than it might appear. Wherein does the sufficiency of Scripture lie? What is the biblical basis for the teaching? How does it relate to other means of growth which Scripture itself sets forth?

13

SPIRITUAL GIFTS
FOR SERVICE

We concluded our study of the doctrine of sanctification by seeing how the Holy Spirit works through various means of growth—Bible study, preaching, the ordinances, prayer, fellowship, and the exercise of faith—to glorify Jesus Christ by bringing us to maturity in Him. In all these things we saw the centrality of the church: Growth in grace occurs in the context of the body of Christ. The growth of the believer and the growth of the body are closely related—indeed, they are inseparable, for God's ultimate purpose is the growth of the whole body into a holy temple to the glory of Jesus Christ (Eph. 2:19–22). So the place where the doctrine of ecclesiology intersects with the doctrine of sanctification is the doctrine of spiritual gifts, which essentially answers two basic questions. How does the Holy Spirit use the church to promote the growth of the believer? And how does the Spirit use the growth of the believer to build up the whole church? The answer to both is that He does it by giving spiritual gifts to every believer to create a mutuality of ministry within the body of Christ. To understand the nature and function of spiritual gifts is to see why this is so.

Four Synonyms

One of the best passages for studying the nature of spiritual gifts is 1 Corinthians 12:4–7, which gives us four synonyms, each highlighting one facet of the whole concept:

> Now there are varieties of gifts, but the same Spirit. And there are varieties of ministries, and the same Lord. And there are varieties of effects, but the same God who works all things in all persons. But to each one is given the manifestation of the Spirit for the common good.

Quite clearly the four verses give parallel statements about the same idea, expressed by the terms *gift, ministry, effect,* and *manifestation* of the Spirit. There are many varieties of these gifts/ministries/effects/manifestations. They all proceed from the same Source (the Trinity, and in particular the Spirit), and each member of the body has at least one for the common good of the whole. A partial list of these gifts follows, with much emphasis on their common Source—the Spirit—and their common purpose—the edification of the body. In this context each of the four synonyms has something to teach us about what the Lord is doing through His Spirit in His church.

Gifts of the Spirit

First and most familiarly, spiritual gifts are gifts of God's grace. The Greek word used for gift (*charisma*) is related to *charis,* the word for grace. Since salvation is by grace alone, it is a free gift received by faith alone (indeed, the same word for gift is used with reference to salvation in Romans 6:23). Salvation itself is a *charisma* resulting from God's *charis,* a gift of His grace. It is fascinating that the same word is used for the practical outworking of that grace in service to the body of Christ. The Spirit who brings the grace of God into our lives in the gift of salvation also brings that same grace through our lives to others in the spiritual gift(s) with which He endows us for service.

The first fact about spiritual gifts then is that they are expressions and practical extensions of the grace of God. We possess them by virtue of His unmerited favor. They are not ours by right or by nature but come to us undeserved like all aspects of the great gift of grace of which they are a part. Like all other aspects of that great *charisma*, they were won for us by Christ on the cross (Eph. 4:7–8) and are communicated to us by His personal Emissary, the Holy Spirit (1 Cor. 12:11). We cannot take any credit for having or exercising them. Gifts of grace are really gifts and all grounds of boasting are rigorously excluded (Rom. 3:27). It is therefore one of the greatest ironies of church history that the possession (or non-possession!) of certain gifts has so often been the occasion for so much of the ugliness of spiritual pride and one-upmanship.

An obvious question which arises when we discuss a spiritual gift is, "To whom is it given?" The answer might seem equally obvious: to individual Christians. Indeed, the gifts are described as given "to one . . . to another" (1 Cor. 12:8). We have neglected the other recipient suggested by the phrase "for the common good" (v. 7) with unfortunate results. The whole tenor of the passage suggests the gifts are not for the individual but for the body, and the individual believer is merely a steward of a gift intended to benefit others rather than self.

I think the following is a helpful illustration. Suppose the children in my neighborhood wish to play baseball. They have a vacant lot, time, and inclination, but are hampered by a total lack of equipment. Out of my sheer goodness and generosity (you can tell this story is getting hypothetical) I decide to supply their need. I purchase enough gloves for half of them (since only half are in the field at any one time—they can share), a bat, and a ball. Because I know that for everybody to be responsible for something is to have nobody responsible for it, I distribute these items, not to the group in general, but to specific individuals. I have thus given the ball, in my deepest intention, to the team; in practicality, I have given it to Jimmy for the team. If he decides to withhold it because he is mad at some of the other players, he will have totally frustrated my purpose in giving the ball in the first place. If he is my own child he will be punished; I may take the ball away from him and give it to someone else. Nevertheless, some damage will have been done. The team will have suffered, and some of the players may quit in disgust, never to return—taking some of the gloves with them!

The little allegory above hardly needs interpretation. Nearly everyone will sadly recognize in it episodes in the history of his own church, if not in his own life. Jimmy has the ball, Tommy has the bat, and Sam has the water cooler; if any one of them doesn't show up, the team suffers, and may not be able to function at all. It is one of the greatest proofs that God is a God of grace that He continues to give His gifts in spite of the use we have made of them. We, too, frequently have taken gifts intended for the good of the body and used them for our own glory or as instruments of manipulation. Thus, instead of being built up as a holy temple to the glory of Jesus Christ, the church dishonors Him. Nothing more severely grieves and quenches the Spirit who gives the gifts than this.

Ministries from the Spirit

My spiritual gift(s) then are given not primarily to me but through me to the church. That realization makes the next designation follow naturally: They are ministries (1 Cor. 12:5). The Greek word is *diakonia*, which means ministry or service. It is the same word from which we get the English *deacon*, a servant of the church. If, as is probable, Acts chapter 6 represents the founding of the diaconate, the original deacons had the practical ministry of waiting on tables so that poor widows could be fed equitably. That is certainly the connotation of the word as we have it here. Not all Christians are called to the office of deacon, but all are called to the function of service to the body and are given spiritual gifts to enable them to perform that function. A spiritual gift is a ministry. It is best conceived of as a divinely given ability to serve in some specific area of need in the body, to the end that it is built up and its Head is glorified.

Effects of the Spirit

One question that is frequently raised about spiritual gifts is their relation to natural talents and abilities. Part of the answer to that question is suggested by the next name Paul gave them: They are effects of the Holy Spirit's ministry in and through the believer (v. 6). The Greek word is *energematon*, literally "energizings." If the basic pattern of the Spirit's operation which we have seen since our study of inspiration and illumination holds true, we would expect the Spirit to work through the natural abilities and talents which are also His gifts to us, "energizing," enhancing, and blessing them as they are dedicated to His service. This is what normally happens. I know of nobody with the gift of teaching, for example, who is a gifted teacher only of Christian doctrine and living in the church, but who becomes totally inarticulate and unorganized when he has to give a secular presentation in the boardroom of his business. People with the gift of helps tend to be helpful people in general, even when they are not functioning in the context of the body.

Surely then there has been a great deal of unjustified mysticism in the discussion of the gifts, with a tendency to create dichotomy between spiritual gifts and natural talents. The classic Old Testament passage on the subject lends itself to a view of continuity. In Exodus 31 when God was equipping His servants for building the tabernacle, God said to Moses in verse 6 that "in the hearts of *all* who are skillful" it was He who had put the skill; then He also "called by name" Bezalel and Oholiab and "filled [them] with the Spirit of God in wisdom, in understanding, in knowledge, and in all kinds of craftsmanship" so that they might oversee the work (v. 3). Here then are spiritual gifts, if you will, for architecture, carpentry, stone-cutting, and metalwork; Bezalel, the foreman, no doubt also had the gift of administration. He and Oholiab probably did an excellent job in their construction work even when they were not laboring on the tabernacle. The pattern seems to be natural gifts (all skill comes from God, v. 6) dedicated, consecrated, and enhanced by the Spirit for use in the Lord's service.

Not all the gifts mentioned in the New Testament can be described in this way, but many more can than is sometimes recognized. We might say that any natural endowment which is laid on the altar of Romans 12:1 and dedicated for the Spirit's use in the service of God's people becomes a *spiritual* gift which the Spirit can then bless and work through to accomplish things which could not be accounted for on a merely natural basis.

Whether all the gifts fit this pattern is open to question, but this would seem to be the basic pattern of the Spirit's work in general and of the gifts in particular. Spiritual gifts then are more than natural talents, but not necessarily distinct from them. The basic pattern is continuity rather than dichotomy, and this recognition should go a long way toward easing the burden of people who have difficult in discerning what their spiritual gifts are.

Manifestations of the Spirit

Paul's final synonym for spiritual gifts is that they are manifestations of the Spirit (1 Cor. 12:7). One of the signs of His presence in an individual or a church is the proper functioning of spiritual gifts in building up the body to the glory of Christ. Note that it is the gifts in general, not any particular one, which are called the manifestation of the Spirit. The sign of the Spirit's fullness in an individual's life is not speaking in tongues but any gift being humbly used to serve others. The sign of His presence in a local church is some reality of "every-member ministry." The mentality which assigns all the work of the church to the professional staff and fosters legions of spectators in the pews is then one of the most powerful quenchers of the Spirit.

The Gifts Themselves

Paul gives us a representative list of gifts: wisdom, knowledge, faith, healing, miracles, prophecy, distinguishing of spirits, tongues, interpretation of tongues (1 Cor. 12:–10). Ephesians 4:11 introduces a somewhat different list: apostles, prophets, evangelists, and pastor-teachers. Romans 12:6–8 begins still another list: prophecy, service, teaching, exhortation, giving, leadership, mercy. First Corinthians 12:28 starts yet another list: apostles, prophets, teachers, miracles, healing, helps, administration, tongues.

The fact that these four lists overlap but are not identical suggests that there is in fact no set number of gifts available. The gifts in Exodus 31 were not needed in the first century church, and so naturally are not mentioned; they are needed by many churches today, and are no doubt given. Paul's lists are representative samples, suggestions of the general kinds of things which can function as spiritual gifts. There is no indication that they are intended to be exhaustive—conceivably one's gift might be something which does not even appear in the lists. Musical talent is never mentioned, but surely it can function as a spiritual gift in the twentieth century as well as in the first. I once had a layman with what I called the gift of technology. He loved to tinker with electronic equipment, and he dedicated that knack to making our primitive sound system function on a level no one else could have approached. The whole point is that there is no need to do mental gymnastics trying to fit his gift into one of Paul's categories, which were apparently only intended as suggestive examples to give us the idea. The Holy Spirit varies the precise inventory of gifts available in response to the changing needs of the church. Some, such as teaching, evangelism, administration, exhortation, helps, and giving are always applicable; others come and go.

Discerning One's Gift(s)

It seems to me that a great deal of our popular teaching on this subject has actually had the effect of bringing people into bondage and making it unnecessarily difficult for them to discover what their spiritual gifts are. Every believer has at least one (1 Pet. 4:10); some have several; probably no one has them all. But the way to discover what your gift is is not to concentrate on Paul's lists of gifts but to be sensitive to needs within the body and ask yourself how God has positioned you to meet them. Exercising your spiritual gifts is the path to fulfillment as a Christian, but the whole point of them is ministry, service, edification, meeting needs. Yours does not have to be something different from your natural gifts and abilities; it does not have to be one which appears in the lists (though they are certainly good places to start); it does not even have to be the same thing at all times. Anything God has given you which you can use to meet a need in the body can be your spiritual gift. You discover it by serving, by caring, living the life of the body. When you find that God consistently blesses your efforts in a certain area you can confidently conclude that there lies one of your gifts.

You do not wait to serve until you somehow mystically discover your gift; you discover it by serving. If you do a little work in an area where you are not gifted in the process, God will forgive you! In fact, we are required to do so all the time. Not everyone, for example, has the gift of evangelism, but that does not excuse anyone from being a witness for Jesus Christ. Not everyone has a Red Cross lifesaving badge either, but when someone is drowning you don't quibble about that lack. Instead, you throw a rope. Naturally, when you discover your gifts you will major in those areas, but that does not mean you will not be helping in other areas from time to time. If the guy with the glove has gone off in a huff, somebody might just have to catch bare-handed so the game can go on. The key perspective is to remember that the gifts exist for the sake of the game. When the game and the welfare of the team are in the forefront of our minds, then the gifts will function as the Spirit who gave them designs: to glorify the Lord Jesus Christ.

There is then probably a need for more flexibility in our understanding of the gifts, especially in the light of the fact that we are not even told what some of them were. It amazes me how confidently some of our teachers can so rigorously define and subtly delineate the New Testament gifts in the absence of any apostolic explanation other than the appearance of a name in a list. How do we know, for example, that the "word of knowledge" meant a divinely given diagnosis of an ailment unknown to anyone in the congregation when there is not one word to that effect in any New Testament text? Even granting that such a gift is operative in some modern congregations (and while many stories have obviously grown in the telling, others are hard to discount), how do we know that this is what Paul was referring to when he does not tell us? Obviously, we *don't* know, and when we don't know we ought to be honest enough to be still.

Prophecy can mean many things in biblical usage, from predicting the future to giving a "Thus saith the Lord!" to merely applying previously revealed truth to a new situation. That seems to be the meaning in 1 Corinthians 14:29, where the congregation is supposed to pass judgment on the prophecies— hardly something you would be prepared to do with those of

172

Isaiah or Elijah! You get the same perspective in 1 Thessalonians 5:20–21. The point is that, while we know less about the precise nature of New Testament gifts than some teachers claim to know, we know as much as we need to in order to serve the Lord with whatever He has given us. In the meantime we ought to serve Him humbly with them and beware of falling into the kind of "confident assertion" Paul condemned in 1 Timothy 1:7.

Summary

We do know that spiritual gifts are ministries, abilities to serve, effects of, and manifestations of the Holy Spirit in our lives, given so we can help each other grow in the Lord so that the church as a body is built up as a result. We know that there are many gifts but one Spirit who gives them. We know that some are more important than others (prophecy more than tongues, for example), and that we are to seek the greater ones (1 Cor. 14:1). We know that all are needed and no one is to despise another, for all are gifts of God's grace and all work together to one end. We know that every believer has at least one gift. The way to discover yours is to get your hands dirty in practical service. We know that God's ultimate purpose is to glorify His Son in the salvation of sinners and the joining of them together in one body of which the Son is the Head. We know that the Holy Spirit serves that purpose by convicting, calling, regenerating, and sanctifying them, and by baptizing them into that body. The Spirit then equips them for life and service in it by imparting to them spiritual gifts

> for the equipping of the saints for the work of service, to the building up of the body of Christ, until we all attain to the unity of the faith, and of the knowledge of the Son of God, to a mature man, to the measure of the stature which belongs to the fulness of Christ. . . . from whom the whole body, being fitted and held together by that which every joint supplies, according to the proper working of each individual part, causes the growth of the body for the building up of itself in love. (Eph. 4:12–16)

Questions for Further Study

1. What are the four designations of spiritual gifts in 1 Corinthians 12:4–7? Define each carefully.

2. What does each word contribute to our understanding of spiritual gifts?

3. How does the giving of these gifts relate to the Spirit's ministry of bringing glory to Jesus Christ by acting as His personal Agent and Representative?

4. How do the various lists of gifts in the New Testament relate to one another? What implications arise from comparing them?

5. What is the most practical approach to discerning one's spiritual gift(s)?

14

WHAT ABOUT TONGUES?

It is one of the great ironies of ecclesiology, one of the great tragedies of church history, and one of the great triumphs of Satan that a doctrine so conducive to the health and unity of the body of Christ as that of the spiritual gifts should have become the occasion for an outpouring of divisiveness, fear, and polarization. Nevertheless, such has been our experience in the twentieth century. It is the well documented nature of heresy that errors tend to breed their opposites. From neglect comes excess; from excess comes fear, denial, and rejection; from all these comes polarization, the hardening of positions, and the squandering of spiritual energy. Logically, the debate is over the place of the so-called supernatural, miraculous, or extraordinary gifts. Practically, the focal point seems to be the emotionally charged issue of tongues. The emotion attached to the issue has skewed our whole view of the Person and work of the Holy Spirit out of biblical balance, with error of doctrine and practice aplenty on both sides. Let's see if we can sort through some of the confusion in the light of a holistic view of the Spirit's ministry.

Have Tongues Ceased?

First we must examine the case for cessationism, the view that miracles in general and tongues in particular ceased by divine plan after the apostolic age. If the Bible teaches that miracles are not for this age, then everything becomes very simple: All manifestations such as glossolalia (speaking in tongues) are counterfeit at best, if not downright demonic. If cessationism holds up, no further discussion is necessary.

A Theological Argument

The case for cessationism depends on two basic arguments, a theological one and a biblical one. The theological argument holds that the purpose of miracles is to authenticate revelation, to prove that the prophets and apostles really did speak for God and that Jesus really was the Messiah. Even in biblical times miracles did not occur indiscriminately but tended to cluster around critical moments in salvation history when God was bringing about deliverance, judgment, and a new revelation of Himself, particularly at the Exodus and the time of Christ and the founding of the church.

Once the foundational revelation was complete with the passing of the apostles and the closing of the canon of Scripture, miracles have performed their function and can be expected to drop out of the divine economy for the world until the next great crisis, the second coming of Christ. That there is at least some truth in the premise of this argument would be hard to deny. Peter appealed in his Pentecost sermon to God's having "attested" Jesus to the Jews by "miracles and wonders and signs" (Acts 2:22). The resurrection plus the Pentecostal tongues heard by all the foreign visitors should "let all the house of Israel know for certain" that Jesus is the Christ (2:36). Certainly one of the purposes of the miracles of the New Testament was to attest and authenticate true revelation from God. But the conclusion that miracles therefore ceased when authoritative revelation ceased, i.e. with the completion of the New Testament, would follow only if we could establish that authenticating revelation was the only purpose which miracles served. And nobody could maintain that thesis without turning a blind eye to a great deal of New Testament material.

Jesus performed miracles of healing and multiplication of food out of compassion (Matt. 14:14). He healed the man born blind for the glory of God (John 9:3). It is needless to pile up examples once the point has been made: authentication. While it surely was one of the major purposes of miracles (John said Jesus performed His signs so we would believe [20:30–31], was not the only one. Since God is still compassionate and since Jesus still desires to glorify the Father (John 17:1), then the miraculous could still very well have a role to play in God's dealings with people today. The most we can conclude that, with one of the major reasons for miracles no longer applicable, some lessening of emphasis on their role in God's economy after the closing of the canon should not be totally surprising. But cessation is simply not proved by the argument.

We must be careful about how we speak of a de-emphasis of the role of miracles. If our above treatment of regeneration is faithful to Scripture, for example, then every new birth of a child of God is just as miraculous—just as incapable of occurring in the normal course of nature—as Jesus' physical resurrection of Lazarus. The Christian faith remains a shockingly supernatural religion for even the most ordinary saint whose life contains nothing of the spectacular and sensational, once the whole ministry of the Holy Spirit is understood. If what we might call "sign miracles" (the outwardly dramatic and spectacular displays of the supernatural) are not everyday and commonplace occurrences, there might be other explanations than lack of faith on the part of the church. (In fact, if they became commonplace they would lose their character and effectiveness as signs!) Yet they cannot be ruled out for today, at least on the basis of the theological argument alone.

A Biblical Argument

We turn then to the textual argument, which is founded on an interpretation of 1 Corinthians 13:8–10.

> Love never fails; but if there are gifts of prophecy, they will be done away; if there are tongues, they will cease; if there is knowledge, it will

be done away. For we know in part, and we prophesy in part; but when the perfect comes, the partial will be done away.

Here surely is a passage which speaks directly of the cessation of tongues. We now "know" and "prophesy" partially, but when the perfect comes these things will no longer be needed. Partial knowledge means that the Bible is not yet all written; the "perfect" (the Greek word, *teleion*, can mean something like complete) is the completed New Testament canon. So the sensational gifts, including tongues, ceased with the completion of the Bible, and all such phenomena reported today are spiritual frauds or counterfeits. Or so this most influential of interpretations goes.

Evaluation

This venerable and influential argument is seriously flawed and erroneous. One's suspicions are aroused immediately by the fact that the argument proves too much. One of the things which has to cease with the closing of the canon is knowledge. It seems strange that we should be given complete knowledge to the end that there should therefore be no knowledge at all. Even if it means that knowledge as we now know it will be transcended by a deeper kind of "knowing" (as seems likely to me), that is hardly something that can be said to have happened when the New Testament was finished. And a brief glance at a slightly larger context deals this now weakened interpretation its death blow.

Paul is contrasting present imperfection of knowledge with some future perfection which is coming. The question is, when is it coming? Verse 11 continues the same train of thought by offering an analogy to the imperfect/perfect contrast: Paul's childish thinking is like the present imperfect knowledge, which is to that as adult thought is to the knowledge, which is coming. He reaches the climax of his argument in verse 12, which concludes the series of parallel contrasts. Now/imperfect/childish knowledge, we see dimly in a mirror, but then/perfect/adult knowledge, we will see Jesus face to face and know Him as we are known. The provision of the full Bible is a wonderful thing, but it does not let me know Jesus the way He knows me. I will do that when I walk no longer by faith but by sight (face to face) on the day He returns. According to the full context then, the day that tongues will cease is not the day the last apostle died or the last page of Scripture was written, but the day Jesus comes back.

The simple, blanket condemnation in advance of all glossolalia is then unbiblical. That does not necessarily mean that all or any tongues being spoken today are truly gifts of the Holy Spirit, honoring to Jesus Christ, and edifying to His body. We cannot prove that tongues have ceased, but this does not commit us to naive and uncritical acceptance of all the claims and practices of what remains a problematic and divisive movement in the church. Such claims, experiences, practices, and phenomena must be evaluated on their merits as they stack up against the whole teaching of Scripture on the Spirit's ministry in general and the gifts in particular rather than being dismissed out of hand. It also means that we must beware of hasty generalizations. But some general principles for conducting such evaluations can be laid down from Scripture as we try to assess the modern tongues movement as a whole.

The Significance of Tongues

First and foremost, we must recognize that, whatever we may make of the tongues we hear today, they simply do not have the significance attributed to them by classic Pentecostal theology. Whatever they may be, they are not the definitive sign of the baptism and fullness of the Holy Spirit. We have already seen in Chapter 10 that there is no biblical justification for holding to a definitive second crisis experience of any kind. In fact, the particular Pentecostal version of that experience as the baptism of the Holy Spirit evidenced by speaking in tongues is plainly contradicted not only by much explicit teaching but even by many of the very passages urged as proof texts for it. John the Baptist's foundational prophecy proves that Spirit baptism is a way of speaking about the Spirit's coming to indwell the believer at the time of conversion. Few would claim that tongues is the sign of the initial conversion to Christ.

If the Bible does not teach the kind of subsequent Spirit baptism which classic Pentecostalism envisions, then obviously tongues cannot be the sign of it. But specific Pauline teaching on tongues as a spiritual gift also contradicts the notion. God places the members in the body—each with differing gifts for the edification of the whole—sovereignly according to His own desires (1 Cor. 12:18). The whole point is that people should have different gifts. This design is confirmed in 1 Corinthians 12:30 by a series of questions: Do all heal? Do all speak in tongues? Grammatically, the passage employs a construction known to every second-semester Greek student as the "rhetorical question expecting a negative answer." Not everybody speaks in tongues, and not everybody is supposed to. But everybody should seek to be filled with the Holy Spirit (Eph. 5:18), whether such filling is conceived as a crisis experience or not. If tongues is the sign of the filling, then everybody should seek to speak in them, but that would make the doctrine of filling directly contradictory to Paul's teaching on tongues as a gift. We cannot have it both ways. If tongues is a spiritual gift it cannot be the sign of Spirit baptism.

Whatever we may make of the practice of glossolalia, this theology of tongues is not only unbiblical but often unChristlike. It arbitrarily elevates one of the Spirit's gifts into a test of spiritual advancement, not only without scriptural sanction but contrary to the clear teaching of Scripture. And it can promote the ugliest kind of legalistic spiritual pride, with its implication that people who have not received this one particular gift are thereby obviously lacking in their experience of the fullness of the Spirit's ministry. The emphasis tends to shift from the gifts' function of edifying the Body and glorifying the Lord to whether or not a person has received this one gift. It is a theology which has often been divisive and destructive.

A Truce Proposal

It is no wonder then that so many conservative evangelicals are closed to the practice of this gift in their own fellowships or even to the potential validity of it outside them, even when they are not committed to cessationism. They are instinctively suspicious of any practice whose doctrinal underpinnings are so far off base and whose effects are diametrically opposed to everything the ministry of the Holy Spirit is all about. And they are right to be. It is noteworthy that a growing number of charismatics no longer hold to this view of the significance of tongues. Any possibility of the gift's becoming acceptable to the body of conservative believers as a whole probably is, and definitely ought to be, tied to the forthright abandonment of that theology by those who claim to be so gifted. This then is the truce proposal which is increasingly being put on the table: We will stop assuming that you are demonic if you will stop assuming that we are unspiritual. Once the doctrinal error on both sides is cleared, we can get down to looking at tongues in a way which has a chance of being fresh, biblical, and constructive.

Two Types of Tongues

Upon further examination, we run into a curious fact which has not received sufficient emphasis. There seem to be two very different types of tongues in Scripture, only one of which is prominent among speakers today. The tongues of Pentecost in Acts 2 were known human languages understood by people who were actually present and spoken by believers who had not learned them in the normal laborious way. In the tongues, believers spoke to others so that all heard the gospel in their own languages. (The debate over whether the miracle took place in the mouths of the apostles or the ears of the hearers seem to me a silly one: What difference does it make whether it was the gift of tongues or of interpretation? Besides, while Acts 2:6, 8, and 11 emphasize the hearing, verse 4 clearly states that the apostles spoke with the tongues.)

In the church of Corinth, no one was present who understood the languages spoken, and they were spoken, not to people, but to God (1 Cor. 14:2). What could be more opposite? The whole point of the Acts tongues was to do away with the need for interpreters; in Corinth, the tongues created a need for interpreters, with the result that Paul forbade their use in public worship unless such interpreters were present (14:28). The Acts tongues edified others; the Corinth tongues edified only the speaker (14:4). In fact, the word *tongue* is the only thing the two accounts have in common. Every recorded attribute of the tongues makes them opposites.

Now this is a curious fact indeed. One is tempted to conclude that the tongues of Pentecost ceased in the very midst of the apostolic age, and were replaced by something else. At the very least, it is hard to resist the conclusion that we are dealing with two different phenomena. And it is important to notice that the modern tongues movement has manifested almost if not exclusively the Corinthian type of tongues. My friends who claim the gift of tongues all describe it as a personal "prayer language" addressed to God (1 Cor. 14:2). None of them has ever led anyone to the Lord who knew no English but spoke only a foreign human language. And their testimony is quite typical. Yet, ironically, the movement justifies its existence almost wholly by appeals to the Book of Acts. It is not self-evident that the Book of Acts has any relevance at all to the tongues being spoken today; it seems to me to be talking about a different phenomenon entirely. But the Book of 1 Corinthians is extremely relevant. One might almost say that the modern tongues movement began, not in the Azusa Street revival of 1906, but in the city of Corinth in the fifties of the first century. If that is so, then the same conclusions must be drawn about it that Paul drew in his extended treatment of the issues in 1 Corinthians 12–14.

Tongues as a Natural Phenomenon

Before we turn to those conclusions, though, it is helpful to provide a context for them by noticing some of the things which can be learned about tongues by observation. One of the most important is to realize that glossolalia is not necessarily a supernatural phenomenon. (See J. I. Packer's excellent treatment and documentation of this fact in *Keeping in Step with the Spirit*, esp. p. 281, n. 22.) It is behavior which can be learned by any individual with the right susceptibilities, whether a believer or not. It frequently occurs in pagan religions. A friend of mine knew a converted Hindu who was horrified by glossolalia. "There is nothing Christian about it," he said. "I can take you to Hindu temples where it is done all the time." It seems to be a state in which normal emotional and rational inhibitions are released, expressing itself in strings of unrelated and often highly repetitive syllables which do not manifest the characteristics of real language at all. To the ungifted, it sounds more like stuttering than a foreign language.

The fact that glossolalia is a natural phenomenon does not mean it cannot be a spiritual gift; many of the gifts, as we saw in the last chapter, are natural abilities enhanced, empowered, blessed, and used by the Spirit. The fact that it is a natural phenomenon reinforces the lesson of Scripture that it has no connection with spirituality at all. You cannot conclude that a person who speaks in tongues is filled with the Spirit—or even converted, even a Christian—any more than you can conclude that a person who is a gifted and articulate communicator is a fellow believer on that basis alone, that is, the fact that he appears to have the gift of teaching. Tongues are not necessarily of the devil or of the Holy Spirit either. Tongues can perhaps open people up to either, but the gift *per se* has no spiritual significance whatever. Charismatics who accept people as brothers in Christ on the basis of their use of the gift apart from any specific doctrinal or other commitments should take warning from these facts. Their trust is grievously misplaced.

The Corinthian Instructions

What place then does the gift of tongues have in the Holy Spirit's ministry in the church today? How should those who have the gift practice it? How should those who do not relate to those who do? Since the tongues being spoken today bear such a marked resemblance to the gift practiced in ancient Corinth, the answers to these questions lie in following the specific instructions for the use of the gift which Paul gave to the original charismatics in 1 Corinthians 14. And those instructions are really quite simple to follow, if not to understand. They are four simple rules: (1) Do not forbid tongues speaking outright (v. 39b). (2) In public worship, only two or three at the most should speak (v. 27a). (3) If they do speak, they must take turns—only one at a time (v. 27b). (4) They should only speak if there is someone present who understands the language being used (vv. 27c–28).

The one principle which underlies all these rules is that all things must be done for edification (v. 26). Therefore, tongues cannot be forbidden outright because they can edify the individual who speaks in them to himself and God (vv. 4a, 28b). But their use is to be severely restricted and discouraged in public services because they do not tend to the edification of the body as a whole (vv. 4–19). Even there Paul did not absolutely rule out their use, but his restrictions have, for all practical purposes, the effect of doing so. In the Pentecostal services I have visited, the application of rules 2 and 3 would have completely squelched everything that was going on. The irony is then that on both sides of the issue people who pride themselves on being Bible believers have been in direct violation not only of the teaching but also of the commands of Scripture, the one group in their flagrantly unbiblical practice and the other in their forbidding of any practice of the gift. But surely the ministry of the Holy Spirit ought to promote obedience to the commands of Christ's apostle who was the Spirit's instrument in His ministry of speaking for Christ!

The Value of Tongues

It is hard for some of us—uptight Western rationalists that we are—to understand why Paul left any room for the exercise of such a problematic gift at all, even in private use. We must start by being obedient enough to accept the fact that he does allow for it, and positively states that the Spirit uses it to edify some people. Here, as a person who has not been granted to know the benefits of this gift by experience, I can only offer a speculation based on the general nature of the phenomenon and the testimonies of those who do experience it. It may be that in some people the release of emotional inhibitions which accompanies the experience may be used by the Spirit to break down emotional barriers in their personalities which keep them from being able to feel what they struggle to believe. If it does so, then the ability to feel forgiven, accepted, and loved by God would definitely be a great boost to their spiritual lives. This would account for the fact that they frequently report a sense of being released by the experience to greater spiritual power for service and greater devotion to God.

The ancient rhetoricians understood that to move the will it is necessary to call the emotions to the aid of the intellect, and something like that may be what the Spirit does for some people through the gift of tongues. If so, it would be in keeping with His essential ministry of making Jesus real to us. The genuine gift, then, would be known by its tendency to glorify Jesus Christ, the counterfeit by its tendency to call attention to itself. That a spiritual gift can be counterfeited by the enemy should not surprise us. Effective teaching can be heretical, and speaking in tongues can be nothing more than emotional self-indulgence. But if that does not mean we should silence all teachers, neither does it mean we should forbid everyone to speak in tongues.

Practical Conclusions

The bottom line then is that people who practice the gift of tongues as a prayer language in their private devotions should receive no hassles from the church, whether it comes from an erroneous cessationism or from a misguided fear of the unknown. They, on the other hand, should not put themselves forward to press the issue of practicing their gift in public worship when to do so would be inappropriate—which would be any time when no interpreter is present in a given congregation. We should avoid conflict, learn to live with one another, and get on with serving the Lord. Once the errors of cessationism on the one hand and a false connection of tongues with the baptism of the Holy Spirit on the other are laid to rest, there is nothing further to be gained by fighting each other over the gift of tongues. The Holy Spirit works in some individuals through the gift of tongues; He works in some churches in spite of it. Often the gift of tongues works directly against the very Spirit who is assumed to inspire it and who wishes to use it as all the other gifts, not to tear down but to build up the body of Christ for the glory of its Head.

Questions for Further Study

1. Summarize the arguments for cessationism. Are they valid? Why or why not?

2. What are some implications of the fact that tongues occur as a natural phenomenon in pagan religions?

3. Evaluate the standard Pentecostal explanation of tongues from a biblical perspective. Does rejecting that explanation mean we must condemn all use of the phenomenon?

4. Summarize Paul's rules for the use of tongues in public worship (1 Cor. 14). What is the general principle which governs their application?

5. Give some thought to how you would apply these rules in a Christlike spirit if tongues were suddenly to break out in a public service of your church.

6. What positive values might tongues have which might have led Paul to command us not to forbid them outright?

15

INDWELLING AND SEALING

The ministry of the Holy Spirit is to glorify Jesus Christ by acting as His personal Agent and Representative in the work of redemption. We have been examining the way He does this in applying to believers the salvation wrought by Christ: inspiring Scripture to inform the sinner of that redemption, illuminating his mind to understand that revelation, convicting him of his sins and calling him to faith in the Savior, regenerating him and sanctifying him, uniting him to Christ and to His body the church, and working through that body to promote growth (practical sanctification) by giving spiritual gifts. In all these activities the Spirit seeks to glorify Christ by bringing about the actual salvation and transformation of sinners, thus blazoning forth on the pages of history the love and grace of God in their altered destiny, His justice in the price paid for it in the atonement, and His character in their own renewed lives in which individualized portraits of Christ are being formed (Gal. 4:19). Two concepts which are basic to almost every aspect of the great sweep of that work have been assumed up to this point. In this chapter they are to be made explicit: indwelling and sealing.

187

Indwelling

The term *indwelling* is frequently used of the Holy Spirit's relationship to the believer. What exactly does it mean? Its biblical basis lies in passages such as John 14:17, in which Jesus promised the disciples that the Spirit who was "with" them would be "in" them after Pentecost. In 1 Corinthians 3:16 the believer is called a "temple" in which the Spirit "dwells." Similar language is used in 2 Timothy 1:14. Likewise Christ is said to live in us (Gal. 2:20) and God to "work" in us (Phil. 2:13). We have already come to understand that God is represented to us by Christ and Christ is represented in us by the Holy Spirit. So all such language can be related to this same doctrine of the "indwelling" of the Spirit.

What does it mean to say that the Holy Spirit of God "lives" or "dwells in" a human being? As a member of the Godhead, without the limitations of human nature adopted by the Second Person, the Holy Spirit is omnipresent—His presence cannot be escaped or evaded, even in hell (Ps. 139:7–8). In some sense He must be present even in the lives of non-Christians. The language of indwelling must be more than a restatement of the doctrine of divine omnipresence—though that attribute is not irrelevant, as it allows Him to be present as Christ's Representative in the lives of all His people simultaneously, as the now incarnate Christ could not be without His aid. (All the biblical pictures of Christ after the ascension seem to assume that He has permanently taken on the limitations of human nature so that He can continue to function as the Head of the restored human race in His role as Second Adam.)

The Metaphor of the Temple

The language of indwelling, to be meaningful, must refer to more than just location; it must account for the difference in mode between God's presence in heaven and in hell, in the Christian and in the sinner who is still a rebel. This means that we are dealing with metaphorical language. That is just to say that it is a verbal picture to help us understand the relationship we have with the Spirit. To grasp the meaning of it we must view it pictorially, and the picture we must form is, in the first place, that of the Old Testament tabernacle or the temple of Solomon, where God's presence dwelt among His people.

The temple was made like a nest of boxes: There was a court-yard, inside which was the holy place, which led finally to the innermost holy of holies where sat the ark of the covenant. There, over the mercy seat which covered the ark, between the outstretched wings of the cherubim carved on it, was the symbolic location of the presence of God. At times it was the actual location of the Shekinah, the visible glory of God, as when "the cloud covered the tent of meeting, and the glory of the Lord filled the tabernacle" and Moses was not able to enter when the tabernacle was dedicated in the wilderness (Ex. 40:34f.).

Solomon was well aware that even the highest heaven could not contain the omnipresent Yahweh (1 Kings 8:27), but his prayer at the dedication of the temple also showed that the temple—particularly the holy of holies—symbolized God's special presence with His people: They would pray toward this place, and God would hear in heaven and forgive and heal. In terms of His relationship to His people, the presence of the omnipresent God was focused between the cherubim, so that they prayed toward that room and the high priest entered it once a year bearing blood to make atonement. It was the special locus of God's presence in the lives of His people, and in that sense the Shekinah could be said to "dwell" there.

But it is there no longer, nor would it be even if the temple were still standing. For when Christ died on the cross, everything changed. He entered into the real, archetypal holy place in heaven, of which the earthly temple was only a picture, bearing, not the blood of bulls and goats but His own blood, making in actual fact, once for all, the atonement which the old high priest had only foreshadowed (Heb. 9—10). When He did so, the veil of the temple, which had separated the holy of holies from the rest, protecting mankind from the burning purity of God's holiness, was dramatically torn asunder, making the way open to God's presence immediately by faith. Now believers are protected and covered by the blood of Christ and may come into God's presence without fear. So when Paul said in 1 Corinthians 3:16 that we are temples of God and the Spirit dwells in us, he was making the most profound statement imaginable about our access to God and the way we relate to Him. My body has replaced the holy of holies as the focal point of God's presence among human beings. And so has yours if you belong to Christ.

Implications of Indwelling

This truth has tremendous implications both for evangelism and for how I conceive my own relationship with God. Solomon hoped the temple would be a rallying point for evangelism of the Gentiles, showing a clearer understanding of the Abrahamic covenant with its provision for blessing all peoples than most of his posterity had (Gen. 12:1–3, 1 Kings 8:41–43). It is where God's presence is concentrated; it is the place to which you look to establish a relationship with this God. So today, while God is by no means limited to working in this way, the best way to expose people to the God and Father of our Lord Jesus Christ as a living presence is to bring them into contact with Christians who are indwelt, not just formally, but fully, by the Holy Spirit. The Shekinah flickers low in the life of anyone who belongs to Christ at all (Rom. 8:9); we ought to aspire to be full of the Spirit so that His glory shines out for all to see. We are the temple of God, indwelt by His Spirit. And what is true individually (1 Cor. 3:16) is even more powerfully true of us corporately, when the church is gathered (Eph. 2:21–22).

The picture of the believer as a temple where God dwells also has great implications for our understanding of the relationship we have with God through Jesus Christ, who sends the Spirit as His Representative in our lives. To picture the Spirit as relating to us by living in us is to suggest three qualities of that relationship: its intimacy, its permanency, and its immediacy.

Intimacy. The relationship we have with Jesus Christ as He is brought into our lives by His personal Emissary, the Holy Spirit, is in the first place one of great intimacy. Indwelling suggests the total interpenetration of our being—and indeed there is no part of the inner person with which the Spirit does not deal in the most personal and private way. In our most intimate communion with another human being there are barriers which are never completely and perfectly overcome. We must infer thoughts, feelings, and intentions from the outward signs given by our bodies, which are simultaneously bridges and barriers between us. But the Holy Spirit has direct access to our minds, our emotions, and our wills, seeing them as they truly are, without masks. His presence quickens us with new life in regeneration; in illumination and sanctification He progressively transforms every aspect of our personalities, making our own thoughts, feelings, and intentions fully our own as in our yielding to Him they become fully His. This is the great mystery which theologians call the "mystical union" between the believer and Christ; the indwelling Holy Spirit is the medium by which it takes place.

Permanence. The language of indwelling also speaks of a relationship which is stable and permanent. The words which are translated "dwell" are built on the word for house: An *oikos* is a house, and the verbs for dwell are *oikeo* and *enoikeo.* They mean to move into a house to take up permanent residence, to set up housekeeping, not just to stay there. You unpack the boxes, put your clothes in the drawers and on the hangers, and put your pictures on the walls. You settle into this place and make it home. You use another word for staying at an inn or a friend's house; you sojourn there, but you dwell at home. The full permanence of the relationship becomes more clear when we look at the doctrine of sealing, but it is implied here as well. And the domestic associations of the word complement the more exalted temple imagery to emphasize the personal nature of the relationship.

Immediacy. Finally, indwelling means immediacy. The Old Testament has been called a "dispensation of distance." Don't touch Mt. Sinai, you'll die; don't touch the ark, carry it by poles, lest you die; send the high priest into the holy of holies once a year, bearing blood. But now because of Christ, we who were far off have been made near (Eph. 2:13). How near? Nearer than you can conceive! The closest Scripture can come to describing it is with the language of indwelling. God is not far away, He is not remote and inaccessible; He is immediately accessible to you, as near as your own innermost thoughts, because when you receive Jesus Christ as your personal Savior and Lord He sends

His own personal Agent, the Holy Spirit, to dwell in your heart—not to be physically or spatially "located" there, but to enter into a personal relationship with you which is as intimate, permanent, and immediate as that.

Consecration

It is no wonder then that Paul drew the implication from the imagery of temple/indwelling that we should be as dedicated, consecrated, set apart for the service of God—sanctified, in other words—as the Old Testament temple was.

> The one who joins himself to the Lord is one spirit with Him. Flee immorality. . . . Do you not know that your body is a temple of the Holy Spirit who is in you, whom you have from God, and that you are not your own? For you have been bought with a price: therefore glorify God in your body. (1 Cor. 6:17–20)

The immediacy between us works both ways; He is immediately grieved by the least attachment to sin which we allow to come into our inner beings. It is one of the highest testimonies to the elegance of God's plan for our salvation that the greatest incentive to personal holiness is also the provision which makes it possible for us to make progress in it: the indwelling Spirit of God.

This unique and wonderful relationship with Jesus Christ through His Spirit which we enter into at conversion underlies everything we have said about illumination and sanctification—it is indeed what makes these ministries possible. The indwelling presence of the Spirit has another related effect on both our standing and our state which is in some respects the capstone of the whole transaction of salvation. It is called the doctrine of sealing.

Sealing

The doctrine of the sealing of the Holy Spirit is based on passages such as 2 Corinthians 1:21–22, which says that the one who "establishes" us in Christ is God, who "also sealed us and gave us the Spirit in our hearts as a pledge." More fully, Ephesians 1:13–14 explains it this way:

> In Him [Christ] you also, after listening to the message of truth, the gos-
> pel of your salvation—having also believed, you were sealed in Him
> with the Holy Spirit of promise, who is given as a pledge of our inherit-
> ance, with a view to the redemption of God's own possession, to the
> praise of His glory.

Paul returns to the idea in Ephesians 4:30, exhorting us not to
"grieve the Holy Spirit of God, by whom you were sealed for the
day of redemption." In some way the Holy Spirit is a seal or
pledge which has relevance for our final redemption on the Last
Day. Interestingly, sealing is not something the Holy Spirit *does*;
rather the language seems to indicate that He *constitutes* the seal
or pledge. We are sealed by virtue of His being given to us as a
pledge on the part of the Father. To understand what this language means, we must consider the function of seals in biblical
culture.

Seals in ancient times had basically two purposes: authentication and protection. A letter, for example, would be closed with
hot sealing wax, and while that wax was still soft the sender
would impress into it his signet ring, leaving in it a symbolic
mark which everybody knew as unique to him. The same thing
might be done for a contract or a covenant, much as a notary
public impresses such documents with his seal today. The presence of the writer's official seal on the document then proves
that it is authentic: It is official, the real thing. That seal can then
be shown to all doubters as proof of authenticity, much like a
person's signature today.

Such a seal also conveniently served to protect the contents of
the document from tampering: There was no way a letter sealed
in this way could be opened without detection. As long as the
seal is unbroken there is no need for suspicion. Interestingly,
other things besides documents could be protected in the same
way: Matthew 27:66 shows Pilate authorizing a seal on Jesus'
tomb. The disciples could not steal the body without breaking it.
Unfortunately for Pilate and the high priests, they did not
reckon with the possibility of angels who might not be
impressed with their official seal! But their intent shows at least
how seals were supposed to work.

By calling the indwelling Holy Spirit God's seal on the
believer, then, Paul suggests that among the benefits we receive

from Him are authentication and protection. The gift of the Spirit is God's pledge that the covenant of grace is official and binding. How do we know that the contract is complete, that God means to keep His promise of salvation on the basis of faith in Christ alone? How do I know that I am included? I know it because Jesus has sent the Holy Spirit to indwell me. His presence as evidenced by His work is the seal, God's signature written in the blood of Jesus Christ on the deed.

How do we know that we will persevere to the end in faith and finally be saved? Again, the Holy Spirit in us is not only God's seal on the contract but also a pledge, a down payment. From another perspective we could ask, how do I know that I am truly a believer, that my faith is authentic? We have the Holy Spirit as credentials from God saying that we are truly His. We see this principle operating several times in the Book of Acts, where the coming of the Holy Spirit to someone's life was taken as proof that he was to be received as part of the community of the faithful (10:44–47; 11:15–18).

Practical Questions About Sealing

The doctrine of sealing obviously has great implications for our understanding of the assurance of salvation, which we will examine in the next chapter. The presence of the Spirit in our lives both authenticates us as truly redeemed and protects us in that state. For the rest of this chapter we need to address some practical questions about how the doctrine of sealing actually works.

Are All Believers Sealed?

The first question is: Have all truly regenerate believers received the sealing with the Holy Spirit? And the answer is clearly yes. Ephesians 1:13 says in a general statement addressed to the whole body that "having also believed, you were sealed." Nothing could be plainer. If you have believed on Jesus with true saving faith, you have been sealed; when you believed you were sealed. (Dr. David Martyn Lloyd-Jones's rather elaborate attempts to evade the plain meaning of the text here is about the only point at which his usually clear and masterful exposition of

Ephesians is not helpful.) The Holy Spirit is the seal. There is no more possibility of being a true Christian without the seal than there is of being one without the Spirit's work in your life on Christ's behalf.

Are There Signs of Sealing?

Question number two: Are there clear and evident signs that the sealing has taken place? Again, the answer is yes. Imagine that I were to hand you a document which I claim has been notarized, but your most minute investigations fail to turn up any evidence of the impression of the notary public's seal. An invisible seal is contrary to the whole nature and purpose of sealing; it would be useless, superfluous, and irrelevant. And nothing about the Holy Spirit's work can be described in those terms. The whole idea of an invisible seal would have rendered Peter's argument for Gentile salvation at the Jerusalem Council without force: Unless it were evident that "God therefore gave to them the same gift as He gave to us also after believing" he would have been just backing up one empty claim with another one (Acts 11:15–18).

What Are the Signs of Sealing?

Question number three: What are the signs of sealing? If there are clear and evident marks impressed on us by the seal of the Holy Spirit, what are they? It is useful first to see what they are not. They are not, for example, a particular spiritual gift such as speaking in tongues. First Corinthians 12:7–11, 30–31 proves beyond a doubt that all believers are not intended to speak in tongues. Ephesians 1:13 assumes that all are sealed with the Spirit. So consequently, tongues cannot be the expression of the seal.

How then does the Spirit seal us? Let's put the question this way: What is it about the Spirit's presence in our lives that marks us out as genuine believers? It is the whole work which the Spirit does to apply to us the work of Christ for our salvation. It is conviction, calling, regeneration, illumination, and sanctification. It is His whole ministry: enabling faith, creating faith, and responding to faith.

That is what the seal is in general terms. It is also helpful to notice some of the specific features which should, according to Scripture, be evident in a person who bears the seal. No doubt others could be found, but the following list contains some of the more important ones and should suffice to give us the idea. They flow from the whole understanding of the Spirit's mission and work which we have been developing, and thus do not need extended comment here. They include:

A. *The conviction of sin* (John 16:8). Not all who are convicted come to faith, but faith in the full New Testament sense includes a recognition of one's own sinfulness and of Jesus as Redeemer from sin.

B. *Love for the Word of God* (John 15:26; 16:13; Eph. 1:13, "listening"). A sure evidence of the Spirit's work is an increasing interest in the text He inspired. Not that no believer will ever be inconsistent in his study, puzzled, frustrated, or even repelled by Scripture; but if he is truly indwelt by the Spirit he will keep coming back to it. To neglect it permanently is to show no contact with its Author.

C. *Faith in Christ* as resurrected Lord (Eph. 1:13, "believed"; 1 Thess. 1:5, "full conviction"; Rom. 10:9, "believe"; 1 John 4:2–3). Not just intellectual assent (though not less than that), but a trust that commits, which casts one's weight on Christ alone as our only hope of redemption; the fruit of the doctrine of "calling."

D. *A Spirit of glad submission to the lordship of Christ* (Rom. 10:9, "as Lord"; 1 Cor. 12:3, "no one can" but by the Spirit). Not that every believer will understand from the outset every implication of Christ's lordship, or that any believer will be perfectly obedient; but Jesus will be Lord at least in principle, and increasingly so in reality if His Agent is indeed at work in a person's life. A consistent bent to anything less is the mark of a different spirit.

E. *Substantial and increasing victory over sin and temptation* (2 Cor. 5:17, a "new creature"; Gal. 5:16–17; 1 Cor. 6:9–11, "such were some of you"). To fall into sin, or to have serious ongoing struggles with sin, are not signs of false profession; but to wallow in sin comfortably as a consistent and chosen life-style is not the mark of a person indwelt by the Spirit of holiness.

F. *A spirit of confidence and boldness in prayer* (Gal. 4:6; Rom. 8:26–27, "Abba! Father!"). Part of the Spirit's ministry is to make real in our experience the access to the throne room (Eph. 2:18) won for us by Christ on the cross.

G. *Love for God and other believers* (Rom. 5:5, "Love . . . poured out within our hearts through the Holy Spirit"; 1 John 2:9–10; 4:7–21). One is tempted to quote half the Bible here. We love Him because He first loved us; He shows His love in this, that while we were yet sinners He loved us and gave His Son for us (1 John 4:19; Rom. 5:8). Love is indeed a fruit of the Spirit (Gal. 5:22). You cannot really believe that you have been forgiven by God at the price of His Son's blood and not love Him for it; you cannot love God and hate anyone that He loves.

H. *Boldness in witnessing for Christ* (Acts 1:8; 4:31; 2 Tim. 1:7). The incidental manifestation of the coming of the Spirit at Pentecost was speaking in tongues; the definitive, essential, and abiding manifestation then and since is boldness in testimony to our faith in Jesus.

I. *A life focused on the glory of God as our highest aim* (Eph. 1:14, "to the praise of His glory"). The ultimate focal point and end of the work of the Holy Spirit is to glorify Jesus Christ—"He shall glorify Me" (John 16:14). So the ultimate mark born by those He seals, indeed the final summation of the impression He makes, is a life which increasingly manifests the same orientation.

Many other things could be mentioned including the fruit of the Spirit, commitment to a specific, local, Bible-believing church, and a minimal level of correct doctrinal understanding. Many of them are implied by items listed here. Surely these qualities are among the indelible and unmistakable marks made on the soul by the impress of the indwelling Holy Spirit. Only by

His work can they truly be present in fallen humanity; therefore, they are the infallible sign of authentic Christianity when they appear together. Their visible presence is God's official seal of approval, saying to the believer and to the world, "This is My child." Their total absence in any professing believer is cause for the greatest concern. We cannot be saved by trying to manufacture these qualities in ourselves, nor is there a certain "standard" we must come up to in order to pass muster. But no one can be regenerated and indwelt by the Holy Spirit of God without manifesting them at least to a certain extent.

Is the Seal Always Equally Visible?

That observation leads us to our final question: Is the seal equally visible in all truly saved people? Here the answer is unfortunately but clearly no. The impression of the seal goes deeper in some people than others. Growth in grace is a mysterious and unpredictable process affected by many factors. Some people mature faster than others. False or inadequate teaching and discipling, stumbling blocks put in the path by other professing believers, simple sinful choices can retard the growth which should take place. Consequently, in some people who are truly saved the marks of the seal are either faintly imprinted or have been covered over by the dust of neglect and sin. Judging others is a tricky business, and we should be slow to do it, even when ministry responsibility makes it necessary. But these are the characteristics of a person who shows evidence of the Lord's work in his life. Being saved, regenerated, indwelt by the Spirit of the living God makes a difference, and this is the difference it makes. For a person to claim to be saved without manifesting any of these marks is simply to delude themselves. Therefore, let a man examine himself, whether he be in the faith.

What the world—what the *church*—needs more than anything else is a generation of believers who understand that the official seal of authentic Christianity is nothing less than the whole work of the Holy Spirit as Scripture describes it in the normative Christian life. Let us renew our commitment to the Lord who sends that Spirit to us even now, asking Him to make that seal shine brightly in us to the glory of Jesus Christ.

Questions for Further Study

1. What is meant by the term *indwelling*? How does it relate to the imagery of the Old Testament temple? Where is the "focal point" of God's presence today?

2. How were seals used in first-century times? What does it mean to say that the indwelling Spirit is the "seal" of our salvation?

3. Are all believers sealed? Can you prove your answer from Scripture?

4. What are some of the specific marks impressed on the soul by the seal of the Spirit?

5. Are these marks causes or effects of salvation? Why is it important to distinguish the two?

16

THE HOLY SPIRIT
AND ASSURANCE

The ministry of the Holy Spirit is essentially to bring the salvation purchased for us by Jesus Christ into our lives in such a way that Jesus is glorified in us. Doubtful and tentative Christian living achieves that goal only very imperfectly; we give glory to Christ for our salvation with full vigor only if we know that we are in fact saved by Him. Therefore, the Holy Spirit is definitely interested in promoting that assurance in those who are true believers and in enabling them to clearly distinguish that assurance from presumption, or false assurance. Doing so is a major aspect of His work because success here is a catalyst which causes things to progress more effectively in other areas. The more confident I am of my relationship with the Savior, the more easily and naturally I find myself relying on Him as sufficient for my every need.

The Grounds of Assurance

The assurance of salvation is a firm and joyous and well-grounded conviction and confidence that I am a child of God, that my sins are forgiven, that I am accepted and beloved by the Father, and that I have therefore passed out of judgment and condemnation and become the possessor of eternal life. It is possible to be saved without having this assurance—witness the publican of Luke 18:9ff., who did not even have enough confidence to lift up his eyes to heaven but who, according to no less an authority than Jesus Himself, was justified. You can be saved without being assured of your salvation, but assurance is one of the benefits of salvation available by faith to all believers. The crucial questions are: How do we appropriate it and how do we tell the difference between real assurance and presumption? Both questions are answered by the realization that the Holy Spirit works to give us assurance by applying to our minds and hearts certain well-defined biblical grounds of assurance.

The Promises of God

What then are the biblical grounds or sources of assurance? The first is simply the promises of God. He has promised salvation to us on the simple condition of faith in Christ, and since He cannot lie, we must believe that this is a promise He will keep. Therefore, one of the chief ways of finding and shoring up assurance is by meditating on the promise of God in the light of His eternal and unchanging character. He has told us that He loves us so much that He sent His only begotten Son so that *whosoever* believes in Him will not perish but have eternal life (John 3:16). He has promised that everyone who calls upon the name of the Lord will be saved (Acts 2:21). He promises no condemnation for those who are in Christ (Rom. 8:1). He says that, if you confess Jesus as Lord with your mouth and believe in your heart that God raised Him from the dead, you will be saved (Rom. 10:9–10). Jesus Himself invites us to come to Him and promises that the one who comes will never be cast out (John 6:37). And the list goes on and on.

What is the Holy Spirit's role in this process? The texts we have mentioned come from Him, for He inspired them in the first place. When we read them in faith He applies them to our lives in accordance with the doctrine of illumination as we studied in Chapter 4. In response to our faith He creates a greater and stronger and more vibrant faith, able with surer hands to grasp the truth of Scripture in its application to our own lives. And logically, this should be enough, for both the promises and the conditions are clear. But because Satan has a vested interest in attacking our assurance in order to paralyze our Christian lives, things get more complicated. Satan raises doubts and scruples to us: How do you know you really believed? That you were really sincere when you accepted Christ? You've messed up enough times since your supposed conversion—maybe it didn't really "take." So a further work of the Spirit is often necessary to make the transfer from the abstract truth to a personal and effective conviction of its application. And the Spirit has adequate means to meet that challenge.

The Sealing of the Spirit

One of the chief means He uses is the sealing discussed in the last chapter. We learned that seals were used both for authentication and protection, and both aspects of their use are relevant to the doctrine of assurance. It is as if the mere presence of the Spirit is such a radical phenomenon that it carries its own conviction. His ministry is known by its effects: Conviction of sin leading to faith in Christ and some progress in sanctification are the marks of God's ownership and protection. These things are the distinctive ministry of the Holy Spirit and cannot be produced apart from Him. Their presence at all is *prima facie* evidence of at least some spiritual reality. If with honesty you can say on any level of imperfection that, "Yes, I really do love Jesus and believe in Him," you may know that such a commitment is simply not possible for unregenerate persons.

If the seal of the Spirit—conviction of sin, love for God, His Word, and His people, faith in Christ which embraces Him as Lord and Savior—is the mark of authenticity when it is present even faintly, it is also the guarantee of protection, a pledge that the work begun, whatever its present state of imperfection, will not be laid aside or abandoned by God until it is completed

(Phil. 1:6). In Ephesians 1:13–14, the seal of the Spirit is called a pledge of our redemption. The word translated "pledge" is a fascinating one: It is the Greek *arrabon*. It means a pledge in the sense of a down payment, earnest money, a first installment on the payment of a debt. This word was used in the ancient papyri to refer to a non-refundable deposit which closes the deal and obligates both parties to complete the transaction. If the purchaser fails to complete his payments, the *arrabon* is forfeited; if he fulfills the contract, it counts as the first payment.

If Paul is using the word *arrabon* in its normal sense, then he is saying that when God gives to us His Holy Spirit, He is giving us thereby the first installment or down payment on all the blessings of heaven and thus freely obligating Himself to finish the payments. Thus the doctrine of sealing has tremendous implications for the assurance of salvation: Not only does it help us to identify the marks of genuine and authentic faith, but also it gives those who have that faith the utmost confidence in their future. If I do have faith in Christ now, how can I be sure that I will continue to have it and so finally be among the redeemed on the last day? I know how fickle and changeable I am. The answer is that, once we have become God's children, our perseverance in the faith no longer depends entirely on us. God has committed Himself in the strongest possible terms to do whatever is necessary to ensure our final salvation once He has sealed us with the Holy Spirit.

Clearly, when a person commits himself to anything, the more precious the item he offers as surety, the more serious is the commitment thereby expressed. The commitment God makes to our salvation reminds me of one made by Judah in Genesis 43—44. Joseph had told his brothers (who did not yet recognize him) that they could not return to Egypt to buy more grain unless they brought Benjamin with them but Israel was reluctant to let him go. Finally, Judah promised that he himself would be "surety" for Joseph (43:8-9). We find out in the next chapter what that meant: When Joseph threatened to keep Benjamin as his slave, Judah pled for his brother, offering his own life in exchange for Benjamin's. "For your servant became surety for the lad to my father" (44:32). This was the act that convinced

Joseph that his brothers had really had a change of heart, so that he immediately revealed himself to them. To give your self in pledge and follow through is the strongest commitment which can be made.

Now the pledge God makes to us is very much like the one Judah made to his father. God has already given His Son; now He pledges His Holy Spirit as well. And we must remember that the *arrabon* is a non-refundable deposit; it is forfeited if the purchase is not completed. This means that if a believer in Jesus Christ who has been sealed with the Holy Spirit were to suffer eternal punishment, the Holy Spirit would have to suffer it too—which is obviously unthinkable. It is something which God simply could not allow. Therefore, do not fear! The God who has given you His Holy Spirit will do whatever it takes to see to it that you do persevere in faith and finally come to Heaven. Once He has sealed you with the Holy Spirit, there is no turning back.

It is crucially important not to misunderstand what is being said here. The doctrine of "eternal security" as sometimes taught is one of the most misunderstood teachings of Scripture. The Bible does teach that those who are truly saved are saved forever. Rightly understood, we can say "once saved, always saved." But this does not mean that a person who shows no signs of commitment to Christ and His church can be confident of going to heaven on the basis of an "experience" he supposedly had in the past. We are not saved by an experience but by grace through faith, and saving faith produces a changed life. The older designation for this doctrine conveyed the right idea: "the perseverance of the saints." Those who are truly saved persevere to the end in faith and the Christian life.

God will complete the work He has begun in true believers (Phil. 1:6); those who are truly saved will show it by manifesting the marks of the Spirit's seal and by being faithful to the end; those who are not truly saved will show it by falling away (1 John 2:19). If staying saved depends on our faithfulness, as those who oppose this teaching must insist, then full assurance is not logically possible because I might fall away at some later date, thus throwing myself into the category of those that John said were "not really of us" (1 John 2:19). But if my final salvation depends ultimately on God's faithfulness, then I can be confident indeed. The perseverance of the saints depends on the preservation of the saints, and in the sealing of the Holy Spirit God has committed Himself to pursuing that preservation with everything omnipotence can do.

This then is what the doctrine of sealing contributes to assurance. The ground of my security in the faith is not the fact that I made some sort of profession at some point in the past, but the fact that I manifest, even if poorly, the signs of real faith in Christ now. Ultimately, my assurance is grounded on God's faithfulness to His promises and to the work of the Holy Spirit in my life. If now I know something of the conviction of sin, if now I am staking everything on Christ and His work on the cross as my only hope of forgiveness, if I have any love at all for Him and His Word and His people, if I can no longer live comfortably in sin, if, even though I fail, I really do want to live my life for His glory in gratitude for all He has done, then I can conclude not only that this is genuine, authentic Christianity, but also that it is God's pledge that He will never, ever let me go. His commitment to bringing me to glory is unwavering, unflinching, of the highest order imaginable. A person, on the other hand, who never goes to church, never reads the Bible, and who prays only in emergencies, but who thinks of himself as eternally secure on the basis of having "gone forward" in his youth, may very well be deluding himself. I cannot dogmatically state that he will not be saved "yet so as by fire"; but I can say that he has no biblical ground for the *assurance* of salvation, since he shows no evidence of having ever been truly regenerated and indwelt by the Holy Spirit.

The Witness of the Spirit

The grounds of assurance so far then are the promises of God and the sealing of the Holy Spirit. But there is a third ground which seems harder to evaluate than the rest because, unlike them, it is wholly inward. The promises are publicly and objectively delivered, written in black and white on the pages of Scripture; the impression of the seal can be visible to others as well as oneself (sometimes more clearly to them than to you!).

But the witness of the Spirit is inward and personal, subjective, but no less real. And despite its subjective character, it can be evaluated in terms of its correlation with the other grounds which are partly objective and outward.

What do we mean by the inner witness of the Spirit? Paul said that the Spirit bears witness with our spirit that we are children of God (Rom. 8:16). This is the same "spirit of adoption" by which we cry out, "Abba, Father!" (Rom. 8:15). There seems to be a confidence that we are indeed adopted children of the Father which is communicated directly to us by the Holy Spirit. The first two grounds depend on inference. I read the promises and logically conclude that God will keep them in my case; I see the marks made by the seal of the Spirit and reason from them to the conclusion they imply. But this is direct: "You are mine!" Somehow, inwardly, we just know.

This is the capstone of the Spirit's ministry of assurance. Its direct and inner nature makes it highly personal, highly effective, and, if we can trust it, very precious. But these advantages also conceal a potential pitfall: How do I know that this inner voice is the Holy Spirit and not just wishful thinking on my part? The apostle John discussed the topic in his first epistle which is helpful at that point.

Avoiding Presumption

The one who believes has the witness in himself, and the witness is that God "has given us eternal life, and this life is in His Son" (1 John 5:10–11). Here the testimony of the Spirit seems to be both to the truth of the gospel in general and to its particular application to the believer's life. Indeed, John's whole first letter could be seen as a treatise on the question of assurance: If you believe that Jesus came in the flesh (4:2–3), turn from sin (3:7–10), love the brethren (3:14), and persevere (2:19), you have good grounds for knowing "that you have eternal life" (5:13). Along with these things is the inner witness of the Spirit (5:9–10). But what is really interesting about John's treatment is the relationship between the inner and the outer as revealed in 5:8. "There are three that bear witness, the Spirit and the water and the blood; and the three are in agreement."

The somewhat cryptic nature of this verse makes it difficult to interpret, and any number of explanations have been offered as to what the "water" and the "blood" refer to: The water and blood which flowed from Jesus' side at the crucifixion, baptism and the Lord's Supper, the birth (incarnation) and death (atonement) of Jesus, or the baptism and crucifixion of Jesus are some of the more likely candidates. We cannot go into all the intricacies of the arguments here, but fortunately we do not need to, for all these interpretations have this in common: They refer to external and public—that is, objective—events. That is the point we need for understanding the principles John is enunciating. The Father gives testimony to Jesus as Savior both by external and public events and by the inner witness of the Spirit, and they are in agreement. The way you can evaluate what the Spirit seems to be doing subjectively is by comparing it with what He has done publicly in Scripture and history. If they do not mesh, you had better back off.

What John is saying about the inner witness of the Spirit then is that the same checks which we saw in our study of illumination apply here as well. The Spirit will not contradict Himself; therefore, He will not contradict Scripture. A person who claimed to have the Spirit's inner witness to his salvation but who did not believe that Jesus came in the flesh, did not confess Jesus as Lord and believe God raised him from the dead, or did not manifest any marks of the seal of the Spirit, would be on very shaky ground. But if the outward and objective testimony stacks up, then the inner witness is a powerful confirmation. The point is that the subjective and objective works of God ought never to be divorced. These various forms of testimony which the Spirit gives are valid and effectual precisely because they are in agreement. Otherwise, the Holy Spirit would be working at cross-purposes with Himself.

One good way of summarizing the ministry of the Holy Spirit would be to say that it consists largely of uniting the objective and subjective aspects of salvation in our experience. The inner alone is mere feeling; the outer alone is mere fact. The Holy Spirit is the force that brings the two together, and that is what produces spiritual reality in general and assurance in particular.

That is what energizes the spiritual life and gives power for victory over sin and effective service. That is why one of Satan's most effective strategies for neutralizing the church has been to foster an increasing dichotomy between dry, academic forms of dead orthodoxy on the one hand and a popular Christianity based on mere feeling on the other. We need to relearn the lesson that in real vital Christianity the two must be kept together; the absence or weakness of either side emasculates the whole spiritual life.

If then we can tell the inner witness of the Spirit from our own wishful thinking by its agreement with the outer, we can conclude our discussion of assurance by giving some specific, practical criteria for distinguishing true assurance from presumption. True assurance of salvation which comes from the Holy Spirit must:

> *Be Christ-centered* (1 John 5:11). The witness is that this life is in His Son.

> *Be cross-centered* (Heb. 10:19). Our confidence comes from the blood of Jesus.

> *Issue in a desire to identify with Christ, even in suffering* (Rom. 8:16–17). The Spirit's witness in verse 16 is that we are His children and heirs if we suffer with Him.

> *Issue in a desire to identify with Christ in godly living* (Rom. 8:12). Paul's exhortation not to live according to the flesh begins the argument which leads into the statement of assurance in verse 16.

> *Issue in a life of prayer and praise* (Rom. 8:15). The same Spirit which gives the witness in verse 16 is the One who inspires the cry, "Abba, Father!"

Otherwise, our assurance of salvation is not from the Holy Spirit; it is presumption.

The Holy Spirit wants to glorify Jesus Christ by bringing Him into our lives in such a way that we know He is there and that He saves. As we walk with the Lord, meditate on His Word, and serve Him, we should find that assurance welling up in us as a fountain of spiritual energy impelling us to live for His glory. And thus the work of the Holy Spirit goes forward.

Questions for Further Study

1. What are the biblical grounds of the assurance of salvation? What does the Holy Spirit contribute to each of them? How do they relate to His mission?

2. What do the promises of God contribute to our assurance? Why are they alone sometimes not enough?

3. What is the relationship between sealing and assurance?

4. How can we distinguish the witness of the Spirit from our own wish-fulfillment dreams and impulses?

5. How would you use the material in this chapter to help a person who is wrestling with assurance?

17

THE HOLY SPIRIT
AND CHRISTIAN SERVICE

Throughout our studies we have seen the Holy Spirit as what we might call the Great Enabler. He is the One who brings the power of God into the lives of sinners, enabling them to do things which would otherwise have been impossible due to the chains of their own forging. Because of His ministry, people who by nature were the hopeless slaves of sin and dupes of Satan find themselves turning from dead works to serve the living God. We were made to know God, love Him, worship Him, and serve Him forever, and through the work of Jesus Christ we will fulfill that destiny. He personally purchased pardon, adoption, and every spiritual blessing for us on the Cross, and through His personal Agent, the Holy Spirit, He begins to bring these blessings into our lives even now. We will glorify Jesus Christ and serve Him in worship forever, and find in that the ultimate fulfillment of our natures. And already we begin to experience foretastes of that fulfillment as the Holy Spirit enables us to serve Him in the present.

Power for Service

For this reason one of the benefits provided by the Spirit which has been precious to the saints is power for service. Our ultimate glory is to glorify our Head by what we are and what we do, and every aspect of the Spirit's work has this as its final aim. The end of regeneration is not a passive and dormant new life but an active and victorious one. The end of sanctification is not a static and inert holiness but a living and serving holiness which brings glory to the Savior in the arena of life. Illumination fosters not a merely theoretical and academic knowledge of Scripture but a working knowledge. Spiritual gifts are ministries for service. The end of assurance is not complacency but boldness in living for Christ.

So power for service to Christ and His church ought to be the practical outcome of every aspect of the Spirit's ministry in our lives. While some are called to contemplation as their particular form of service that the insight and love of the whole body might be deepened and its active service be more intelligent, their contemplation will be as spiritual as it is profitable and fruitful for the edification of a serving church (1 Tim. 1:3–6). Spirituality is inward, but it is not ingrown; it is quiet but not quietistic; its end is to fit us for service in the church militant. Anything less is a deficient if not a false spirituality, not focused on the glory of Christ where the Spirit is focused.

The Enabler

So central is service to the Spirit's work that one of His most familiar names speaks mightily to His role in that area. He is called the Paraclete, from the Greek verb *parakaleo* and its noun form *parakletos*. The word is usually translated "comforter," but the connotations of that English word give a false impression of the Greek concept. "Comforter" is much too weak and passive. If a paraclete is a comforter, he does not comfort by patting you on the shoulder but by *strengthening* you to face and deal with the situation which gave rise to the need for comfort. Perhaps a better translation would be *helper*—or the word we began this chapter with, *enabler*.

This concept of the Spirit's role fits in with the meaning of the Greek word for power, *dunamis*. Its associations as the ancestor of English words like dynamite, dynamo, and dynamic are exciting but perhaps misleading; its basic meaning in Greek is simply the ability or capacity to get things done. So the "power" for service which comes from the Enabler is not necessarily something dramatic and "explosive"—it is simply the ability to get things done. What things? Things we could not do without His aid—repenting, forsaking, following, witnessing, and serving. Some of these things cannot be done in the power of the flesh at all; some can be done, but not with the fruitfulness which comes when the Lord is in it.

Of Jesus' Ministry

A number of statements in Scripture give testimony to the Holy Spirit's ministry as an enabler of effective and profitable service. One of the most interesting is Luke 4:14, which says that Jesus' ministry in Galilee was conducted "in the power of the Spirit." Indeed, the Spirit had come upon Him at His baptism in a special way to anoint Him for His earthly ministry. This is intriguing. If the Lord Himself, operating through His unfallen human nature, needed the power of the Holy Spirit for successful ministry, how much more do we! As we follow in Jesus' footsteps, it is heartening to realize that we have the same spiritual resources available to us that He had. Knowing we would need them was one of the reasons why He sent that same Spirit to us.

Of Witness

In Luke's version of the Great Commission, Jesus told the disciples that they would be His witnesses, but they should wait for the promised Spirit who would clothe them with *dumanis* from on high (Luke 24:48–49). Before His ascension Jesus repeated that promise: They would receive *dunamis* when the Holy Spirit came upon them, and they would be His witnesses (Acts 1:8). Quite literally, then, the Holy Spirit gives us the ability to witness for Christ. In Acts 2, He did it by allowing the disciples to speak languages they had never learned. In Acts 4:31 He gave them boldness to speak the Word of God.

Being an effective witness for Christ requires an array of gifts that few people possess including winsomeness and the ability to summarize aptly and succinctly the doctrine of salvation. When we consider the spiritual blindness we are up against and the fact that we live in perhaps the most defensive generation in history about claims to absolute truth, we realize that the ability to be what we are called to be—a witness to Jesus' saving power and an ambassador for Him—is not to be taken for granted. Apart from a profound dependence on the Holy Spirit, it cannot be done in a way which will honor Christ and call people to faith in Him at all. I find the connection between the Holy Spirit and boldness particularly interesting in the light of the natural reticence most of us must overcome in order to speak to people about something as personal as their souls. People who overcome that reticence in the power of the flesh are usually obnoxious. Our deep need for the ability to serve, which only the Holy Spirit can give, is painfully inescapable.

Of Love

As disciples of Jesus we have the command to love one another along with the prediction that our success as witnesses will depend greatly on whether the world is able to see our love (John 13:35; 17:21). But obedience to this command involves a twofold difficulty: The self-sacrificing love of Jesus is a higher thing than is natural to us, and we are put in the position of having to love a great many people who are, frankly, in various stages of unloveableness. Again, we are not able to do what is required for God to be glorified, but the love of God is shed abroad in our hearts by the Holy Spirit (Rom. 5:5). "So let us love, dear love, like as we ought," says Edmund Spenser, for "Love is the lesson that the Lord us taught." It is only the Holy Spirit who can give us the ability to love in that way.

Of Obedience, Prayer, Service

In general, the Holy Spirit strengthens us with *dumanis* in the "inner man" (Eph. 3:16). In other words, we might say that the Holy Spirit gives us spiritual backbone. The inner man joyfully concurs with the law of God but our intentions of obedience are thwarted by the other law working in the members of the body (Rom. 7:22–23). So we might say then that the Holy Spirit enables us to obey God even when it goes contrary to the old nature to do so. He enables us to pray when we cannot do that (Rom. 8:26), and He enables us to serve by giving us spiritual gifts. Wherever you find the grace of God bearing fruit in effective and powerful Christian service which brings glory to Jesus Christ, you may be sure that behind the scenes the Holy Spirit has been active in motivating, guiding, equipping, energizing, and enabling.

Appropriating the Power

How then do we tap into this reservoir of power? How do we stop serving the Lord in the power of the flesh, producing thereby at best a pitiful caricature of the service He requires and deserves? There is really no great mystery about it. To speak of His giving us the power or ability to serve is just one way of speaking about His whole transforming ministry in our lives. Enabling us to serve is no different from enabling us to understand Scripture, repent, exercise faith in Christ, or live holy unto the Lord. So the sources of spiritual power are the same as the sources of spiritual growth in general. It is a life of faith which grows out of a deep daily walk with the Lord. When in that context we consciously depend on Him for the ability to do what He has called us to do, we will find that ability marvelously supplied.

The Key

Faith—learning to trust—is the key. It is as simple and as complicated, as easy and as difficult, as that. It is simple in itself, but difficult because it goes against the grain of our self-centered natures. We believe that apart from Him we can do nothing (John 15:5), but we still find ourselves automatically acting as if we were something in and of ourselves. It helps to remember the basic pattern of the Spirit's work in us which we have seen throughout these studies: He works through our own minds and wills to enable them to do things beyond their natural ability. So we should neither beat our heads against the wall as if intensity of effort would avail, nor should we passively wait for the Spirit to do something in us that we are somehow not involved in. We work out our own salvation because God works in us.

D. Martyn Lloyd-Jones tells us of an old preacher who was expounding Philippians 4:13, "I can do all things through Him [Christ] who strengthens me." He was carrying on an imaginary dialogue with the apostle: "What do you mean, you can do all things? That sounds like boasting." He quoted back to Paul all his own statements of his inability from Romans 7, his claim to be the least of the apostles. How could Paul do all things? Finally, Paul was able to get a word in edgewise and finish the statement: "I can do all things through *Christ*." "Oh, I'm sorry," replied the preacher. "I didn't realize there were two of you." But there are! What I cannot do apart from Christ and what He normally does not do apart from me, we both do together as He enables me through the Holy Spirit. My part is simply to be humbly obedient and willing for all the glory to come to Him.

Three Steps

The key to power is the same key that unlocks every other aspect of the Christian life: simple faith in Christ. Faith is the victory that has overcome the world (1 John 5:4). It is not a vain confidence we manufacture in ourselves, not a psychological trick we play on ourselves; it is simple trust in Jesus. But since this truth is perhaps too simple for our complicated minds, it might be helpful to analyze it into a series of steps: aspire, ask, act.

Aspire to serve the Lord in the power of the Holy Spirit. We must first be sure that we truly desire spiritual power. It is easy to fool ourselves at this point, for to desire the power that comes from the Holy Spirit is to desire with all our hearts that Jesus receive all the glory from our service. Those are the only terms on which His personal Emissary is interested in aiding us. And it is all too insidiously easy to desire to be used in the Lord's service so that *we* can be noticed and receive the praise of others. We do not have to be perfect for God to use us—if that were true, Jesus would be the only hero of the faith in the Bible, and Hebrews 11 would have to be cut out—but we do have to be *real*. There must be a real desire to live for His glory alone, and we must often pray for our motives much as the man in the gospels prayed: "Lord, I believe; help my unbelief." Lord, I aspire; help my mixed motives. We have biblical precedent that Jesus responds positively to such a prayer as this (Mark 9:24).

Ask for divine enablement. Consecrate yourself before the Lord to His service, confessing your unworthiness and inadequacy, but rejoicing in the grace of God which confers on you the honor of being His servant nonetheless (1 Tim. 1:12), and asking Him to use you for His glory. Renew this commitment daily, even hourly, thus maintaining a constant state of readiness when an opportunity for service is providentially laid in your path. If you are called to an office or ongoing responsibility in the church, approach it in the same spirit, and in faith expect God to work through you.

Act on the basis that the ability has been given. This is the acid test which reveals whether faith is really faith or whether it is only theory. Though the results may or may not be what counts as "success" in the eyes of human beings, if your heart is right before God, He will be glorified, and that is all that matters.

The Place of Miracles

A question which is increasingly being raised is whether the power thus received includes the power to work miracles. As we saw in our study of spiritual gifts, such manifestation certainly cannot be ruled out today. On the other hand, my impression from reading the New Testament is that, with the possible exception of the apostles, the authority to perform miracles at will was not the norm even in the first century. I would suggest that we need to be open to the possibility that God might use us even in miraculous ways, but not be disillusioned if dramatic works of power in that sense are not our everyday experience. Such supposedly ordinary acts as genuine repentance are decidedly supernatural, enabled by the Holy Spirit of God Himself.

Probably the most credible exponent of miraculous healing today is John Wimber of Vineyard Christian Fellowship. The Vineyard movement is known for an often unbalanced emphasis on "signs and wonders," but Wimber can sometimes sound quite balanced indeed. He made an interesting statement in a recent interview which sheds some light on this whole area. "I have laid hands on people who were blind, and they now see. I also have laid hands on a larger number of blind who do not see and who got no particular benefit, evidently, from my prayers" (John Wimber et.al., "The Holy Spirit: God at Work," *Christianity Today,* 19 March 1990, 28). Not only is this a refreshing honesty, so different from the hype which characterizes many faith healers and discredits their claims, but it rings true to our position in eschatological history, as Wimber explains:

> Since I adhere to theologian George Ladd's teaching concerning the kingdom of the "already" and the "not yet," I believe we are already empowered to give sight to the blind, but we are not going to give sight to *all* the blind. We are not going to give sight to the bulk of the blind because we are still in the "not yet" (ibid).

In other words, we have in the Holy Spirit a foretaste of the joys of the kingdom, a down payment but not the final restoration of all things, which is "not yet." God has not yet brought the time in which all tears will be wiped away. In the present, believers, no matter how much faith they may have, are not automatically exempted from identifying with the world in the suffering caused by sin. God will sometimes heal miraculously to encourage us and to demonstrate His love and power, but evil and all its consequences will not finally be defeated and removed until the Lord returns.

Not all suffering is the direct result of personal sin; some is simply part of living in a fallen world. So lack of faith or personal sin are not the only reasons why a person might not be healed. We need to avoid both the false spirituality which puts God in a box and limits His power and the equally false spirituality which cruelly assumes that if anyone is not healed it is his own lack of faith which is at fault. Youth evangelist Rich Hodge, whose ongoing bout with cancer gives him credibility, puts it well: "Dare to ask God for *anything,* but leave the results up to Him."

Glorification

Wimber's use of the language of "already" and "not yet" reminds us that, as fulfilling in this life as serving the Lord is, an even greater fulfillment awaits us when we will serve Him in worship before His throne forever. Then our worship, our love, and our service will finally be perfected; we will know Him as we are known, for we will see Him as He is. At that time the work of the Holy Spirit will be brought to completion; His final act as Christ's Representative in our lives will be to bring us, now fully and completely prepared, before His face. This culmination of the process of redemption is called glorification: Those whom the Father foreknew He predestined to be conformed to the image of Christ. To accomplish that destiny He sent the Son to make atonement and the Spirit to call us to faith in Him. Those He called, He justified; and those He justified, He glorified (Rom. 8:29–30). Though the moment of glorification awaits the Lord's return, Paul spoke of it already in the past tense of accomplishment: What God has decreed is as good as done.

Glorification is the conclusion of the process that began with conviction and calling and led on through regeneration and sanctification. The Holy Spirit is still the Agent of Christ in bringing it about. The Holy Spirit brought back life to Jesus' physical body in the tomb, with the result that it was raised immortal and glorified. At the resurrection the same Holy Spirit will do the same to us who are in Christ as well. Paul caught the exhilaration of it in Romans 8:11: "If the Spirit of Him who raised Jesus from the dead dwells in you, He who raised Christ Jesus from the dead will also give life to your mortal bodies through His Spirit who indwells you." We will be like Him, for we will see Him as He is!

First John 3:2 explains the process by which glorification will take place. Just by representing Jesus to us and in us, the Spirit has already begun to transform us into Jesus' likeness. We are already redeemed from the guilt of sin in justification, and in sanctification we are being redeemed from the power of sin. We are being made more like Him. But when we are brought directly into His presence—when we see the glory of God in the face of Jesus Christ, no longer through a glass darkly but face to face—then the transformation will be complete—since we will then be given by the Spirit the strength to see it, one glimpse of that face will cancel and destroy the power of sin in us, and its pull in us, forever. No one has ever put it better than Cowper:

> Had I a throne above the rest
> Where angels and archangels dwell,
> One sin, unslain, within my breast
> Would make that heaven as dark as hell.
> But oh! No foe invades the bliss
> When glory crowns the Christian's head;
> One view of Jesus as He is
> Will strike all sin forever dead.

And He shall reign forever and ever. Amen. Our study of the ministry of the Holy Spirit should end with those words from Revelation, which can never be heard without evoking the magnificent strains of Handel's *Messiah*. That is where all His labors tend: to the glory and everlasting reign of Jesus Christ. Christ is the center of all the Spirit's ministry, as He works to point us to Jesus, to bring us to Jesus, to join us to Jesus, to conform us to Jesus, and finally to leave us with Jesus Christ, to whom be glory in the church, world without end, Amen.

Questions for Further Study

1. Carefully define *paraclete* and *dunamis*. Use a theological dictionary or Greek lexicon to check your work. What are the practical implications of these definitions for Christian service?

2. What are some of the things the Spirit enables us to do which we could not accomplish without Him? How do they relate to His mission?

3. How does the believer avail himself of the power for service which the Holy Spirit provides? Why does the church so frequently seem to flounder when this power is promised and available?

4. What role is played by miracles in God's economy today? Outline a responsible approach to this issue in keeping with your understanding of the Spirit's ministry.

5. What is meant by the doctrine of "glorification"? How does it fit in with the Spirit's ministry as a whole?

POSTSCRIPT

If we have learned one thing from this study of the person and work of the Holy Spirit, it is that all doctrine about the Holy Spirit, all experience of the Holy Spirit, and all walking with the Holy Spirit must come back to this inescapable reference point: The heart and soul of His character and the whole aim and quintessence of His work is to glorify the Lord Jesus Christ. It is from this standpoint that the state of spirituality in the church must be evaluated as she prepares—should the Lord tarry—for ministry in a new millennium. And it is from this standpoint that we find her in need of radical revival on both sides of the chasm which separates traditional evangelicals from Pentecostals and charismatics—in need, that is, of an intensification (or outpouring) of the work of the Holy Spirit as it is presented in Scripture in all its fullness.

The Pentecostal and charismatic movements have simultaneously forced the rest of us to pay attention to the doctrine of the Holy Spirit once again and made it difficult for us to do so by the unbiblical excesses of which they have often been guilty. Traditional evangelicals should thank these movements for bringing the Spirit to the church's attention and apologize to them for our neglect of His ministry. If the tongues movement has been a reaction to dead orthodoxy which threw out some of the orthodoxy along with the deadness, the "orthodox" have partly themselves to blame. Both streams of evangelical Christianity have failed in significant ways to glorify the Lord who bought them.

Pentecostal and charismatic spirituality frequently dishonors Christ in basically three ways. First is an unbiblical and false subjectivism in which the Holy Spirit becomes divorced from the grammar of the text He inspired. A particular type of emotional experience rather than faithfulness to Scripture becomes determinative, the touchstone of Christian belief and practice. Second, this subjectivity leads to a false ecumenicalism in which shared experience rather than a shared commitment to the faith once delivered to the saints defines the boundaries of what is considered the believing church. Third, there is a built-in tendency toward imbalance wherever the classic Pentecostal theology of the gifts is believed. The focus becomes not, "Do you know the Lord?" but "Have you received the Spirit evidenced by tongues?" The Holy Spirit Himself, as we have seen, is far more interested in the first of those questions; His whole ministry exists to enable us to answer yes on an even deeper level. A focus on even a valid spiritual experience for its own sake rather than on the glory of Jesus Christ is contrary to the Spirit's whole nature and purpose.

Traditional evangelicals, on the other hand, have often been guilty of a profound neglect of spiritual life in general and the doctrine of the Holy Spirit in particular. I know people who, in their fear of being identified with the abuses of Pentecostalism, are almost afraid even to mention the Holy Spirit. I must confess to having at one time been one of them. When we do acknowledge His existence we often dishonor the Lord by being content with correct doctrine apart from seeing that doctrine live in our own spiritual lives. Dead orthodoxy is the great breeding ground of both fanaticism and practical, if not actual, atheism. One kind of person decides it is better to be a pyromaniac than one of God's Frozen People; another kind concludes that fire is a myth after all. He knew it all along. Orthodoxy is the truth of

God; it is such a powerful force that only the orthodox can discredit it, and we have done so grievously. The rising tide of both fanaticism and atheism today can at least partly be blamed on a too-often smug, complacent, self-satisfied, and decadent church.

The solution is for both groups to return to an emphasis on spiritual reality—on Christian experience as interpreted and evaluated by a correct interpretation of Scripture. Both groups have departed from the wholeness of the ministry of the Holy Spirit in relating the whole person to Jesus Christ as the One who sums up all existence (Eph. 1:10). We have departed from it in different directions, and we have got to get back to it if we expect to have the spiritual reality it will take to minister in the post-Christian twenty-first century—or if we just expect to really know the Lord.

It is not enough for traditionalists to become more open to emotion and for charismatics to change their doctrine. That kind of shallow compromise misses the point entirely. We have to become humble enough to admit that neither of us really knows that much of spiritual reality and wholeness of vision, and desperate enough to hunger for it as our necessary food. We must stop pretending we are rich and admit we are naked, hungry, and blind, that despite the material prosperity of our churches we have become so spiritually impoverished that our very survival depends on a new Reformation and a Third Great Awakening. It is not enough to know that tongues are not the sign of the fullness of the Holy Spirit; we must know that repentance, faith, boldness in witness, a servant spirit, godliness, love, joy, peace, patience, kindness, goodness, faithfulness, gentleness, and self-control *are* and begin increasingly to manifest them in our lives through faith and reliance on His work—to the glory of Jesus Christ.

The way home is to pray for revival. While we are praying for revival, we must return to the basics of our own spiritual lives in faithful use of the means of growth, refusing to be satisfied with anything less than at least a modicum of reality there. If enough of us do that, it just might be that in the sovereignty of the Spirit the revival we seek will come. Even if revival does not come on a national scale, we at least will be able to say that we have known what real Christianity is. Having known it, we will be able by God's grace to pass it on to at least some others, who will keep the torch alive until revival comes or the Lord returns. We will hear Jesus Himself say, "Well done, thou good and faithful servant." In saying that to us, our Master will also be saying to the Spirit He had sent to be His personal Representative in our lives, our link with Him until that very moment, "Mission accomplished." Amen.

PENTECOST

(Compared with Later Imitations)

Stronger than a hawk, the Dove
Swept by, and in the eddies of
His passing, tongues of flame were fanned
And men fell to the ground unmanned.
They stuttered as their wits were lost
And thought it a new Pentecost:
The merely inarticulate sigh
Of His furious passing by.
But when He stopped to build His nest
First in the apostolic breast,
A different language was expressed
In fit words, honed and well disposed;
Those were not drunk as men supposed,
But spoke true tongues they had not learned:
Thus the true tongues of fire burned.
Men heard about their sins and grieved;
They heard the gospel and believed,
For each one heard of Jesus' blood
In his own tongue—and understood.
Does that Dove's nesting in the heart
Drive it and the mind apart?
Never! Rather, say He brings
The two together 'neath His wings.
The mind alert was not the cost
Of the primal Pentecost,
Where true wit was not lost, but gained
When the showers of blessing rained.

—D.T.W.

FOR FURTHER READING:
AN ANNOTATED BIBLIOGRAPHY

Because this book is aimed at pastors and serious students rather than scholars (though I hope some scholars may appreciate the synthesis of the vision offered), I have not burdened the text with footnotes and I have tried to keep technical discussions to a minimum. Readers who are familiar with the literature on the Holy Spirit will easily note my great indebtedness to many of the works listed below. Readers who are inspired to further study will find a large mass of froth, as well as much that is worth pursuing. The following list is a brief introduction to that second category. It makes no pretensions to being complete, comprehensive, balanced, unbiased, or any such thing; it is simply a survey of books which I have personally found to be helpful and which I recommend on that basis.

I have not included obvious steps such as checking the relevant chapters of Calvin's *Institutes* and the better modern systematic theologies—standard works such as Hodge, Berkhof, Strong, Miley, Erickson—or the relevant articles in standard reference works such as the *International Standard Bible Encyclopedia*, the *Zondervan Pictorial Encyclopedia of the Bible*, *The New Bible Dictionary*, *The Holman Bible Dictionary*, the *New Dictionary of Theology*, or the *Evangelical Dictionary of Theology*. Interested students will also find it profitable to look up the key Greek words in the *New International Dictionary of New Testament Theology*. Such works are too obviously relevant to be needed in the listing. I have also omitted references to works on particular doctrines, such as inspiration, which are touched on here, and have concentrated only on books dealing directly with the Holy Spirit or Christian spirituality. What follows then is my personal Hall of Fame of books which meet those limited criteria. As the child said to Augustine, "Take up and read!"

Alexander, Donald L., ed. *Christian Spirituality: Five Views of Sanctification*. Downers Grove, IL: InterVarsity, 1988. Interesting symposium in which five writers present their views of sanctification and critique each other's contributions.

Bruner, Frederick Dale. *A Theology of the Holy Spirit: The Pentecostal Experience and the New Testament Witness*. Grand Rapids: Eerdmans, 1970. One of the single most useful books on the subject. The first half surveys Pentecostal teaching, and the second half examines it in the light of a careful interpretation of the Book of Acts. An appendix offers selections from primary sources of Pentecostal theology. Bruner has a special gift for following the train of thought through the biblical text.

Carson, Donald A. *Showing the Spirit: A Theological Exposition of 1 Corinthians 12—14*. Grand Rapids: Baker, 1987. Outstanding treatment of one of the central texts. Careful, accurate exegesis with judicious, balanced commentary.

Dunn, James D. G. *Baptism in the Holy Spirit: A Re-examination of the New Testament Teaching on the Gift of the Spirit in Relation to Pentecostalism Today*. London: SCM Press, 1970. Considered by many to be the definitive treatment. Solid, cogently argued; a standard.

Edwards, Jonathan. *A Treatise Concerning Religious Affections*. Edited by John E. Smith. New Haven: Yale, 1959. Classic work in defense of the first Great Awakening, explores how to distinguish real working of the Spirit from counterfeits. Acute, perceptive, profoundly biblical; indispensable.

Griffith, Thomas W. H. *The Holy Spirit*. 1913; repr. Grand Rapids: Kregel, 1986. Thorough treatment of biblical data by great turn-of-the-century evangelical Bible teacher. Dated, but still worth reading.

Grudem, Wayne. *The Gift of Prophecy in the New Testament and Today*. Westchester, IL: Crossway, 1988. Fresh and exciting biblical study; makes the reader keep asking, "Why didn't I ever see that before?"

Hendry, George H. *The Holy Spirit in Christian Theology*. Philadelphia: Westminster, 1965. Contains much good discussion, especially of the relation between the Spirit and the Son. Chapter on inspiration is weak.

Howard, David M. *By the Power of the Holy Spirit*. Downers Grove, IL: InterVarsity, 1973. A derivative study dependent on Stott, Bruner, etc., Howard is valuable for the missionary perspectives he brings to the topic.

Inch, Morris A. *Saga of the Spirit: A Biblical, Systematic, and Historical Theology of the Holy Spirit*. Grand Rapids: Baker, 1985. One of the more worthy modern attempts at synthesis. Tries to cover too much ground for the space allotted, resulting in thin treatment at spots.

Jeffrey, David Lyle, ed. *A Burning and a Shining Light: English Spirituality in the Age of Wesley*. Grand Rapids: Eerdmans, 1987. More classic texts relevant to our topic than will be found under one cover anywhere else. Jeffrey's historical introduction has excellent analysis of spiritual conditions just prior to the revival which remind us of our own seemingly hopeless day.

Kuyper, Abraham. *The Work of the Holy Spirit*. 1900; repr. Grand Rapids: Eerdmans, 1973. Massive, magisterial; will strike some as too speculative.

Law, William. *A Serious Call to a Devout and Holy Life*. Edited by John W. Meister. Philadelphia: Westminster, 1955. Eighteenth-century classic; the title says it all.

Lloyd-Jones, D. Martyn. *Joy Unspeakable: Power and Renewal in the Holy Spirit*. Edited by Christopher Catherwood. Wheaton: Harold Shaw, 1984. The doctor is always profitable reading, a model of what exposition should be. While I dissent from his view of sealing in this study, I believe he is calling a real experience by a wrong name. And nobody describes the reality better.

---------------------. *Revival*. Westchester, IL: Crossway, 1987. J. I. Packer says, "I do not think our age has seen any more powerful or profound treatment of revival than this book." He's right.

---------------------. *The Sovereign Spirit: Discerning His Gifts*. Wheaton: Harold Shaw, 1985. Sequel to *Joy Unspeakable*.

McArthur, John. *Charismatic Chaos. Spiritual Depression: Its Causes and Cure*. Grand Rapids: Eerdmans, 1965. Contains much that is relevant to our topic.

Morgan, G. Campbell. *The Spirit of God*. London: Hodder and Stoughton, 1916. Practical study by the great British expositor and mentor of Lloyd-Jones.

Murphree, Jon Tal. *The Love Motive: A Practical Psychology of Sanctification*. Camp Hill, PA: Christian Publications, 1990. Recent practical study from a moderate Wesleyan perspective contains much that will be useful to people of other persuasions as well.

Owen, John. *The Holy Spirit: His Gifts and Power*. Grand Rapids: Kregel, 1954. The classic older treatment by the great seventeenth-century Puritan divine. The right stuff.

Packer, J. I. *Keep in Step with the Spirit*. Old Tappan, NJ: Revell, 1984. Of the recent studies, one of the best all-around.

Ryle, J. C. *Holiness*. Old Tappan, NJ: Revell, n.d. Old standby from the great nineteenth-century evangelical Anglican bishop.

Schaeffer, Francis A. *True Spirituality*. Wheaton: Tyndale, 1971. Excellent book on spiritual reality by a man who lived it. Schaeffer considered this book the foundation of all his work.

Stott, John R. W. *Baptism and Fullness: The Work of the Holy Spirit Today*. Downers Grove, IL: InterVarsity, 1976. The best short treatment available.

Thomas á Kempis. *The Imitation of Christ*. New York: Grosset & Dunlap, n.d. Written in the 1400's, `a Kempis represents pre-Reformation medieval piety at its best.

Warfield, Benjamin B. *Perfectionism*. Edited by Samuel G. Craig. Philadelphia: Presbyterian and Reformed, 1958. For serious students. Contains much minute analysis of second-blessing or deeper-life type groups.

Wesley, John. *A Plain Account of Christian Perfection*. London: Epworth Press, 1968. The definitive treatment of the Wesleyan Holiness teaching.

Williams, Charles. *The Descent of the Dove: A Short History of the Holy Spirit in the Church*. Grand Rapids: Eerdmans, 1972. Interesting perspectives from the close friend of C. S. Lewis. Unique.

Wimber, John. *Power Evangelism*. With Kevin Springer. San Francisco: Harper & Row, 1986. Challenging inside account of the "signs and wonders" movement.

SUBJECT INDEX

SCRIPTURE INDEX